Religion and Law in Cyprus

Religion and Law in Cyprus

Fourth Edition

Achilles C. Emilianides

This book was originally published as a monograph in the International Encyclopaedia of Laws/Religion Law.

Founding Editor: Roger Blanpain
General Editor: Frank Hendrickx
Volume Editor: Wouter Druwé

Wolters Kluwer

Published by:
Kluwer Law International B.V.
PO Box 316
2400 AH Alphen aan den Rijn
The Netherlands
E-mail: lrs-sales@wolterskluwer.com
Website: www.wolterskluwer.com/en/solutions/kluwerlawinternational

Sold and distributed by:
Wolters Kluwer Legal & Regulatory U.S.
920 Links Avenue
Landisville, PA 17538
United States of America
E-mail: customer.service@wolterskluwer.com

ISBN 978-94-035-1758-2

e-Book: ISBN 978-94-035-1768-1
web-PDF: ISBN 978-94-035-1778-0

The Author

Achilles C. Emilianides is Professor and Dean of the School of Law of the University of Nicosia and a practising advocate and senior partner of the firm A&E C. Emilianides, C. Katsaros and Associates LLP. He has been elected as a Founding Member and Secretary-General of the Cyprus Academy of Sciences, Letters, and Arts, as an ordinary member of the European Academy of Sciences and Arts, and as a member of the UNESCO Conciliation and Good Offices Commission. He further represents the Cyprus Academy to ALLEA (All European Academies). He holds a PhD in Law and an LLM from the Aristotle University of Thessaloniki and an LLM from Leicester University. He is the Consulting Editor of the Cyprus Review and the Chair of the Royal Commonwealth Society Cyprus Branch. His publications in the IEL series, published by Kluwer, are: *Constitutional Law in Cyprus* (3rd, 2024), *Family and Succession Law in Cyprus* (3rd, 2024), *Labour Law in Cyprus* (3rd, 2024), *Competition Law in Cyprus* (2021), *Tort Law in Cyprus* (2021), *Civil Procedure in Cyprus* (2020), *Religion and Law in Cyprus* (3rd, 2019), *Media Law in Cyprus* (2nd, 2019), *Private International Law in Cyprus* (2015).

The Author

Table of Contents

List of Abbreviations

AKEL	Progressive Party of Working People
CJEU	Court of Justice of the European Union
CLR	Cyprus Law Reports
CyBC	Cyprus Broadcasting Corporation
DIKO	Democratic Party
DIPA	Democratic Alignment
DISY	Democratic Rally
ECHR	European Convention on Human Rights
ECtHR	European Court of Human Rights
EDEK	Movement for Social Democracy
EEC	European Economic Community
EHRR	European Human Rights Reports
EOKA	National Organisation of Cypriot Fighters
EPP	European People's Party
EU	European Union
FCNM	Framework Convention for the Protection of National Minorities
GDPR	General Data Protection Regulation
MEP	Member of the European Parliament
MoU	Memorandum of Understanding
RSCC	Reports of the Supreme Constitutional Court of Cyprus
RTA	Radio Television Authority
'TRNC'	'Turkish Republic of Northern Cyprus'

List of Abbreviations

Preface

This study consists of an extensive analysis of the Cypriot legislation, case law and legal theory concerning law and religion. This is the fourth edition of this work – the first edition having been published in 2011, the second in 2014 and the third in 2019. Cypriot Law of Religion is unique due to the turbulent history of the island. The principal characteristics of the system of coordination between the Republic of Cyprus and the various religions and creeds can, therefore, be properly understood only through knowledge of the country's history and social framework. While each chapter retains its autonomy, the reader might benefit significantly from reading beforehand the general introduction, which provides the basis for an understanding of Cypriot history and religious social data.

I am especially indebted to the late Prof. Charalambos Papastathis for teaching me the significance of law and religion and who was the first person to systematically study law and religion in Cyprus. This volume is dedicated to his memory. I would also like to thank my colleagues at the European Consortium of Church and State Research for enabling continuous comparative reflection on the various aspects of Cypriot law and religion within the European Union (EU) framework, as well as my colleagues at both the University of Nicosia and my law firm for facilitating my research in the field of law and religion, as well as their perspectives and comments. My colleagues at the University of Padova, especially Giuseppe Giordan, have opened new horizons through the focus on religion of our joint PhD on Human Rights, Society and Multilevel Governance. Ioannis Konidaris and his team at Nomokanonika have been a constant source of inspiration. My personal assistant Andria Andreou worked tirelessly on the index of this book. The International Encyclopaedia of Laws were kind enough to include this monograph in their Encyclopaedia of Religion Law. Without them and the publisher, Kluwer Law International, this volume would have never been written. Last but not least, I would like to thank my family and friends for their support during all these years, without which nothing else would be of significance. Unfortunately, this new edition was published following the passing of my beloved parents Constantinos and Zeta, and therefore, this time, I did not have the opportunity to benefit from their comments on my work and their overall presence in my life.

General Introduction

§1. General Background of the Country

I. Geography

1. Cyprus, officially the Republic of Cyprus, is the third largest Mediterranean island after the Italian islands of Sicily and Sardinia. Cyprus is situated in the Eastern Mediterranean, at a distance of 300 km to the north of Egypt, 90 km to the west of Syria, 60 km to the south of Turkey and 360 km to the northwest of Greece. It covers an area of 9,251 sq. km (3,572 sq. mi) and has 648 km of coastline. Cyprus is divided into six districts, namely Nicosia, Limassol, Famagusta, Larnaca, Paphos and Kyrenia. The capital of the island is the town of Nicosia. Cyprus also has two mountain ranges: the Pentadaktylos range, which runs along the entire northern coast and the Troodos massif in the central and southwestern parts of the island. Between the two ranges lies the fertile plain of Messaoria.[1]

II. Constitutional History

A. *The Struggle Towards Independence*

2. The constitutional history of Cyprus is characterized by continuous attempts to overthrow, modify or replace the constitutional structure.[2] In a referendum held on 15 January 1950 and organized by the Church, more than 95% of the indigenous Greek population voted in favour of the Union (Enosis) of the island with Greece; however, the British colonial Government rejected the Greek position, with the then Minister of State for Colonial Affairs, Henry Hopkinson, declaring that Cyprus should never be allowed full independence.[3] On 1 April 1955, the National Organisation of Cypriot Fighters (EOKA) led by George Grivas (alias Dhigenis), a Greek Cypriot who was a colonel in the Greek army, declared an armed insurrection

1. A. Sophocleous, *An Introduction to the History and Geography of Cyprus* (Nicosia: Nikoclis Publishing, 1995, in Greek).
2. *See* in general A. Emilianides, *Beyond the Constitution of Cyprus* (Thessaloniki: Sakkoulas 2006, in Greek); K. Chrysostomides, *The Republic of Cyprus: A Study in International Law* (The Hague: Martinus Nijhoff, 2000).
3. *See* in detail A. Emilianides, 'The Cyprus Question Before the House of Commons: 1954–1955', in *Great Power Politics: Foreign Interventions and Domestic Perceptions* 11–31 (M. Kontos et al. eds, Newcastle upon Tyne: Cambridge Scholars Publishing, 2014).

against the British, demanding the Union (Enosis) of the island with Greece.[4] The political leader of the Greek Cypriots was Makarios III, who was also the Archbishop of the Greek Orthodox Church. This was due to the fact that during the British rule of Cyprus, the Orthodox Church constituted the nation-leading political organization of the Greeks of Cyprus under foreign sovereignty, also known as the Ethnarchy.[5]

3. Emergency measures were introduced by the British colonial Government, including detention without trial, arrest without warrant, curfews, hanging of suspected EOKA fighters, as well as collective punishments. Makarios and three other leading figures of the Greek Cypriots were exiled to the island of Seychelles by the colonial Government in an effort to force the Greek Cypriots to accept its constitutional proposals.[6] During this period, the Turkish Resistance Organisation (TMT) was established, its aim being the partition of the island (taxim). Turkey, with the encouragement of the United Kingdom, became involved in Cyprus, and negotiations ensued between the United Kingdom, Greece and Turkey. Several proposals for a constitutional settlement were rejected[7] since the Greek Cypriots insisted that they should be allowed to exercise their right of self-determination.[8] However, on 11 February 1959, the Zurich Agreements for the final settlement of the Cyprus dispute were concluded between Greece and Turkey. The Agreements, which were in fact imposed on the people of Cyprus, were then signed in London by the leaders of the two communities of Cyprus, Archbishop Makarios and Fazil Kutchuk, and the Government of the United Kingdom.

B. The Establishment of the Republic of Cyprus

4. The Republic of Cyprus was established as an independent and sovereign republic on 16 August 1960, when its Constitution came into force and British sovereignty over Cyprus, as a crown colony, ceased.[9] The Cypriot Constitution was

4. SIMAE (Council for the Preservation of Historical Memory of the EOKA Struggle), *Fifty Years on from the EOKA Struggle* (Nicosia: Ministry of Education, 2006, in Greek); R. Holland, *Britain and the Revolt in Cyprus: 1954–1959* (Oxford: Clarendon Press, 1998).
5. *See* A. Gavrielides, *The Ethnarchic Rights and the Referendum for Union with Greece* (Nicosia: 2nd ed. 1972, in Greek).
6. *See* A. Emilianides (ed.), *The Reports of the European Commission of Human Rights with Respect to Cyprus. App. 176/1956 & 299/1957* (Nicosia: Ministry of Education and Culture, 2008, in Greek); Ethnarchy of Cyprus, *Violations of Human Rights in Cyprus: A Factual Documentation* (Nicosia: 1957).
7. *See* E. Hatzivassiliou, *The Cyprus Question 1878–1960: The Constitutional Aspect* (Minneapolis: University of Minnesota, 2002).
8. *See* S. Loizides, *The Right to Self-Determination and the Cyprus Question* (Athens: 1957); S. Loizides, *The Cyprus Question and the Law of the United Nations* (Nicosia: Ethnarchy of Cyprus, 2nd ed. 1954); C. Tornaritis, *The Right of Self-determination with Special Reference to the Republic of Cyprus* (Nicosia: 1973).
9. Cyprus Act, 1960, s. 1, Republic of Cyprus Order in Council 1960 S.I. 1960 No. 1368, *Cyprus: Presented to Parliament by the Secretary of State for the Colonies, the Secretary of State for Foreign Affairs and the Minister of Defence*, Cmnd. 1093, July 1960.

signed by Sir Hugh Foot, the then-British Governor of the Colony of Cyprus, representatives of Greece and Turkey, as well as Archbishop Makarios and the Turkish Cypriot Fazil Kucuk. The latter two had already been elected as the first President and Vice-President of the Republic, respectively. The establishment of the Republic was the outcome of the Zurich and London Agreements of February 1959, on which the fundamental provisions of the Constitution were based.[10] As a result, the constitutional structure of Cyprus was essentially decided without the participation of the people of Cyprus.[11] Consequently, the people of Cyprus considered that the constitution had been imposed on them.

5. The structure provided by the Zurich Agreement was considered as a compromise between the Greek demand for union with Greece and the Turkish demand for partition of the island. Further, the United Kingdom retained – and continues to retain – '*sovereignty*' over two Base Areas, one in Akrotiri and the other in Dhekelia, which cover 250 sq. km (99 sq. mi) of the land area of the island of Cyprus.[12] The Constitution is unique in its perplexity and in the multiplicity of safeguards that it provides for the principal numerical minority of the island, namely the Turkish Community.[13] It has been correctly argued that the constitutional rules embodied in the Constitution might as well have been conceived by a constitutionalist and a mathematician in a nightmarish dialogue.[14] Apart from the constitutional structure, two additional international treaties were signed, which became part and parcel of the package deal agreed upon in Zurich; those were the Treaty of Alliance, according to which Greek and Turkish contingents would be permitted to be stationed on the island,[15] and the Treaty of Guarantee according to which Greece, Turkey and the United Kingdom would act as the guarantor powers of the independence, territorial integrity and constitutional order of the Republic of Cyprus. Article IV of the Treaty of Guarantee, which refers to the right of unilateral intervention of the guarantor powers, has been intensely criticized as being contrary to international

---

10. A. Emilianides, *The Zurich and London Agreements and the Cyprus Republic*, Vol. II, 629–639 (Athens: *Melanges Seferiades*, 1961); P. Tzermias, 'Der Neue Status Cyperns', *Archiv des Öffentlichen Rechts* 84, 459–489 (1959); G. Vlachos, 'L' Organisation Constitutionelle de la Republique de Chypre', *Revue International de Droit Comparé* 3, 526–559 (1961); P. Liakouras, 'Looking Back to See Forward: The 1959 Zurich and London Accords and the Constitutional Order of Cyprus', *Etudes Helléniques* 10, 47–61 (2002).
11. *See* in detail A. Emilianides, T*he Secret Negotiations. The Establishment of the Republic of Cyprus (1959–1960)* (Athens: Papazisi/CECL 2022, in Greek).
12. A. Emilianides, *A Long-Drawn out Game of Chess. The Confidential Negotiations on the British Bases* (Nicosia: Hippasus, 2021, in Greek); S. Theodoulou, *Bases militaires en droit international: le cas de Chypre* (Manheim: Bibliopolis, 2006); A. Pellet, 'The British Sovereign Areas', *Cyprus Yearbook of International Law*, 57–72 (2012); L. Loucaides, 'The Legal Status of the British Base Areas and the Right to Territorial Waters', *Cyprus Law Review* 27, 4175–4178 (1989) (in Greek); S. Theodoulou, *The Legal Status of the British Military Base Areas in the Territory of the Republic of Cyprus* (Nicosia: 1995, in Greek); L. Papaphilippou, *The Legal Status of the British Base Areas in Cyprus: Nature and Extent of the Sovereignty of the British Authorities* (Nicosia: 1993, in Greek).
13. *See* P. Polyviou, *The Problem of Cyprus: Constitutional and Political Aspects* (Nicosia: 1974).
14. A.S. De Smith, *The New Commonwealth and Its Constitutions* 282 (London: Stevens & Sons 1964).
15. C. Tornaritis (ed.), 'The Treaty of Alliance and the Agreement for Its Application', in *Constitutional and Legal Problems of the Republic of Cyprus* 33–39 (Nicosia: 2nd ed. 1972).

law.[16] In any event, it was accepted that the use of military force by the guarantor powers without the prior approval of the Security Council of the UN was not permitted.[17]

6. Based on the principle of bi-communality, Cyprus is a unitary state comprising two communities:[18] the Greek Community and the Turkish Community. According to Article 2 of the Constitution, the Greek Community comprises all citizens of the Republic who are of Greek origin and whose mother tongue is Greek, who share the Greek cultural tradition, or who are members of the Greek Orthodox Church. On the other hand, the Turkish Community comprises all citizens of the Republic who are of Turkish Origin and whose mother tongue is Turkish, who share the Turkish cultural traditions, or who are Muslims. Citizens of the Republic who did not fulfil any of the above criteria opted to belong either to the Greek or the Turkish Community within three months of the date of the coming into operation of the Constitution. A citizen of the Republic must, therefore, belong, or opt to belong, either to the Greek or the Turkish Community; however, no foreigners may belong to either Community.

7. The principle of bi-communality permeates the whole constitutional structure, according, in many respects, an equal status to the Greek Community, representing 82% of the population, and the Turkish Community, representing 18%.[19] It was therefore provided that a Greek Cypriot President should be elected by members of the Greek Community, while a Turkish Cypriot Vice-President should be elected by members of the Turkish Community. The President and the Vice-President would exclusively exercise the executive power on specific matters and retain broad powers of veto on decisions of the Council of Ministers concerning foreign affairs, defence and security. A similar veto right was accorded to the President and the Vice-President, with respect to the laws enacted by the House of Representatives. It was further provided that the Council of Ministers would comprise seven Greek Cypriots appointed by the President and three Turkish Cypriots appointed by the Vice-President. At the same time, the Public Service would be composed on the basis of a seven-to-three analogy, while the Public Service Commission – which has

16. *See* G. Zotiades, *Intervention by Treaty Right. Its Legality in Present Day International Law* (Thessaloniki: 1965); A. Jacovides, *Treaties Conflicting with Peremptory Norms of International Law and the Zurich and London Agreements* (Nicosia: 1966).
17. D. Constantopoulos, 'The Right of Intervention', *International Relations* 6, 41–47 (1964); N. Emiliou, 'The Prohibition of the Use of Force in International Law and the Cyprus Problem', *Modern Greek Studies Yearbook* 10–11, 171–203 (1994–1995); J. Wolfe, 'The Treaty of Guarantee: Intervention and Intercession in Cyprus', in *International Law Conference on Cyprus,* 33–49 (Nicosia: Cyprus Bar Council, 1979).
18. C. Tornaritis, 'The Constitution of Cyprus', *International Relations* 6, 28–40 (1964); T. Tsatsos, *Observations on the Constitution of Cyprus* (Athens: A. Sakkoulas 1965); M. Dendias, 'L' Arrangement du Problème de Chypre: Regime Constitutionelle et International et Garanties de la Republique de Chypre', *Festchrift für Prof. W. Schätzel,* 88 ff. (Düsseldorf: 1960).
19. G. Papademetriou, 'The Constitutional Problem of the Republic of Cyprus', *Cyprus Law Tribune* 39, 850–856 (1991) (in Greek); N. Antonopoulos, 'Les Tendances Constitutionelles des États Avant Accédé Récement à l' Independance: La Constitution de la République de Chypre', *Revue Hellénique de Droit International* 15, 307–326 (1962).

the power to appoint, promote, transfer and exercise disciplinary control over civil servants – would consist of ten members out of which seven shall be Greek Cypriots and three, Turkish Cypriots. If the issue concerned the question of whether to fill a vacant post with a Greek Cypriot or a Turkish Cypriot, a minimum number of votes from either Community would be needed.

8. The House of Representatives would consist of fifty Representatives; once again, 70% of the members of the House of Representatives were to be elected separately by the members of the Greek Community, while 30% were to be elected separately by the members of the Turkish Community. The President of the House of Representatives would be a Greek Cypriot, elected from among the Greek Cypriot Representatives, while the Vice-President would be a Turkish Cypriot, elected from among the Turkish Cypriot Representatives. Any amendments to the electoral law, the passing of laws concerning municipalities and laws imposing taxes or duties, would require a separate majority among Greek and Turkish Cypriot representatives, present and voting. In addition, the amendment of non-fundamental constitutional provisions would require a two-thirds majority of the representatives of each Community, voting separately. The Constitution also provided for two Communal Chambers: a Greek Communal Chamber and a Turkish Communal Chamber, which would have legislative power in educational, cultural, religious and other matters of a purely communal nature.

9. It was further provided that the judicial power was to be exercised by the Supreme Constitutional Court, the Supreme Court and their subordinate courts. The Supreme Constitutional Court should be composed of a non-Cypriot citizen as President and two members, a Greek Cypriot and a Turkish Cypriot, all appointed jointly by the President and the Vice-President. The Supreme Court would consist of two Greek Cypriot judges and one Turkish Cypriot, while the President of the Court would also be non-Cypriot. The bi-communal element was evident in the judiciary; it was provided that a judge trying a civil or criminal case should belong to the community of the parties or that of the accused, and if the parties or the accused and the injured party belonged to different communities, then the court should consist of judges belonging to both communities. The composition of the security forces was also based on increased proportions: an army of 2,000 men should consist of 60% Greek Cypriots and 40% Turkish Cypriots, while the Police and Gendarmerie would be composed on the basis of a seven-to-three analogy.

C. The 1963 Collapse and Its Aftermath

10. Not surprisingly, the Zurich Agreement failed to establish cooperation between the Greek and Turkish Communities on the island[20] and proved to be

20. *See* A. Emilianides, *The Parliamentary Co-existence of Greeks and Turks in Cyprus* (Nicosia: Epifaniou, 2003, in Greek).

unworkable in practice.[21] In 1963, the then President of the Republic of Cyprus, Archbishop Makarios, transmitted to the then Turkish Cypriot Vice-President, Fazil Kucuk, a thirteen-point memorandum, whereby he suggested the revision of certain articles of the Constitution, which had impeded the smooth functioning of the Republic of Cyprus. Makarios suggested, *inter alia*, the abolition of separate majorities in the House of Representatives and of veto rights of the President and Vice-President of the Republic, as well as the unification of the system for the administration of justice and the abolition of the Greek Communal Chamber.[22] The Government of Turkey rejected such proposals even before the Turkish Community had submitted any comments on them. There was an outbreak of violence on the island, which led to a constitutional breakdown.[23] In 1964, a United Nations Peace-keeping operation came to the island and has remained there since.[24] The Security Council of the United Nations, with Resolution 186/1964, and the General Assembly of the United Nations on 18 December 1965, called upon all States to respect the sovereignty, unity, independence and territorial integrity of the Republic of Cyprus and to refrain from any intervention with it.[25] The Government of the Republic of Cyprus continued to be recognized by the international community as the only legitimate representative of the Republic.[26]

11. As a result of the bi-communal violence that broke out in Cyprus in December 1963, there existed a state of armed rebellion against the established Government of the Republic, which led to armed clashes between organized groups resisting the authority of the State, loss of life, damage to property, interruption of communications and assertion of authority and actual physical control over areas of State territory by the insurgents and their political leaders. The Turkish Cypriot Vice-President, the three Turkish Cypriot ministers, as well as the fifteen Turkish Cypriot members of the House of Representatives vacated their offices. Furthermore, the President of the Supreme Constitutional Court, a German citizen, and the President of the High Court, a Canadian citizen, both resigned.[27] In view of the

21. C. Tornaritis, *Peculiarities of the Constitution of Cyprus and Effect on the Normal Function of the State* (Nicosia: 1980, in Greek); T.W. Adams, 'The First Republic of Cyprus: Review of an Unworkable Constitution', *Western Political Quarterly* 19, 475–490 (1966); C. Papastathopoulos, 'Constitutionalism and Communalism: The Case of Cyprus', *University of Toronto Law Journal* 16, 118–144 (1965).
22. *See* C. Tornaritis, *Cyprus and Its Constitutional and Other Legal Problems* 67 ff. (Nicosia: 2nd ed. 1980); D. Bitsios, *Cyprus: The Vulnerable Republic* 121 ff. (Thessaloniki: Institute for Balkan Studies, 1975); A. Emilianides, *Beyond the Constitution of Cyprus* 88 ff. (Thessaloniki: Sakkoulas, 2006, in Greek).
23. *See* S. Kyriakides, *Cyprus: Constitutionalism and Crisis Government* (Philadelphia: University of Pennsylvania Press 1968).
24. A. Papadopoulos, *Peace-Making and Peace-Keeping by the United Nations: Cyprus a Case Study* (Nicosia: 1969); G. Kaloudis & P. Lang, *Role of the UN in Cyprus from 1964 to 1979* (London: Peter Lang 1991); A. Emilianides, 'The United Nations Forces Function, Its International Conflicts and Civil Strifes', in *Melanges Bridel* 147–168 (Lausanne: Imprimeries Réunies, 1968).
25. SC Resolution 186/64. There followed twenty-eight Security Council Resolutions up to 1974, affirming SC Resolution 186/64.
26. *See* further C. Tornaritis (ed.), 'The Legal Position of the Present Government of the Republic', in *Constitutional and Legal Problems in the Republic of Cyprus* 43–55 (Nicosia: 1972).
27. Forsthoff had actually resigned since May 1963.

above, the two highest tribunals of the Republic had ceased to function. No appeals, criminal or civil, could be adjudicated upon, and no constitutional jurisdiction or any revisional jurisdiction in administrative law matters could be exercised.

12. The administration of justice, as well as the very existence of the Republic of Cyprus, was in immediate danger.[28] In view of the aforementioned problems, the House of Representatives enacted the Administration of Justice (Miscellaneous Provisions) Law 33/1964, according to the provisions of which a newly established Supreme Court would exercise the jurisdictions and powers of the Supreme Constitutional Court and the High Court, *until such time as the people of Cyprus may determine such matters.*[29] The remaining five members of the two former highest tribunals of the Republic (three Greek Cypriots and two Turkish Cypriots) would constitute the Supreme Court, with a Turkish Cypriot, Judge Zekia, holding the position of the President of the Court. The above Law was held to be constitutional by the Supreme Court in the case of *Ibrahim*[30] on the basis of the doctrine of necessity.[31] The Court held that the doctrine of necessity was a direct result of the rigidity and narrow ambit of the Constitution of 1960 and that it would be inconceivable that a state should destroy itself because of its Constitution.

13. It was, therefore, held that Article 179 of the Constitution, which states that the Constitution is the supreme Law of the Republic, ought to apply subject to the proposition that where it is not possible for a basic function of the state to be discharged properly, or where a situation has arisen which cannot be adequately met under the existing provisions of the Constitution, then the appropriate organ may take such steps within the nature of its competence as are required to meet the necessity. Hence, it was understood that the doctrine of necessity is not a supra-constitutional principle; on the contrary, it forms part of Article 179 of the Constitution as an implied principle. The doctrine of necessity, based upon the principles *salus populi suprema lex esto* and *necessitas non habet legem*, was a direct result of the rigidity and narrow ambit of the Constitution of 1960.

14. In essence, the Supreme Court held that there are four prerequisites in order to determine whether the doctrine of necessity could be applied in a particular case, namely: (i) an imperative and inevitable necessity or exceptional circumstances; (ii) no other remedy to apply; (iii) the measure taken must be proportionate to the necessity; and (iv) it must be of a temporary character limited to the duration of the

---

28. *See, inter alia, The Attorney-General of the Republic v. Ibrahim* [1964] CLR 195.
29. Preamble of Law 33/64.
30. *The Attorney-General of the Republic v. Ibrahim* [1964] CLR 195.
31. For the Cypriot doctrine of necessity *see* A. Emilianides, C. Papastylianos & C. Stratilatis, *The Republic of Cyprus and the Doctrine of Necessity* (Athens-Thessaloniki: Sakkoulas 2016, in Greek), P. Polyviou, *The Case of* Ibrahim, *the Doctrine of Necessity and the Republic of Cyprus* (Nicosia: Chryssafinis & Polyviou 2015), C. Kombos, *The Doctrine of Necessity in Constitutional Law* (Athens-Thessaloniki: Sakkoulas 2015), C. Tornaritis, *The Principle of Necessity and the Cypriot Legal System* (Nicosia, 1978, in Greek); L. Papaphilippou, *The Doctrine of Necessity and Cypriot Constitutional Order* (Nicosia: 1995, in Greek). A. Emilianides, 'Accession of the Republic of Cyprus to the EU, the Constitution and the Cypriot Doctrine of Necessity', *Cyprus Yearbook of International Relations* 65–82 (2007).

exceptional circumstances.[32] The Supreme Court is responsible for determining whether the aforementioned prerequisites are satisfied, taking into account that the doctrine of necessity is applied so as to safeguard the constitutional rights and freedoms. The *Ibrahim* case forms the foundation for the case law of the Supreme Court with regard to the doctrine of necessity and was cited with approval in a number of international cases.

D. The 1974 Turkish Invasion

15. Inter-communal talks began with the aim of achieving a satisfactory solution to the Cyprus Problem.[33] However, in July 1974, the Republic of Turkey, one of the guarantor powers of the independence, sovereignty and territorial integrity of Cyprus, invaded the country with its armed forces and occupied the northern part of the island. Turkey alleged that its invasion had the purpose of restoring constitutional order on the basis of the provisions of the Treaty of Guarantee following a coup against President Makarios by the Greek military government (junta), which was then in power in Greece;[34] an allegation, which, however, was correctly not accepted by the international community.[35] Resolution 360/74 expressed the official contempt on behalf of the Security Council for the unilateral military force undertaken against the Republic of Cyprus, while Resolution 3212/74 of the General Assembly of the United Nations demanded that all foreign armed forces leave at once from the Republic of Cyprus and that any foreign intervention with the Republic of Cyprus's affairs should cease immediately. The latter Resolution was endorsed by Resolution 365/74 of the Security Council.[36]

16. As a result of the Turkish invasion, the Greeks and other Christians of the region were displaced to the southern part of the island. The Turks of the southern part of the island were forced to move to the north. The area occupied by Turkey amounts to 36.4% of the territory of the Republic of Cyprus and is the richest part of the island in natural and productive resources. The Turkish invasion resulted in grave human suffering and material economic loss, and its effects are still evident today, with more than one-quarter of the population of the island being displaced persons and more than 1,000 people still being classified as 'missing persons'. Turkish military troops amounting to 43,000 and armed with the latest military weapons

32. *The Attorney-General of the Republic v. Ibrahim* [1964] CLR 195, at 264.
33. *See* P. Polyviou, *Cyprus in Search of a Constitution: Constitutional Negotiations and Proposals* (Nicosia: 1976).
34. For the Turkish position *see* Z. Necatigil, *The Cyprus Question and the Turkish Position in International Law* (Oxford: Oxford University Press 2nd ed. 1993).
35. *See* I. Brownlie, 'The Prohibition of the Use of Armed Force for the Solution of International Differences with Particular Reference to the Affairs of the Republic of Cyprus', in *International Law Conference on Cyprus* 198–213 (Nicosia: Cyprus Bar Council, 1979); R. McDonald, 'International Law and the Conflict in Cyprus', *Canadian Yearbook of International Law* 19, 3 ff. (1981); D. Constantopoulos, *The Turkish Invasion of Cyprus from the Aspect of International Law* (Thessaloniki: 1978).
36. Similar Resolutions of the Security Council from 1974 to 2004 amount to eighty-seven.

continue to be based illegally on the island, while settlers are being brought to Cyprus in an effort to change the demographic character of the island.[37]

17. In 1983, the Turkish-occupied area declared itself as the 'Turkish Republic of Northern Cyprus' ('TRNC'), although that entity is recognized only by Turkey. The Security Council of the United Nations has condemned the declaration of the so-called 'TRNC' with Resolution 541/83, in which it declared that such declaration was legally invalid.[38] The Security Council called upon all Member States to abstain from recognizing any other state in Cyprus apart from the internationally recognized Republic of Cyprus. The fact that the government of the Republic of Cyprus is the only internationally recognized government has also been recognized by various decisions of international Courts, such as the Court of Justice of the European Union (CJEU)[39] and the European Court of Human Rights (ECtHR).[40] The so-called TRNC was held to be a subordinate administration to Turkey. The ECtHR has confirmed in both the *Loizidou* judgment and the interstate judgment of *Cyprus v. Turkey* that:

> Turkish armed forces of more than 30,000 personnel are stationed throughout the whole of the occupied area of Northern Cyprus, which is constantly patrolled and has checkpoints on all main lines of communication.

It was further observed that:

> It is obvious from the large number of troops engaged in active duties in northern Cyprus … that her army exercises effective overall control over that part of the island. Such control, according to the relevant test and in the circumstances of the case, entails her responsibility for the policies and actions of the 'TRNC'.

---

37. *See* C. Tornaritis, *The Turkish Invasion of Cyprus and Legal Problems Arising Therefrom* (Nicosia: 1975); L. Clerides, 'Violations of Human Rights by Turkey during the Invasion in 1974 and Continuing Violations Today', *Cyprus Law Review* 17, 2669–2680 (1987) (in Greek); Cyprus Bar Association, *Turkey's Violations of Human Rights in Cyprus. Findings of the European Commission of Human Rights and Continuing Violations by Turkey* (Nicosia: 1995).
38. *See also* L. Clerides, 'The Legal Invalidity of the Unilateral Declaration of an Independent State from the Turkish Cypriot Leadership', *Cyprus Law Review* 7, 1198–1203 (1984) (in Greek); K. Ioannou, 'Observations on Certain Legal Aspects of the New Cyprus Crisis', *Cyprus Law Review* 3, 491–497 (1983) (in Greek).
39. Case C-432/92, *R v. Minister of Agriculture, Fisheries and Food*, ex p. *S. P. Anastasiou (Pissouri) Ltd and Others* [1994] ECR I-3087.
40. *Loizidou v. Turkey*, Judgment of 23 Mar. 1995 and 18 Dec. 1996; *Cyprus v. Turkey*, Judgment of 10 May 2001. *See* further L. Loucaides, 'The Judgment of the European Court of Human Rights in the Case of Cyprus v. Turkey', *Leiden Journal of International Law* 15, 225–236 (2002); G. Cohen & Jonathan, 'L' Affaire Loizidou devant la Cour Européenne des Droits de l' Homme: Quelques Observations', *Revue Général de Droit International Public* 46, 123–144 (1998); R. White, 'Tackling Political Disputes Through Individual Applications', *European Human Rights Law Review* 1, 61–72 (1998); H. Dipla, 'Responsabilité de l' État en Droits de l' Homme: L' Arrêt de la Cour de Strasbourg en l' Affaire Loizidou c. Turquie', *Revue Hellenique de Droit International* 50, 17–42 (1997).

E. The Cyprus Problem Today

18. The Turkish occupation of Cyprus continues to the present day, and therefore, the Republic of Cyprus is prevented from exercising its powers over the occupied territory. A number of constitutional provisions which refer to the Turkish Community are temporarily not in force due to the abnormal situation prevailing on the island. The application of the doctrine of necessity has been accepted by the Supreme Court of Cyprus so that the Parliament may enact laws even contrary to those provisions of the constitution, which are temporarily not in force because of the Cyprus Problem. Several attempts to achieve a solution to the Cyprus Problem have so far failed. On 24 April 2004, the fifth and final version of the plan of the Secretary-General of the United Nations, Kofi Annan, for the comprehensive solution to the Cyprus Problem was submitted for approval in separate simultaneous referenda. If the plan had been accepted, a new state of affairs would have come into being by the *United Cyprus Republic,* replacing the Republic of Cyprus.

19. The Plan was rejected by the people of Cyprus since 75.83% of the members of the Greek Cypriot Community voted against it, while 65% of the Turkish Cypriot Community voted in favour of it. Therefore, the so-called Annan Plan is, according to its own provisions, null and void and shall have no legal effect. There is little doubt that the Annan Plan was a misguided attempt to solve the Cyprus Problem and that it was fundamentally flawed since its drafters did not aim to solve problems in a permanent and stable manner but rather to find short-term compromising solutions.[41]

20. Cyprus became a full member of the EU on 1 May 2004.[42] However, the application of the *acquis communautaire*, the complete body of EU Law, in the occupied areas has been suspended until a solution to the Cyprus Problem is found. What is more, the *acquis* does not apply at all in the British Sovereign Base Areas.[43] Following his election in 2008, President of the Republic, Demetris Christofias, pledged to restart negotiations with the representative of the Turkish

---

41. C. Palley, *An International Relations Debacle: The UN Secretary-General's Mission of Good Offices in Cyprus 1999–2004* (Oxford: Hart Publishing 2005), A. Syrigos, *The Annan Plan: The Legacies of the Past and the Prospects of the Future* (Athens: Patakis, 2005, in Greek), A. Emilianides, 'Beyond the Servant State Paradigm: The Cyprus Problem Revisited', *Institute of International Relations Yearbook,* 107–126 (2003–2004); A. Emilianides et al., *The Annan Plan: Five Critical Essays* (Athens: Ypsilon/Egean, 2003, in Greek); C. Chrysogonos, 'UNSG's Proposal for a New Cypriot Constitution', *Geostratigiki* 1, 45–57 (2003)(in Greek).
42. *See* S. Laulhé-Shaelou, *The EU and Cyprus: Principles and Strategies of Full Integration* (Leiden: Brill, 2010); A. Markides, 'The Cyprus Problem as a Legal Problem within Europe', *Revue Européenne de Droit Public* 12, 1195–1214 (2000); A. Syrigos, 'Cyprus and the EU: Sovereign State, Negotiations and Objections from an International Law Point of View', in *Cyprus and the European Union* 91–106 (A. Theophanous, N. Peristianis & A. Ioannou eds, Nicosia: Intercollege Press 1999); L. Loucaides, 'European Community and the Cyprus Problem', *Cyprus Law Review* 34, 5241–5255 (1991), A. Sepos, *The Europeanization of Cyprus: Polity, Policies and Politics* (London: Palgrave Macmillan 2008), A. Theophanous, *The Cyprus Question and the EU: The Challenge and the Promise* (Nicosia: Intercollege Press 2004).
43. S. Laulhé-Shaelou, 'Focus on Territorial Exclusion and Sui Generis Territories in the EU: The British Bases in Cyprus. A Special Case', *Cyprus Yearbook of International Law,* 73–110 (2012).

Cypriot Community, Mehmet Ali Talat, in an attempt to find a solution to the Cyprus Problem; however, negotiations failed to produce results.[44] Subsequent President Nicos Anastasiades also carried out lengthy negotiations with the representatives of the Turkish Cypriot Community; however, the negotiations reached a deadlock.

21. The failure of the Constitution of Cyprus with regard to the unworkable division of political power between two arithmetically unequal communities does not imply that the Cyprus Problem was due to religious differences. On the contrary, it is suggested that the Cyprus Problem has never had any religious connotations; the Christian population of Cyprus has never disputed that the Muslims of Cyprus should have the right to administer their own religious affairs, including education, cultural, spiritual and matrimonial matters, and other matters of a purely communal nature. The Muslims of Cyprus actually used to participate in the celebration of religious holidays with the Christians of Cyprus; thus, it would seem that the need for religious tolerance between Christians and Muslims of Cyprus has never been disputed. The Cyprus Problem is therefore of a political nature and has its roots in ethnic conflict and the strategic or geopolitical interests of foreign powers in Cyprus, not in religious differences.

III. Constitutional Structure

A. General Overview

22. Cyprus has a written constitution codified in a single document that takes precedence over all other national or international laws.[45] Cyprus is a unitary state with a central government comprising the two communities of the island. Following the constitutional crisis of 1963, the Greek Communal Chamber was self-dissolved. On the basis of Law 12/1965, the legislative competencies of the Greek Communal Chamber were transferred to the House of Representatives, while its administrative competencies with respect to educational matters were transferred to the Ministry of Education (as it was then named); the remaining competencies of the Greek Communal Chamber were transferred to the Council of Ministers. Law 12/1965 was justified on the basis of the doctrine of necessity.[46] As a result, all competencies currently belong to the central government. Cyprus' system of government is a presidential democracy based on the rule of law. There is a strong division

44. *See* A. Emilianides, M. Kontos & G. Kentas, *A Marked Deck: The Confidential Documents of the Negotiations between Christofias and Talat* (Nicosia: Power Publishing 2010, in Greek).
45. With respect to the constitution of Cyprus *see* A. Emilianides, *Constitutional Law in Cyprus* (The Hague: Kluwer 2nd ed. 2019); C. Kombos, *Cypriot Constitutional Law* (Athens: Nomiki Vivliothiki 2021, in Greek), A. Markides, 'The Republic of Cyprus', in *Constitutional Law of 10 EU Member States: The 2004 Enlargement* 3–77 (C. Kortmann, J. Fleuren & W. Voermans eds, The Hague: Kluwer 2006); G. Pikis, *Constitutionalism, Human Rights, Separation of Powers. The Cyprus Precedent* (Leiden: Martinus Nijhoff, 2006); A. Loizou, *Constitution of the Republic of Cyprus* (Nicosia: 2001, in Greek); C. Tornaritis, *The State Law of the Republic of Cyprus* (Nicosia: Cyprus Research Centre, 1982, in Greek).
46. *Cypiom Ltd v. The Police* [2003] 2 CLR 459 (in Greek). *See also Georgiades v. The Republic* [1966] 3 CLR 252.

of the executive, legislative and judicial powers based on checks and balances; thus, the principle of separation of powers is considered an implied constitutional principle of supreme importance.

23. A significant number of constitutional provisions are considered to be fundamental and are not subject to change at all. These articles have been incorporated from the Zurich-London Agreements and form the essentially bi-communal identity of the constitution. The other articles of the constitution can only be changed if two-thirds of the Greek Cypriot representatives and two-thirds of the Turkish Cypriot representatives vote in favour. Following the constitutional crisis of 1963, it has been accepted that the House of Representatives may modify the non-fundamental articles of the Constitution by a majority of two-thirds of its Greek Cypriot members only by invoking the doctrine of necessity,[47] so long as any such amendments are not contrary to the international obligations of the Republic of Cyprus, and more importantly the European Convention on Human Rights (ECHR) and EU Law. This should not mean that the temporary character is no longer an element of the Cypriot doctrine of necessity; it should, however, imply that the doctrine of necessity should have the stability of the Republic as its primary purpose in view of the degree and quality of the actual necessity.[48]

24. Cyprus has a pluralistic system of political parties. Political parties are a fundamental element of public life, and their function is an essential element of the constitutional order. Cypriot citizenship is acquired by birth, by registration or by naturalization. A child acquires Cypriot citizenship by birth if he/she is born in Cyprus and one of his/her parents is a Cypriot citizen. If the child is born abroad, he/she may acquire Cypriot citizenship by registration. A foreigner may become a citizen of Cyprus, even if neither of his/her parents is a Cypriot citizen, so long as he/she is naturalized. Any person who becomes a citizen of the Republic after independence has to opt to become a member of either the Greek Community or the Turkish Community. Married women belong to the Community of their husband, while children under 21 belong to the Community of their father unless the latter is unknown and the child has not been adopted, in which case they belong to the Community of their mother.

B. Executive Branch

25. All Cypriots over the age of 18 have the right to vote in elections; however, a person may not be elected as a member of the House of Representatives unless

47. *Nicolaou v. Nicolaou* [1992] 1 CLR 1338 (in Greek); *Koulountis v. The House of Representatives* [1997] 1 CLR 1026 (in Greek), *Charalambides and Another v. Republic and Another*, Administrative Appeal 99/2016, Judgment of 4 Apr. 2018 (in Greek).

48. *See* A. Emilianides, *Beyond the Constitution of Cyprus* 151 ff. (Thessaloniki: Sakkoulas 2006, in Greek); A. Emilianides, 'Accession of the Republic of Cyprus to the EU, the Constitution and the Cypriot Doctrine of Necessity', *Cyprus Yearbook of International Relations* 65–82 (2007); E. Venizelos, *The Cyprus Problem, the Cypriot Constitutional Order and the Accession to the European Union* 97–121 (Athens: A. Sakkoulas 2000, in Greek).

he/she is at least 21 years old, and he/she may not be elected as President unless he/she is at least 35 years old. The President is the Head of State and represents the Republic in all its official functions; he/she belongs to the Greek Cypriot Community and is elected for a five-year term directly, by universal suffrage and secret ballot. Thus, contrary to the parliamentary system, the Head of State is not elected by the House of Representatives but directly by the people and need not be supported, at any given time, by the majority of the members of the House of Representatives. The President appoints and dismisses the members of the Council of Ministers and has vast executive powers. The Constitution also provides for a Turkish Cypriot Vice-President who is the Vice-Head of State and has similar powers as the President. Following the constitutional crisis of 1963, the office of the Vice-President remains vacant.

26. The Council of Ministers exercises executive power alongside the President. The Constitution provides that the Council of Ministers is composed of seven Greek Cypriots and three Turkish Cypriots who shall be designated respectively by the President and the Vice-President of the Republic. Following the constitutional crisis of 1963, all ten Ministers are Greek Cypriots and are appointed by the President. An eleventh Ministry of Education, Sport and Youth has replaced the dissolved Greek Communal Chamber; the Minister of Education, Sport and Youth has the same voting rights as other Ministers. Ministers are chosen from outside the House of Representatives. Currently, in addition to the Ministry of Education, Sport and Youth, there are the following Ministries: (a) Interior; (b) Finance; (c) Foreign Affairs; (d) Defence; (e) Justice and Public Order; (f) Agriculture, Rural Development and the Environment; (g) Transport, Communications and Works; (h) Health; (i) Labour and Social Insurance; (j) Energy, Commerce and Industry. The decisions of the Council of Ministers are reached by an absolute majority of the Ministers, with the President heading the Council of Ministers without having a right to vote.[49] There are also the following Deputy Ministries: (a) Shipping, (b) Tourism, (c) Research, Innovation and Digital Policy, (d) Social Welfare, and (e) Culture, Deputy Ministers (including the Deputy Minister to the President, as well as the Government Spokesperson and Deputy Government Spokesperson) are not members of the Council of Ministers and do not have a right to vote.

C. Legislative Branch

27. The House of Representatives exercises the legislative power of the Republic.[50] The constitution provides that 70% of the Representatives shall be elected separately by the members of the Greek Cypriot Community and 30% separately by

49. *See* C. Tornaritis, 'The Legal Position of Ministers in the Republic of Cyprus', *Cyprus Law Tribune* 1, 7–16 (1967) (in Greek); C. Tornaritis, 'May the President of the Republic Submit a Proposal to the Council of Ministers Himself?', *Cyprus Law Tribune* 5–6 (1977) (in Greek).

50. *See* D. Melissas, *The Organisation of Political Power in the Cypriot State* (Athens: A. Sakkoulas 1996, in Greek); A. Michaelides, 'The House of Representatives of the Republic of Cyprus', *The Parliamentarian* 60, 67–71 (1979); C. Tornaritis, *The Republic of Cyprus and Its House of Representatives* (Nicosia: 1978).

the members of the Turkish Cypriot Community. Following the constitutional crisis of 1963, the offices of the Turkish Cypriot Representatives remain vacant. The House of Representatives currently has fifty-six Representatives, while the twenty-four seats of the Turkish Cypriot Representatives remain vacant. The Representatives are elected for a term of five years in free, general and direct elections. The right to introduce bills belongs to both the Representatives and the Ministers; however, bills relating to an increase in budgetary expenses can be introduced by Ministers only. Laws may be enacted by a simple majority vote of the Representatives present and voting. Laws come into operation upon their publication in the official gazette of the Republic.

D. *Human Rights*

28. Part II of the Constitution of Cyprus, which guarantees fundamental rights and liberties, is modelled on the ECHR. However, the provisions of the ECHR have been extended and enlarged in some respects, with a number of social and economic rights added in order to meet the basic requirements of modern society.[51] The rights are generally guaranteed to every person, although only citizens are protected against extradition or deportation. For Cyprus, human rights are of fundamental importance to legal thinking. Fundamental rights are binding on all public authorities under any circumstances. The courts have the power to declare that any law or administrative action which is contrary to fundamental rights is unconstitutional and invalid. While fundamental rights are not unlimited, no fundamental right may be disregarded completely. The constitution expressly provides that even in those circumstances where fundamental rights may be limited, such limitations must be prescribed by law. In addition, any limitations to fundamental rights must be reasonably justified and must respect the principle of proportionality.

29. Fundamental rights and liberties safeguarded in Part II of the Constitution include: the right to life and corporal integrity, the prohibition of torture or degrading treatment or punishment, the right to a decent existence and to social security, the prohibition of slavery or servitude or forced or compulsory labour, the right to liberty and security, the right to a fair trial, the right to free movement and residence, the right to respect for the family and private life, house and correspondence, the right to freedom of thought, conscience and religion, the right to freedom of speech and expression, the right to education, the right to marry and found a family, the right to peaceful assembly and association, the right to property, the freedom from taxation unless such is imposed by law, the right to practice any profession or carry any occupation, trade or business, the right to enter into legal

51. *See* P. Evangelides, *The Republic of Cyprus and Its Constitution, with Special Regard to the Constitutional Rights* (Bamburg: Difo – Druck GmbH, 1996); C. Paraskeva, *Cypriot Constitutional Law: Fundamental Rights and Freedoms* (Athens: Nomiki Vivliothiki, 2015, in Greek); C. Tornaritis, *The Human Rights as Recognised and Protected by Law with Special Reference to the Law of Cyprus* (Nicosia; 1967); M. Triantafyllides, 'A Comparison of the Provisions for Civil and Political Rights in the Cyprus Constitution with Relevant Internationally Adopted Provisions', *Cyprus Law Tribune* 6, 3–7 (1968); Z. Nedjati, *Human Rights and Fundamental Freedoms* (Nicosia: 1972).

contracts, the right to strike, the right to equality before the law and the prohibition against discrimination, the right to petition the authorities, and the right to vote and stand for election.

E. The Judicial System

30. The judiciary is independent of the executive and legislative organs and is a powerful factor, both in legal and social life.[52] The highest Cypriot court was, until July 2023, the Supreme Court of Cyprus, which functioned, following the constitutional crisis of 1963, both as the Supreme Constitutional Court[53] and as the Supreme Appellate Court of the Republic. Many of the Court's decisions have been of the highest legal and political impact. However, since 1 July 2023, there are once again two distinct highest courts, the Supreme Constitutional Court and the Supreme Court, as well as a second-instance Appellate Court. The Appellate Court has jurisdiction to hear and determine all appeals from lower courts in civil and criminal matters. The hearing of the appeal is based on the record of the proceedings kept in the lower court. The Appellate Court only hears oral evidence in exceptional and very rare circumstances. In the exercise of its appellate jurisdiction, the Appellate Court may uphold, vary or set aside the decision appealed from, or it may order a retrial.

31. The Supreme Court further used to have the exclusive jurisdiction to hear any recourse filed against a decision, act or omission of any person, organ or authority exercising executive or administrative authority. A decision, act or omission may be annulled on the ground that it is in excess or abuse of any power vested in the administrative organ or contrary to the provisions of the Constitution.[54] The exclusive jurisdiction to hear these administrative law recourses has since January 2016 been transferred to the newly established Administrative Court, whereas the Appellate Court shall exercise appellate jurisdiction in such cases, and the Supreme Constitutional Court shall exercise jurisdiction to hear appeals in a third degree or to hear appeals directly where, *inter alia*, there are conflicting previous judgments of the Appellate Court or the legal point in question is of great importance. The

52. *See* C. Clerides, *The Cypriot Legal System* (Athens: Nomiki Vivliothiki, 2018, in Greek); J. Josephides, 'The Judicial System of Cyprus', *Cyprus Today* 9, 14–20 (1971); P. Michaelides, 'The Cypriot Legislation on Judiciary', *Aspects of Cypriot Law*, I, 67–124 (Nicosia: Asselia, 1981, in Greek).
53. *See* S. Papasavvas, *La Justice Constitutionelle à Chypre* (Paris: Economica, 1998).
54. *See* in general A. Emilianides, *Constitutional Law in Cyprus* (The Hague: Kluwer 2nd ed. 2019); N. Charalambous, *Cypriot Administrative Law Textbook* (Nicosia: 3rd ed. 2016, in Greek); C. Paraskeva, *Cypriot Administrative Law* (Athens: Nomiki Vivliothiki, 2017, in Greek); C. Paraskeva, *Cypriot Administrative Procedure Law* (Athens: Nomiki Vivliothiki, 2020, in Greek); A. Angelides & S. Angelides, *Administrative Procedural Law* (Nicosia: Cyprus Bar Association, 2nd ed. 2020, in Greek), C. Melides, 'Administrative Law', in *Introduction to Cyprus Law* 87–117 (Andreas Neocleous & Co LLC eds, Limassol, 3rd ed. 2010); A. Angelides, *The Law on General Principles of Administrative Law and the Subsequent Case – Law of the Supreme Court* (Nicosia: House of Representatives, 2008).

Supreme Constitutional Court also has jurisdiction to determine questions of constitutional law referred to it. As an electoral court, the Supreme Constitutional Court has exclusive jurisdiction to hear and determine petitions concerning the interpretation and application of electoral laws, with the exception of municipal elections. In addition, the Supreme Court has exclusive jurisdiction to issue the prerogative writs of Habeas Corpus, Mandamus, Certiorari, Quo Warranto and Prohibition.[55]

32. There are seven types of subordinate courts in Cyprus, namely the District Courts, the Assize Courts, the Administrative Court, the Family Courts, the Rent Control Courts, the Labour Disputes Courts, the International Protection Administrative Court and the Military Court. There is one District Court in each district of Cyprus, and they exercise civil and criminal jurisdiction. District Courts are composed of Presidents of the District Court, Senior District Court Judges and District Court Judges, all of whom are appointed by the Supreme Council of Judicature, which is composed of the Supreme Court judges. In their civil jurisdiction, they can examine any action whose cause arose within the district where the court is situated or in which the defendant or one of the defendants in the action resides. In their criminal jurisdiction, they can adjudicate on any criminal offence committed within their districts which has not been specifically assigned to the jurisdiction of the Assize Courts.

33. The Assize Courts have jurisdiction to try criminal offences; each Assize Court is composed of three judges who try serious criminal offences for which the sentence of imprisonment for life or imprisonment for more than five years may be imposed. The Administrative Court exercises jurisdiction in all administrative law recourses. The International Protection Administrative Court, however, exercises jurisdiction on administrative resources made by asylum seekers and relating to the Refugee Law 6(I)/2000. Family Courts have jurisdiction in all family law matters, including divorce, alimony, family property, custody, or adoption. Rent Control Courts have jurisdiction in claims concerning evictions, rent adjustments and any other matters which arise in relation to statutory tenancy. Labour Disputes Courts have jurisdiction to entertain claims concerning disputes between employers and employees with respect to matters concerning employment and labour law. Finally, the Military Court exercises criminal jurisdiction over the members of the National Guard in accordance with the Military Criminal Code and Procedure.

F. Legal System

34. No law or administrative act may be inconsistent or contrary to the Constitution. All courts have jurisdiction to declare a Law as unconstitutional.[56] Since the

---

55. P. Artemis, *Prerogative Orders* (Larnaca: 2004, in Greek); C. Tornaritis, 'The Prerogative Orders under the Constitution and the Law of the Republic of Cyprus', *Proceedings of the Second International Cyprological Conference*, Vol. III, 641–650 (Nicosia: Society for Cypriot Studies, 1987).
56. C. Tornaritis, *Constitutional Review of Laws in the Republic of Cyprus* (Nicosia: 1983); E. Venizelos, 'The Judicial Control of the Constitutionality of Laws in Greece and Cyprus: A Parallel Overview', *Cyprus Law Review* 39–40, 5845–5856 (1992) (in Greek); E. Nicolaou, *The Control of Constitutionality of Laws and Distribution of Competencies of the Organs of the State in Cyprus*

Fifth Amendment of the Constitution in 2006, EU Law has been considered an integral part of the Constitution; therefore, no provision of the Constitution may invalidate the Law of the EU, irrespective of whether such Law arises from the Treaties or from secondary legislation, such as a Regulation, or Directive. It should be noted that EU Law is acknowledged as an intra-constitutional principle and not as a supra-constitutional principle; therefore, EU Law acquires, similarly to the doctrine of necessity, constitutional status and cannot be invalidated due to the existence of contrary constitutional provisions.[57]

35. Apart from the Constitution and the Laws made under the Constitution, all the Laws which were in force prior to independence continue to be in force until amended or repealed, as the case may be; such Laws are construed and applied with any such modifications which are necessary to bring them into conformity with the Constitution.[58] Furthermore, the principles of common law and equity apply in the Republic of Cyprus. Previous judgments of the Supreme Court are binding on lower courts; thus, case law is of great significance with regard to the interpretation of legal provisions. The legal rule which must be applied is the *ratio decidendi* or the legal principle on which the previous decision was founded. The ratio of the case is distinguishable from obiter dicta, which are statements on principles of law made in the course of a decision but on which the decision does not depend. It is noted, however, that previous case law is only binding so far as a subsequent law with different content has not been enacted.

36. Under Article 169 §3 of the Constitution, treaties, conventions and agreements concluded by decision of the Council of Ministers and approved by a law enacted by the House of Representatives have superior force to any municipal law from the date of their publication in the official Gazette, on condition that such treaties, conventions and agreements are applied by the other party thereto; a condition of reciprocity is thus introduced.[59] While the condition of reciprocity cannot, in principle, be invoked in multilateral conventions, such conventions may be held to be self-executing and, thus, applicable, with superior force, in the domestic legal order of the Republic of Cyprus if their provisions create rights for the individuals and govern, and directly affect relations, of the internal life between the individuals,

(Athens: A. Sakkoulas, 2000, in Greek); A. Loizou, 'The Judicial Control of Unconstitutionality of Laws and Legality of Administrative Acts', *Cyprus Law Review* 27, 4161–4173 (1989) (in Greek).

57. *See* A. Emilianides, 'The Constitution of Cyprus after Accession', in *Policy Proposals after the Accession of Cyprus in the EU* 110–118 (A. Emilianides ed., Nicosia: Power Publishing, 2005, in Greek); S. Papasavvas, 'The Constitutional Aspects of the Accession of the Republic of Cyprus in the European Union', *Hellenic Review of Community Law* 22, 81–91 (2002) (in Greek); E. Nikolaou, 'The Accession to the European Union and the Constitutional Order of Cyprus', *Hellenic Review of Community Law* 19, 23–33 (1999) (in Greek); E. Venizelos, 'The Cyprus Problem, the Cypriot Constitutional Order and the Potential Accession in the European Union', *Hellenic Review of Community Law* 20, 287–306 (2000) (in Greek); C. Patsalides, 'Accommodating the Principle of Supremacy of Community Law to the Cypriot Legal Order: The Necessity for a Constitutional Amendment', *European Public Law* 12, 363–370 (2006).

58. *Christodoulou v. The Republic* 1 RSCC 1.

59. *See also* C. Tornaritis, 'The Introduction of International Law into the Legal System of Cyprus', *Cyprus Law Tribune* 3, 460–474 (1990).

or the individuals and the public authorities. There is no doubt that the ECHR is self-executing. In the case of *Malachtou*, it was held that:

> It would be incomprehensible for a State not to secure the rights and freedoms defined in section 1 of the Convention of Human Rights on the ground that another party to the Convention violates the Convention even against a national of the first State.[60]

37. The legal system of the Republic of Cyprus is characterized as a mixed legal system,[61] albeit a unique mixed legal system where common law mostly dominates in the field of private law, whereas continental law dominates in the field of public law. The fundamental norms of the system generally adhere to the common law tradition;[62] English cases may, therefore, be cited in Cypriot courts and are often used as guidelines where there is no relevant Cypriot case. However, Article 146 of the Constitution introduced into the Cypriot legal system a system of administrative law compatible with the continental law tradition.[63] The administrative jurisdiction exercised by the Supreme Court derives its principles from the French Conseil d' Etat rather than from any common law principle. Greek Law books are often cited in administrative law cases, as well as in other areas of law, such as family law.[64] Furthermore, the Supreme Court used to draw on the principles arising out of the judicial precedents of the Supreme Court of the United States with respect to constitutional law. Having a substantially codified legal system, Cyprus applies common law principles so far as existing Cypriot legislation is not contradicted.[65]

IV. Economy

38. The constitution does not specify a particular economic system. However, certain basic decisions by the framers of the constitution provide for a set of conditions that have to be met while structuring the economic system. Among them are the freedom of property, the freedom of occupation or profession, the right to enter into a contract and the right to form associations; it is further provided that a person

60. *Malachtou v. Armefti* [1987] 1 CLR 207.
61. A. Emilianides, 'Cyprus: Everything Changes and Nothing Remains Still', in *A Study of Mixed Legal Systems: Endangered, Entrenched or Blended* 215–240 (S. Farran et al. eds, Aldershot: Ashgate 2014); S. Symeonides, 'The Mixed Legal System of the Republic of Cyprus', *Tulane Law Review* 78, 441 (2003); N Hatzimichail, 'Cyprus as a Mixed Legal System', *Journal of Civil Law Studies* 3, 38 (2013).
62. *See* G. Pikis, *English Common Law, Equity and Their Application in Cyprus* (Larnaca: 1981, in Greek); L. Loucaides (ed.), 'The Dependence of Cypriot Law to English Common Law', in Topics *of Cypriot Law* 36–77 (Nicosia: 1982).
63. *See* S. Papasavvas, 'The Osmosis of Continental Public Law and Common Law in Cyprus', *The Constitution* 28, 693–706 (2002) (in Greek).
64. *See* C. Tornaritis, 'Influence of Greek Law on Contemporary Cypriot Institutions', in *Proceedings of the First International Cyprological Conference*, Vol. III, 385–393 (Nicosia: Society for Cypriot Studies, 1973).
65. C. Artemides, 'The Principle of Commitment of Courts to Case-Law in English Common Law', in *Aspects of Cypriot Law*, Vol. I, 219–231 (Nicosia: Asselia, 1981, in Greek).

is bound to contribute towards the public burdens according to his/her means. The right to strike is also constitutionally safeguarded. The Cypriot economy is, in general, based on the free market system, with the private sector being the backbone of economic activity. The Government's role is limited to safeguarding a transparent framework for the operation of market mechanisms, the exercise of indicative planning and the provision of public utilities.

39. Although the blow inflicted on the economy by the Turkish invasion of 1974 was devastating, considering the occupied part at that time accounted for almost 70% of the Gross Domestic Product (GDP), recovery was remarkable. The decline in the volume of production experienced during 1974 was quickly reversed, and by 1977, this surpassed its pre-1974 level. Business confidence returned and was followed by a sharp upturn in investments. By 1979, conditions of full employment had been restored. The rate of unemployment, which approached 30% of the economically active population during the second half of 1974, had been virtually eliminated (1.8%), and the displaced persons were relocated temporarily, pending return to their homes.

40. In the post-1974 period, Cyprus has converted from an exporter of agricultural products and minerals into a services-oriented economy, with tourism and the provision of services being the main pillars of economic growth. International trade is of considerable importance to the economy of Cyprus; Cyprus has been sought after as a base for several *offshore* companies for its highly developed infrastructure, as well as for the tax incentives it offers. On the production side, the lack of raw materials, energy resources and heavy industry for the production of capital goods necessitates the import of such inputs. On the demand side, due to the small size of the domestic market, exports are vital in supplementing the aggregate demand for Cypriot agricultural and manufactured products and services. The main economic partners of Cyprus are the EU member countries, the neighbouring Middle-Eastern countries and the countries of Central and Eastern Europe.

41. Since its accession to the EU, Cyprus has undergone significant economic and structural reforms, which have transformed its economic landscape; tariffs and quantitative restrictions have been eliminated for all manufactured goods and agricultural products originating in EU countries. Trade and interest rates have also been liberated, while price controls and investment restrictions have, as a principle, been lifted. Private financing has been introduced for the construction and operation of infrastructural projects, while the state monopoly in the telecommunications sector has been abolished. EU Law provisions concerning competition and public procurement now form part of Cypriot internal Law, with superior force. As of 1 January 2008, Cyprus has adopted the euro as a national currency. Following a financial collapse in early 2013,[66] Cyprus agreed to a Eurogroup agreement for the recapitalization of the Cypriot banking sector by forcing the depositors in the two major Cypriot banks to bail in. A Memorandum of Understanding (MoU) was signed with

66. C. Ioannou & A. Emilianides, 'How the Cypriot Crisis Came to Be: The Real Causes and Responsibility', *Foreign Affairs: The Hellenic Edition*, 12, 41–51 (2013) (in Greek).

Troika[67] in order to loan the Cypriot economy; the agreement introduced a series of austerity measures on the island. Structural adjustments included public spending cuts and tax increases, reform of the system of distribution of public benefits, as well as a privatization scheme for profitable semi-governmental organizations. Improvement in the financial situation led to the completion of the financial support programme and the eventual exit from the MoU in 2016.[68]

V. Politics

42. The two largest political parties in Cyprus are the communist-oriented Progressive Party of Working People (AKEL), which is a member of the European United Left in the European Parliament and the right-wing Democratic Rally (DISY), which is a member of the European People's Party (EPP); DISY has seventeen seats in the House of Representatives and represents approximately 28% of the voting population, whereas AKEL has fifteen seats and represents approximately 22%. The centrist Democratic Party (DIKO) has nine seats in the House of Representatives and represents approximately 11% of the voting population, while the socialist Movement for Social Democracy (EDEK), the centrist Democratic Alignment (DIPA) and the far-right-wing National People's Front (ELAM) each secured four seats in the House of Representatives and represented approximately 6%–7% of the voting population. The Ecological Movement secured three seats and approximately 4% of the voting population[69] Most of the political debate in Cyprus used to revolve around the Cyprus Problem and attempts for its solution; thus, social, economic or cultural issues regularly received less attention when compared to this. Following the recent prolonged financial crisis, however, economic and social issues came to the forefront of public debate.

43. Current President Nicos Christodoulides was elected as President of the Republic after receiving 51.97% of the votes in the second round of the 2023 Presidential Elections, surpassing the candidate of AKEL, Andreas Mavroyiannis.

---

67. The tripartite committee composed by the European Commission, the European Central Bank and the International Monetary Fund. For the bail-in decision, *see* A. Emilianides & C. Ioannou, 'A Financial Crisis as Limitation to a Fundamental Right to Protection of Deposits under European Union Law', in *Staat – Religion – Recht. Festschrift für Gerhard Robbers* 937–954 (K. von der Decken & A. Günzel eds, Baden-Baden: Nomos 2020); C. Ioannou & A. Emilianides, 'The Haircut of Cypriot Deposits and the Protection of Fundamental Rights', *Cyprus Human Rights Law Review* 2, 141–166 (2013); C. Ioannou & A. Emilianides, 'Cyprus and EU following the Haircut of Deposits', in *Cyprus in a New Era: Geostrategy, Economy, Foreign Policy* 124–153 (C. Ioannou, D. Sotiropoulos & A. Emilianides eds, Nicosia: Foreign Affairs: Hellenic Edition and Hippasus, 2014, in Greek).
68. *See also* O. Christou & C. Ioannou, 'The Restructuring of the Cypriot Welfare System', in *Routledge Handbook of European Welfare Systems* 73–90 (S. Blum et al. eds, London: Routledge 2nd ed. 2020).
69. For a development of political parties in Cyprus *see* S. Zavou, *The Political Parties of Cyprus in the 20th Century* (Nicosia: Epifaniou 2nd ed. 2011, in Greek). For the legal framework *see* D. Melissas, *Political Parties in the Republic of Cyprus: The Development towards Institutionalisation* (Athens: A. Sakkoulas 1996, in Greek).

Christodoulides was officially supported by DIKO, EDEK and DIPA but is not supported by either of the two largest parliamentary parties, i.e., DISY and AKEL. Although Christodoulides, a former Minister of Foreign Affairs in the right-wing Anastasiades Government, used to be a member of DISY prior to announcing his candidacy, he was not supported by his own party, which supported its President Averof Neofytou; when Neofytou failed to proceed to the second round of elections, DISY declined to support either Christodoulides or Mavroyiannis. With regards to economic issues, Christodoulides is, in general, a proponent of liberalization and free market policies and considers himself as ideologically belonging to the EPP.

§2. Social Facts about Religion

I. Population and Religion

44. According to the official census of 1960, the population of Cyprus was 573,666, out of whom 441,656 (77.0%) were of Greek origin and adhered to the Orthodox Christian religion, while 104,492 (18.3%) were of Turkish origin and adhered to the Islamic religion. Further, 3,378 (0.6%) were Armenians, 4,505 (0.8%) were Roman Catholics, and 2,572 (0.5%) were Maronites, while 16,333 (2.8%) belonged to other ethnic groups and were mainly British. The percentage analogies of the population had not been materially affected prior to the Turkish invasion. In 1973, it was estimated that the population of Cyprus reached 631,778 inhabitants. Out of these, 498,511 (78.9%) belonged to the Greek Community, including the Armenians, the Maronites, and the Roman Catholics, 116,000 (18.4%) belonged to the Turkish Community, while 17,267 (2.7%) were foreigners.

45. Since the Turkish invasion, providing precise figures with respect to the population of Cyprus has presented certain difficulties due to the abnormal situation prevailing on the island. The Statistical Service of the Republic of Cyprus has estimated, however, that by the end of 2006, the population of Cyprus was 867,600, out of which 660,600 (76.1%) belonged to the Greek Community, while 88,900 (10.2%) belonged to the Turkish Community. The remaining 118,100 (13.7%) were foreign residents.[70] According to the 2011 official census, the population of Cyprus was 840,407, out of whom 667,398 (79.41%) were Cypriots, 106,270 (12.64%) were European citizens, and 64,113 (7.62%) were third-country nationals (the majority being Asian or Russian nationals).[71] Out of the members of the Greek Community, 2,700 (0.4%) were Armenians, 4,800 (0.6%) were Maronites, and 900 (0.1%) were Roman Catholics. With the exception of a few agnostics, atheists or naturalized citizens, members of Greek origin normally adhere to the Greek Orthodox religion. In view of the fact that many non-Cypriots, such as mainland Greeks, Russians, Romanians and Bulgarians, also adhere to the Orthodox Christian religion, it is estimated that approximately 82% of the total current population of

70. *Source*: Statistical Service of the Republic of Cyprus.
71. The remaining 0.33% were unidentified. Source: Statistical Service of the Republic of Cyprus.

Cyprus are Orthodox Christians. It is further estimated that the number of Roman Catholics residing in Cyprus, if foreigners are also included, is approximately 2%. An official census was also carried out in 2021, but only preliminary results have so far been released; the population seems to have increased to 923,272.

46. The actual number of Turkish Cypriots residing in Cyprus is difficult to estimate with precision. After the Turkish invasion of 1974, there has been an effort by Turkey to change the demographic character of the occupied Northern Cyprus through the implantation of settlers. The indigenous population of the island (Greek and Turkish Cypriots) has always insisted that the possible legalization of the Turkish settlers would not only illegally modify the demographic structure of the island and constitute a constant source of tension but would further threaten the stability and security of the Republic.[72] This view was also adopted by the Council of Europe.[73] It is estimated that 57,000 Turkish Cypriots have emigrated from Cyprus following the invasion of 1974. The number of settlers currently residing in Cyprus is not known. It is estimated, however, that more than 100,000 settlers from mainland Turkey are currently residing in the occupied areas. Illegal settlers are not included in any estimation of the current population of Cyprus. While the Statistical Service of the Republic of Cyprus estimates that the number of Turkish Cypriots currently residing in the occupied areas reaches approximately 88,900, it is suggested that the actual number might be closer to 130,000, as estimated by Turkish Cypriot sources. Turkish Cypriot representatives increase the number to 220,000. Therefore, it is estimated that approximately 12% of the current total population of the Republic, excluding the Turkish settlers, are Turkish Cypriots.

47. In view of the above, it is estimated that approximately 82% of the total population of Cyprus are Orthodox Christians, 13% are Muslims, 2% are Roman Catholics, 1% are Anglicans, 0.6% are Maronites, 0.4% are Armenians, while the remaining population adheres to other religions, or rites, and are mainly Jews, Buddhists, Protestants, Jehovah's Witnesses, or atheists. It is further estimated that approximately 2,000 Cypriots are Orthodox Christians who follow the Old Calendar.

II. Societal Place of Religion

A. *General Overview*

48. According to Eurobarometer 2010, Cyprus was one of the most religious countries in the EU, with 88% of Cypriots declaring that they believe in God and

72. L. Loucaides (ed.), 'Expulsion of Settlers from Occupied Territories: The Case of Turkish Settlers', in *Essays on the Developing Law of Human Rights* 108–138 (Dordrecht: Martinus Nijhoff, 1995); A. De Zayas, 'The Annan Plan and the Implantation of Turkish Settlers in Northern Cyprus', *Cyprus Yearbook of International Relations* 163 ff. (2006); M. Stavrinos, *Settlements as a Crime in International Law* (Parga: 2013, in Greek).
73. Council of Europe, 2 May 2003, Doc. 9799, *Colonisation by Turkish Settlers of the Occupied Part of Cyprus* (Rapporteur Mr Laakso).

8% declaring that they believe there is some sort of spirit or life force. Similarly, the 1998 International Society Survey Program survey suggested that Cypriots show confidence in the Church and religious organizations. From the data of the aforementioned survey, it is observed that while there are small minorities of atheists and agnostics, the great majority of the population declares that they believe, and have always believed, in God. No indication of strong shifts in religiosity during the lives of Cypriots was revealed during the survey. While the overwhelming majority of Cypriots felt that religious leaders should not attempt to influence government decision-making, they also rejected the view that Cyprus would be in a better position if religion was any less influential.[74] Although the 1998 study is now dated, recent surveys, including recent Eurobarometer surveys, have effectively confirmed the small number of people self-identifying as either atheists or agnostics in Cyprus; it would seem, however, that the number of atheists and/or agnostic is gradually increasing, although remaining relatively small.

49. Religion undeniably has a central place in Cypriot society. While Cypriots, either Orthodox or Muslims, or belonging to smaller religions or denominations, cannot be considered religious fanatics in any sense of the term, they pray on a regular basis, and they consider their religious beliefs as an essential part of their identity. Many Cypriots attend religious services regularly or confess their sins to religious ministers. However, the number of Cypriots regularly participating in church activities other than attending religious services is low. Fasting is an essential aspect of the identity of a significant number of Greek Cypriots; in general, fast days for Orthodox Christians are all Wednesdays and Fridays throughout the year (with the exception of fast-free periods), the Nativity Fast (which is the forty days preceding Christmas), the Great Lent (which consists of the fifty days preceding Easter), the Dormition Fast (which consists of a two week period preceding the Dormition of Theotokos, namely the repose of the Virgin Mary), as well as certain special days. During fasting, foods like meat, dairy products, eggs, or even fish, oil and alcohol should be avoided; indeed, Cypriot restaurants, including fast food, often offer meals suitable for Christians who fast. Christians who are preparing to receive the Eucharist do not eat or drink at all from midnight until after receiving the Holy Communion.

B. *The Orthodox Church of Cyprus and Its Position Within the Orthodox Church in General*

50. The Orthodox Church is a Communion comprising the separate autocephalous hierarchical churches which recognize each other as Canonical Orthodox Christian churches. The various autocephalous churches are in full communion with each other so that any priest of those churches may lawfully minister in any of them; each national or local Orthodox Church is, thus, considered to be only a part of the Orthodox Church. There is no single earthly head of all the Orthodox Churches in a manner comparable to the Pope of Rome; however, the highest-ranking Bishop of

74. *Source*: International Social Society Program: Religion II, 1998.

the Eastern Orthodox Church is the Patriarch of Constantinople. The term 'Orthodox' is a Greek word which means 'correctly believing' and was adopted by the Orthodox Church in order to distinguish itself from other denominations. Depending on the mode of its administration, an Orthodox Church may be autocephalous or autonomous. A church is autocephalous when it is spiritually self-sufficient and independent in administration. It is autonomous when it is only independent in administration.

51. At present, the following are autocephalous: the Ecumenical Patriarchate of Constantinople and the Patriarchates of Alexandria, Antioch, Jerusalem, Russia, Serbia, Romania, Bulgaria, and Georgia, together with the Archbishoprics of Cyprus, Greece, Poland, Albania, the Czech Republic, and Slovakia. The Orthodox Churches of Finland and Estonia are autonomous. Autocephalous churches are independent as regards their administration, but within a dogmatic and Canonical framework, deviation from it can lead to heresy or schism. This framework constitutes the spiritual unity of Orthodoxy, which is treated under the headings of dogmatic and Canonical unity. Dogmatic unity consists of following the teachings of the Holy Scripture, respecting tradition, and strict observance of the dogma as defined by the Ecumenical Councils and the local Synods. Canonical unity consists in the observance of at least the most important institutions of Church administration, which were also defined and acknowledged by the same Councils and Synods, as well as through the relations between Orthodox Churches.[75]

52. The Orthodox Church of Cyprus had ranked, until 1593, fifth in order of seniority among the various Orthodox Churches, below the four ancient patriarchates of Constantinople (Ecumenical Patriarchate), Alexandria, Antioch and Jerusalem. From the Orthodox point of view, there would have been five ancient patriarchates had the patriarchate of Rome, which had been first in place of honour among the five patriarchates, not broken off during the Great Schism of 1054, which split the Church into the (Western) Roman Catholic Church headed by the Pope, and the (Eastern) Orthodox Church led by the four eastern patriarchs. Currently, however, the Orthodox Church of Cyprus ranks tenth in order of seniority due to the fact that the younger Churches of Russia, Serbia, Romania, Bulgaria and Georgia have been elevated to patriarchates. The Orthodox Church of Cyprus is thus the only ancient Orthodox Church which is not a patriarchate.[76] The Orthodox Church of Ukraine has recently been recognized by the Patriarchates of Constantinople and

---

75. *See* G. Papathomas, *L' Église Autocéphale de Chypre dans l' Europe Unie, Approche Nomocanonique* (Katerini: Epektasis, 1998); E. Mantzouneas, *Ecclesiastical Law of the Apostolic, Autocephalous Orthodox Church of Cyprus* (Evrichou: 1988, in Greek); C. Pitsakis, 'La Tradition du Droit Canonique de l' Èglise d' Orient dans l' Ordre Juridique Chypriote: Histoire et Survivances Contemporaines', *Yearbook of the Centre of Research of the History of Greek Law* 38, 151–180 (2004).

76. *See* V. Tzortzatos, *The Autocephalous of the Church of Cyprus* (Athens: 1976, in Greek); I. Papaioannou, 'The Autocephalous of the Church of Cyprus', *Orthodoxy* 23, 69–73 (1948), at 134–142 (in Greek); H. Alivisatos, 'The Autocephalous of the Church of Cyprus in Case of Union of Cyprus with Greece', in *Proceedings of the First International Cyprological Conference*, Vol. III, 27–28 (Nicosia: Society for Cypriot Studies, 1973), (in Greek); A. Mitsides, *The Autocephalous of the Church of Cyprus* (Athens: 1976, in Greek).

Alexandria and the Churches of Cyprus and Greece, causing a serious rift with Moscow. The Holy Synod of the Church of Cyprus decided to recognize the Church of Ukraine on 25 November 2020, pursuant to the insistence of then Archbishop Chrysostomos II; the decision was taken by a majority vote of 10-7. The decision caused an internal disharmony between the Archbishop and influential members of the Holy Synod, such as the Metropolitan of Limassol and the Bishop of Kykkos;[77] however, following the Russian invasion of Ukraine and the election of a new Archbishop, unity seems to have prevailed once again with the decision to recognize the Church of Ukraine enjoying steady support from the Holy Synod.

C. The Islamic Tradition of Turkish Cypriots

53. Most Turkish Cypriots favour a secular state despite the fact that they are Muslims, which shows the strong influence of Kemalism in Turkish Cypriot religious affairs. Turkish Cypriots, like most Turkish nationals, are followers of Sunni Islam. The Sunnis (from *sunnah*, tradition) argued that Muhammad had prescribed no definitive procedure for choosing his successors, unlike the Shias (from Shiat Ali, party of Ali), who insisted that his designation of his cousin and son-in-law Ali established a hereditary succession. Sunnis consider the Quran and the *hadith*, a separate collection of the sayings and deeds of Muhammad, to be a complete, comprehensive, and eternally correct source of religious guidance, requiring only deductive elaboration by scholars. Within Sunni Islam, Turkish Cypriots have traditionally followed the Hanafi school of legal interpretation, a rather austere variety of Islam.

54. Turkish Cypriots were among the first to adopt Atatürk's prohibition of Arabic in religious services and to use the Quran in Turkish translation. Since Atatürk's death, Turkish Cypriots have generally followed the religious practices of Turkey. When, in 1951, the Turkish authorities once again allowed the use of the Quran in Arabic and directed that the call to prayers also be in Arabic, the Turkish Cypriots followed. Although there was some fasting during the month of Ramadan, moderate attendance at the Friday prayers and widespread observation of the holy days, few Turkish Cypriots were orthodox Muslims. Most of those who fasted during Ramadan lived an unorthodox life the rest of the year, and Turkish Cypriots did not generally abstain from alcohol as standard Muslim teaching requires but followed traditional Mediterranean drinking customs. In addition, it should be observed that while religious instruction was available in schools, it was not obligatory for Turkish Muslims.[78]

---

77. Nikiforos Bishop of Kykkos, *The Modern Ukrainian Question and its Solution pursuant to the Holy and Spiritual Canons* (Nicosia: Holy Monastery of Kykkos Research Centre, 2020, in Greek).
78. *See* further A. Emilianides, *Annotated Legal Documents on Islam in Cyprus* (Leiden: Brill, 2014); A. Emilianides, 'Islamic Faith as One of the Main Religions: The Case of Cyprus', in M. Moravcikova (ed.), *Islam in Europe* 220–228 (Bratislava: Institute for State-Church Relations, 2005); F. Dassetto, S. Ferrari & B. Maréchal, *Islam in the European Union: What's at Stake in the Future* 93 ff. (Brussels: European Parliament, 2007).

§3. Historical Background

I. Prior to the British Rule

A. Antiquity

55. The history of Cyprus begins with the early Neolithic period, dating back to the 8th or even 10th millennium BC.[79] The Achaean-Mycenaean Greeks arrived on the island at around 1600 BC, and the Achaean civilization was introduced into Cyprus. Greek extensive colonization continued in subsequent years, and by 1000 BC, the island had adopted the Greek city-state system of government, as well as the Greek civilization, culture and way of living. Each city had its own King, who held both secular and religious power, although the people gradually became involved through their assembly. The Mycenaean influence is particularly evident from a rich collection of archaeological findings. The island's predominantly Greek character, therefore, dates from that period.

56. Cyprus was then conquered successively by Assyria in the eighteenth Century BC, then briefly by Egypt and eventually by Persia in 545 BC. During that period, the Greek element remained dominant on the island. Evagoras, King of Salamis, succeeded in uniting all the Kingdoms of Cyprus under his leadership during the revolt against the Persians but was defeated and forced to sign a treaty of submission to Persia. The island was once again brought under Greek rule by Alexander the Great. After Alexander's death, Cyprus came under the rule of the Ptolemies for about two and a half centuries until the island was annexed by Rome in 58 BC. Cyprus thus became a province of the Roman Empire.

B. Roman and Byzantine Era

57. During the early period of Roman rule, Christianity was introduced in Cyprus. On his first missionary journey in 45 AD, Paul, accompanied by Barnabas, a Cypriot, and Mark, landed in Cyprus and preached the new religion there. Arriving at Salamis, they travelled to Paphos, where Sergius Paulus, a Roman proconsul, became the first-ever Roman official to convert to Christianity. The Orthodox Church of Cyprus is, therefore, apostolic since it was founded by Apostle Barnabas, who is considered the Church's first Archbishop.[80] The conversion of Cypriots to Christianity had been completed by the beginning of the fifth century. With the exception of sporadic Arab invasions, Cyprus remained for more than eight and a half centuries, between 325 and 1191, a province of the Byzantine Empire. Thus,

---

79. For an extensive history of Cyprus *see*, *inter alia*, C. Kyrris, *History of Cyprus* (Nicosia: 1985); G. Hill, *A History of Cyprus*, Vols 1–4 (Cambridge: Cambridge University Press 1940–1952).
80. For a history of the Orthodox Church of Cyprus *see* J. Hackett, *A History of the Orthodox Church of Cyprus* (London: Methuen & Co. 1901); V. Egglezakis, *Twenty Studies on the Church of Cyprus* (Athens: Leventis Association, 1996, in Greek).

Christianity was the state religion of the island, similar to other parts of the Byzantine Empire; the ecclesiastical courts of the Orthodox Church applied Byzantine Law and had competencies over religious matters and matters of personal status, including family law matters.[81]

58. When Cyprus was politically attached to Antioch during the early years of Byzantine rule, an attempt was made by the Patriarch of Antioch to subject the Church of Cyprus to his control. However, such an attempt was resisted successfully by the Cypriot Bishops at the Third Ecumenical Synod of 431, which was held at Ephesus. The Eighth Canon of the Third Ecumenical Synod declared that the Church of Cyprus was autocephalous. The autocephalous status of the Church of Cyprus was later confirmed by an edict of the Byzantine Emperor Zeno, who rejected Antioch's claims and granted three imperial privileges to the Archbishop of Cyprus: namely, to hold a sceptre, instead of the regular episcopal crosier, to sign his name in cinnabar and to wear a purple mantle.

59. The Arab invasions of the seventh century forced the Archbishop of Cyprus to flee to Hellespont, where, under the protection of Emperor Justinian II, he established a new city called Nova Justiniana near the city of Cyzicus. The autocephalous status of the Church of Cyprus, as well as the status and privileges of the exiled Archbishop, were once again ratified by the Quini-Sext or Trullian Ecumenical Synod, which was held at Constantinople in 692 AD. When the Arabs were driven out of Cyprus in 698, the Archbishop returned, retaining the title of *Archbishop of Nova Justiniana and All Cyprus*, in addition to the three imperial privileges.

C. Frankish Rule

60. The period of Byzantine rule in Cyprus ended in 1191, when Cyprus came briefly under the rule of the then King of England and crusader, Richard the Lionheart, or Coeur de Lion, who immediately sold Cyprus to the Order of the Knights Templar for 40,000 gold Besants; the transaction was, however, short-lived, and it was cancelled in view of the Cypriot resistance. The island was once again sold, for the second time in the same year, to the King of Jerusalem, Guy de Lusignan, who was a French knight; this time, Richard received 100,000 gold Besants as consideration. The island remained under the rule of the Lusignans for nearly 300 years, from 1191 to 1489, which is considered to be the period of Frankish rule over Cyprus.

81. *See* C. Tornaritis, *The Ecclesiastical Courts Especially in Cyprus* 15 (Nicosia: 1976); D. Seremetis, 'The Administration of Justice in Cyprus During the Byzantine and Post-Byzantine Era', in *Proceedings of the First International Cyprological Conference*, Vol. III, 309 ff. (Nicosia: Society for Cypriot Studies, 1973), (in Greek).

61. During the period of Frankish rule, Roman Catholic (Latin) Christianity became the official religion of the island. However, the greater majority of the population still adhered to the Orthodox Christian religion and were Greeks. Pope Alexander IV issued the *Bulla*, or *Constitutio Cypria*, on 3 July 1260, according to which the then-existing fourteen Orthodox Metropolises were reduced to four so that their number and geographical limits would coincide with the respective Metropolises of the Roman Catholic Church. The legislation during the Lusignan period was the one contained in the Assizes of Cyprus, which were modelled after the Assizes of Jerusalem.[82] However, the ecclesiastical courts of the Greek Orthodox Church applied, with respect to the family affairs of members of the Orthodox Church, the so-called *Hellenic Laws* of Cyprus, which essentially consisted of a codification of Byzantine Law.[83] During the Venetian rule from 1489 to 1571, the Roman Catholic Church remained the dominant church of the island, and the Assizes continued to be the governing legislation.[84]

D. Ottoman Rule

62. The conquest of the island by the Ottomans in 1571 resulted in radical changes in the legal position of the different churches existing in Cyprus. The period of Ottoman rule lasted for more than 300 years, until 1878, and marked the first appearance of adherents of the Islamic faith in Cyprus. The Sheri (Sharia) Law, namely the interpretation of the Qurani Law, was not only the personal law of the Muslims of Cyprus but also the state law, thus replacing the law of the Assizes, which had been the state law during the period of Frankish and Venetian rule. The Sheri Law was applied by the Sheri courts, which were the competent courts for the legal affairs of all people living on the island, irrespective of their religion.[85]

---

82. *See* N. Coureas, *The Assizes of the Lusignan Kingdom of Cyprus* (Nicosia: Cyprus Research Centre, 2002); P. Zepos, 'The Law of Cyprus During Frankish Rule', *Yearbook of the Centre of Research of the History of Greek Law* 23, 123–141 (1976) (in Greek); A. Emilianides, 'Polyarchy in the Frankish Rule of Cyprus', in *Mélanges à la Memoire de Michel Dendias* 7–13 (Athénes & Paris: 1978); T. Papadopoulos (ed.), 'Cypriot Legal', in *Studies*, Vol. I, 1–142 (Nicosia: Foundation of Archbishop Makarios III, 1984) (in Greek).
83. A. Emilianides, 'The Hellenic Laws of Cyprus During Frankish Rule', *Yearbook of the Cyprus Research Centre* 25, 51–74 (2004) (in Greek); A. Emilianides, 'The Hellenic Laws of Cyprus and the Hexabiblos of Armenopoulos', *Yearbook of the Faculty of Law of the Aristotle University of Thessaloniki* 33–38 (1951); D. Simon, *Zyprische Prozessprogramme* (München: Beck, 1973); J. Maruhn, 'Eine Zyprische Fassung Eherechtlicher Titel der Epitome', *Forschungen zur Byzantinischen Rechtsgeschichte* 218–255 (Fontes Minores, IV, 1981).
84. A. Aristeidou, 'Assizes in Cyprus During the Venetian Rule', *Yearbook of the Cyprus Research Centre* 22, 95–101 (2001).
85. M. Zekia, 'A Short Historical Survey of the Laws Administered by the Ottoman Civil and Criminal Courts and of the Constitution of Such Courts during the Ottoman Era in Cyprus during 1571–1878', in *Proceedings of the First International Cyprological Conference*, Vol. III, 457–464 (Nicosia: Society for Cypriot Studies, 1973); V. Bedevi, 'A Survey of the Cyprus Sheri Courts Registers', in *Proceedings of the First International Cyprological Conference*, Vol. III, 29–36 (Nicosia: Society for Cypriot Studies, 1973); H. Inalcik, 'Ottoman Policy and Administration in Cyprus After the Conquest', in *Proceedings of the First International Cyprological Conference*, Vol. III, 119–136 (Nicosia: Society for Cypriot Studies, 1973).

63. The only exception to the exclusive competence of the Sheri courts was the law of personal status and family relations of members of the Orthodox Church. The ecclesiastical courts of the Orthodox Church continued to be the only competent courts with regard to the family relations of their members and continued to apply Byzantine Law. During that period, the Orthodox Church was considered to play the primary role in the preservation of faith, national identity and traditions of the Greek Cypriots.[86] The Roman Catholic Church was virtually abolished, while the members of the said Church were obliged to either present themselves as Orthodox in order to avoid forced conversion to Islam or even to behave in the open as Muslims while secretly retaining their Roman Catholic faith.[87]

64. The right of all Christian Communities to administer their religious and family affairs was eventually recognized following the Tanzimat reform of the Ottoman Imperial rescript, Hatt-i-Humayun, of 18 February 1856.[88] The Hatt-i-Humayun also applied in Cyprus.[89] The Hatt-i-Humayun granted spiritual advantages and exemptions, as well as a form of religious autonomy to the various Christian and non-Muslim religious communities living within the boundaries of the Ottoman Empire. As a result, the Maronites and the Roman Catholics gradually referred their family law disputes to their ecclesiastical courts in Lebanon and Jerusalem, respectively, while the National Constitution of the Armenians was confirmed by a *firman* of the Sultan of the Ottoman Empire.[90]

II. The British Rule

A. The Political Framework

65. The Ottoman Empire assigned the rights of possession and administration of Cyprus over to Great Britain by signing the Convention of Defence Alliance on 4

---

86. *See* T. Papadopoulos, *The History of the Greek Church and People under Turkish Domination* (Variorum: Aldershot 2nd ed. 1990); H. Luke, *Cyprus under the Turks 1571–1878: A Record Based on the Archives of the English Consulate in Cyprus* (London: Oxford University Press, 1921); M. Michael, *The Church of Cyprus During the Ottoman Era* (Nicosia: Cyprus Research Centre, 2005); H. Alasya, 'The Privileges Granted to the Orthodox Church of Cyprus by the Ottoman Empire', in *Proceedings of the First International Cyprological Conference*, Vol. III, 23–26 (Nicosia: Society for Cypriot Studies, 1973); N. Pantazopoulos, *Mythical and Pragmatical Elements in the Concept of Islamic Privileges to the Christians* (Athens: 1970); G. Dionyssiou, 'Some Privileges of the Church of Cyprus under Ottoman Rule', *Yearbook of the Cyprus Research Centre* 19, 327–334 (1992).
87. A. Emilianides, *The Evolution of the Law of the Mixed Marriages in Cyprus since the Frankish Rule* (Nicosia: 1938, in Greek); F. Zanettos, *A History of the Island of Cyprus from British Conquest until Today*, Vol. I, 1035 (Larnaca: 1910, in Greek).
88. G. Dionyssiou, 'The Ottoman Administration of Cyprus and the Tanzimat Reforms', *Yearbook of the Cyprus Research Centre* 20, 361–366 (1994); G. Young, *Corps de Droit Ottoman*, Vol. II, 22ff. (Oxford: 1905); D. Nicolaides, *Ottoman Codes*, Vol. III, 2858–2866 (Constantinople: 3rd ed. 1890), (in Greek).
89. *Parapano and Others v. Happaz* (1893) 3 CLR 69; *Tano v. Tano* (1910) 9 CLR 94. *See also* the observations of G. Serghides, *Internal and External Conflict of Laws in Regard to Family Relations in Cyprus* 32 ff. (Nicosia: 1988).
90. C. Tornaritis (ed.), 'The Legal Position of the Armenian Religious Group', in *Constitutional and Legal Problems of the Republic of Cyprus* (Nicosia: 2nd ed. 1972); Case 172/32 *Takvorian v. Nassibian and Others* (District Court of Nicosia).

June 1878 in Constantinople.[91] With the signing of the Treaty of 1878, the period of British rule in Cyprus officially began. Great Britain was granted the power to enact laws and conventions for the island of Cyprus and to regulate its commercial and consular relations and affairs. An Annex to the Treaty of 1878 provided that such Treaty would be terminated and Cyprus would be restored to the Ottoman Empire, so long as Russia restored Kars, Ardahan and Vatoum to the Ottoman Empire. Thus, while by law Cyprus still theoretically belonged to the Ottoman Empire and could eventually be returned upon the fulfilment of certain conditions, in effect, the real and only sovereign of Cyprus was Great Britain, which exercised the administration of the island.[92]

66. The Anglo-Turkish Mixed Arbitral Tribunal held that the position of Cyprus during that period was analogous to that of a protectorate in the sense that it fell within the designation of a country under the protection of Great Britain, which in fact governed the island.[93] This peculiar situation ceased in 1914, when, immediately after the outbreak of the First World War, Great Britain annexed Cyprus by an Order in the Council of 5 November 1914.[94] While it could be argued that such unilateral annexation was invalid, it was eventually recognized by Turkey in 1923 by Article 20 of the Treaty of Lausanne. By Article 16 of the Treaty of Lausanne, Turkey renounced all rights and titles whatsoever over Cyprus. The island was proclaimed a Crown Colony on 10 March 1925.[95]

67. The administration of Cyprus by Great Britain was a colonial one, without the genuine involvement of the native population. The objective of the colonial administration was to equalize the influence of the votes of the Greek Cypriots in the Legislative Council, who were the majority of the population, with the combined votes of the British officials and the Turkish Cypriots. The colonial Government further had the right not to enforce any decision.[96] Eventually, the Legislative Council was itself abolished as a response to the disturbances of 1931, which culminated in the burning down of the Government House in Nicosia; the demonstrations were the culmination of the disappointment felt by Greek Cypriots towards the

---

91. *See* G. Georgallides, *A Political and Administrative History of Cyprus 1918–1926 with a Survey of the Foundations of the British Rule* 3 ff. (Nicosia: Cyprus Research Centre, 1979); L. Dwight, *Great Britain and the Cyprus Convention Policy of 1878* (Cambridge: Harvard Historical Studies, 1934).
92. G. Tenekides, 'La Condition Internationale de la République de Chypre', *Annuaire Francais de Droit International* 6, 133ff. (1960); M. Dendias, 'L' ile de Chypre dans le Droit International', *Revue de Droit International* 130ff. (1933).
93. *Parounak & Bedros Parounakian v. The Turkish Government*, Annual Digest 1929–1930, Case no. 11.
94. Cyprus Annexation Order in Council of 5 μ i 1914 in J. Howarth & C. Gerahty, *Statute Laws of Cyprus*, Vol. II, 184 (London: 1923); C. Orr, *Cyprus under British Rule* 175 (London: Robert Scott, 1918).
95. Cyprus Gazette 1 May 1925, Notification No. 266.
96. *See* A. Emilianides, 'Justice and Human Rights During British Rule in Cyprus', *Cyprus Law Tribune* 3, 66–96 (2006) (in Greek); S. Symeonides, 'Introduction to Cypriot Law', in *Comparative Law* 375 ff. (F. Frantzeskakis, D. Evrigenis & S. Symeonides eds, Thessaloniki: Sakkoulas, 1978, in Greek). *See also* C. Kyriakides, *The Cypriot Legislative Council (1878–1937). Establishment, Function and Parliamentary Debates. Constitutional Liberties under Restriction and Doubt* (Nicosia: House of Representatives, 2016, in Greek).

colonial Government for what they considered to be a series of arbitrary decisions, as well as the rejection of their plea for Union of the island with Greece.[97] Britain reacted with a degree of military force and administrative repression that combined to sow the seeds of the 1955 liberation struggle.

B. The Legal Status of Christian Religions

68. With respect to religion, Great Britain maintained the existing state of affairs,[98] with the sole exception that the Islamic faith was no longer the prevailing religion. Essentially, the system could be characterized as post-Millet in the sense that the right of all religious communities, either Muslim or non-Muslim, to administer their religious and family affairs without any state intervention was recognized. The system of State-Church relations prevailing in Cyprus was, thus, one of loose separation.[99] This view is indirectly supported by the Supreme Court of Cyprus' judgment in the case of *Stratoura*, where it was held that 'the Orthodox Greek Church is not in any way a State Church in Cyprus nor is it regulated so far as regards matters such as marriage by State laws'.[100]

69. The Orthodox Church maintained its competencies with respect to its internal affairs, including the election of Bishops and the administration of the Church's property.[101] However, following the disturbances of 1931, the Metropolitans of Kition and Kyrenia were deported from the island by the colonial Government, while in 1937, three laws were enacted, which were considered as an intrusion into the Church's autonomy and rights. The enactment of such Laws amounted to a British attempt to restrict the role of the Orthodox Church, which constituted not only the ministering religious organization of the Orthodox Christians of the island but also the nation-leading political coalition of the Greeks under foreign sovereignty.

70. Law 25/1937 provided for the investigation of the affairs and the auditing of the accounts of the churches and monasteries, while Law 33/1937 disqualified anyone who had been deported or had been convicted of sedition or any offence punishable with imprisonment or penal servitude for more than two years, or was not

---

97. *See* P. Stylianou, *The Movement of October of 1931 in Cyprus* (Nicosia: 1984, in Greek); V. Livadas, G. Spanos & P. Papapolyviou, *The Insurrection of October 1931* (Nicosia: 2004, in Greek); G. Georgallides, 'Church and State in Cyprus October 1931 to November 1932: A Systematic Humiliation of the Autocephalous Church of Cyprus', *Yearbook of the Cyprus Research Centre* 19, 361–448 (1992).
98. A. Emilianides, 'Private International Law', in *Symposium on Cypriot Juridical Issues* 90 (Thessaloniki: 1974), (in Greek).
99. C. Papastathis, *On the Administrative Organisation of the Church of Cyprus* 31 (Thessaloniki: 1981, in Greek); K. Chrysostomides, 'Cyprus Ecclesiastical Law', in *Tribute to the Parish of Agion Panton of London* 130 (London: 1968), (in Greek).
100. *Stratoura v. Yakoumi* (1905) 6 CLR, 91.
101. A. Gavrielides, *The Ethnarchic Rights and the Referendum for Union with Greece* 92 (Nicosia: 2nd ed. 1972), (in Greek); C. Tornaritis, 'The Relations Between Church and State According to Cypriot Law', *Review of Public and Private Law* 1, 11 (1967), (in Greek).

a native of the Colony, from election as Archbishop. Further, Law 34/1937 provided that a newly elected Archbishop ought to be approved by the colonial British Government; otherwise, his election should not be consummated by any religious or ceremonial rites. Essentially, Law 34/1937 provided that the election of an Orthodox Archbishop could be invalidated by the decision of a state authority.

71. Attempts to restrict the autonomy of the Orthodox Church were eventually abolished by Law 20/1946 due to the strong reaction of the Church. The right of the Church to elect its Archbishop and generally administer its internal affairs without any state intervention was confirmed by Decision 343/1948 of the District Court of Nicosia.[102] In the aforementioned Decision, it was held that the procedure for electing a Bishop is of a religious character, and thus, the Orthodox Church has exclusive competence on the matter. Thus, the internal affairs of the Orthodox Church were governed by the Canon Law of the Orthodox Church and not by state laws.

72. The 1914 Charter of the Orthodox Church was drafted and put into effect by the Church itself without the intervention of the British authorities.[103] It lasted for sixty-six years until the enactment of the 1980 Charter, which remained for thirty years. The Church of Cyprus was established as a legal entity, not further determining its nature (Article 94). It is safe to assume, however, that the Church considered itself to be a legal entity under private law.[104] The Charter was never vested with state authority, nor was the Church subjected to control on the part of the state, something that ought to have happened if the Church had been considered a legal entity under public law. Acts of the Church that were of a legislative and administrative nature, the decisions issued by ecclesiastical courts on any subject, and marriages celebrated only through a church ceremony were recognized by the state administration and justice system as a result of the aforementioned state of affairs, which was preserved by Great Britain after the annexation of Cyprus.[105]

73. The application of the Canon Law of the Orthodox Church, with respect to the adjudication of the family law disputes of its members, was also recognized. During the early years of British Rule, the Privy Council held that the Canon Law of the various Christian Communities continued to apply in family law cases, as it did according to the Ottoman Law formerly prevailing in Cyprus.[106] The status of

102. Case 343/1948, *Manoli v. Makarios Archbishop of Cyprus* (District Court of Nicosia). *See* A. Gavrielides, *The Ethnarchic Rights and the Referendum for Union with Greece* 72–76 (Nicosia: 2nd ed. 1972), (in Greek).

103. *See* A. Emilianides, 'Meletios Metaxakis and the Charter of the Church of Cyprus of 1914', *Nomokanonika* 2, 21–38 (2016), (in Greek).

104. *See also Autocephalous and Apostolic Orthodox Church of Cyprus v. House of Representatives* (1990) 3 CLR 338 (in Greek).

105. C. Papastathis, *On the Administrative Organisation of the Church of Cyprus* 27 ff. (Thessaloniki: 1981, in Greek); A. Emilianides, *The Cypriot Law of Marriage and Divorce* 47 (Thessaloniki: Sakkoulas, 2006, in Greek).

106. *Parapano and Others v. Happaz and Others* (1893) 3 CLR 69. *See* further A. Emilianides, 'The Parapano Judgment: Conflict of Laws with Respect to Legitimization of Children and Succession in Cyprus During British Rule', in *Five Studies in the History of Private Law* 67–78 (Nicosia: Dikaionomia, 2007).

the Orthodox Church, with respect to the adjudication of family law disputes, was also confirmed by the Administration of Justice Law 38/1935; section 34(c) of Law 38/1935 expressly provided that family law matters would continue to be governed according to the law of the religious community of the parties. Further, section 50 of Law 38/1935 explicitly excluded from the jurisdiction of state courts any marital disputes between members of the Greek Orthodox Church whenever the marriage was celebrated in accordance with a prescribed religious ceremony. Thus, the ecclesiastical courts of the Orthodox Church continued to enjoy exclusive jurisdiction regarding the family law disputes of their members, while the Canon Law of the Church continued to be applicable in those disputes.[107]

74. Smaller Christian religious Communities of the island also continued to enjoy spiritual autonomy with respect to their internal affairs. In Decision 172/32 of the District Court of Nicosia, it was held that the National Constitution of the Armenians continued to apply to Cyprus.[108] Thus, smaller Christian Communities maintained their competencies with respect to their internal affairs, including the election of Bishops and the administration of their ecclesiastical property. Further, the family law disputes of members of the smaller Christian churches would continue to be governed according to the law of the religious community of the parties. In addition, the ecclesiastical courts of the smaller Christian Communities maintained their exclusive jurisdiction with respect to family law disputes of their members until 1935.

75. Section 50 of Law 38/1935 excluded from the jurisdiction of state courts not only any marital disputes of members of the Greek Orthodox Church but also any other matter which, according to the principles of the Ottoman Law that was formerly in force in Cyprus, was subject to the jurisdiction of an ecclesiastical court of the religious community of the litigants. The Supreme Court held that the above reference to 'any other matter' intended to cover matters, such as election of bishops, and not family law matters.[109] Marital disputes of members of the Greek Orthodox Church were expressly excluded; should the legislator have intended to further exclude marital disputes of members of the smaller Christian Communities, this would have also been explicitly mentioned. Thus, since 1935, the state courts have acquired jurisdiction to adjudicate the family disputes of members of the smaller religious communities of the island; state courts should, however, apply the Canon Law of the religious community of the parties. The restriction on the rights of the smaller Christian religious Communities referred only to jurisdiction and not to applicable law.

---

107. *See* further A. Emilianides, *The Cypriot Law of Marriage and Divorce* 48 ff. (Thessaloniki: Sakkoulas, 2006, in Greek); G. Serghides, *Internal and External Conflict of Laws in Regard to Family Relations in Cyprus* 54 ff. (Nicosia: 1988).
108. Case 172/32 *Takvorian v. Nassibian and Others* (District Court of Nicosia).
109. *See* G. Serghides, *Internal and External Conflict of Laws in Regard to Family Relations in Cyprus* 61–62 (Nicosia: 1988); A. Emilianides, *The Cypriot Law of Marriage and Divorce* 91 ff. (Thessaloniki: Sakkoulas, 2006, in Greek).

C. The Legal Status of the Islamic Religion

76. The Treaty of 1878 expressly provided that Great Britain would respect Sheri courts and Sheri Law with respect to the religious affairs of Muslims. In 1902, the Supreme Court of Cyprus held that the phrase 'religious matter' is vague, while ecclesiastical courts in different ages and countries have at times assumed and exercised jurisdiction in almost every kind of matter on the grounds that such matter was religious, or affected religion. It was thus held that matters relating to religion are, in particular, questions which affect or arise out of marriage, divorce, alimony, infancy, wills and inheritance.[110] Section 17 of the Cyprus Courts of Justice Order of 1927 further interpreted the term 'religious matters' as covering all cases concerning marriage, divorce, alimony, hereditary succession, wills and registration of *Vakfs*. The competence of the Sheri Courts with regard to the religious matters of Turkish Muslims was confirmed by section 50 of the Courts of Justice Law 38/1935.[111]

77. On the other hand, the Interim Committee of Turkish Affairs observed in its Report in 1949 that while the matrimonial relations of the Turkish Muslims ought to retain their religious character and derive their origin and basic principles from the Quran, they should also be modified on the basis of Kemalic reforms and of the principles of Articles 82–145 of the Civil Code of Turkey of 1926.[112] On the basis of the observations of the Interim Committee, two laws were enacted: the Turkish Family (Marriage and Divorce) Law 4/1951, Cap. 339 in the 1959 Edition of the Laws of Cyprus and the Turkish Family Courts Law 3/1951, which was eventually replaced by the Turkish Family Courts Law 42/1954, Cap. 338 in the 1959 Edition. According to section 2 of Cap. 338, the term 'religious matters', for which the Turkish Family Courts have exclusive competence, was defined as covering any matters concerning marriage, divorce, alimony and registration of *Vakfs*, but not matters concerning hereditary succession or wills.

110. *Sabri v. Ibrahim* (1902) 6 CLR 1; *Effendi v. Irikzade* (1906) 7 CLR 37; *Abdullah v. Hassan and Others* (1909) 8 CLR 123.

111. *See* further A. Emilianides, 'Islamic Faith as One of the Main Religions: The Case of Cyprus', in *Islam in Europe* 220–228 (M. Moravcikova ed., Bratislava: Institute for State-Church Relations, 2005).

112. Cyprus Government Printing Office, *Interim Report of the Committee on Turkish Affairs: An Investigation into Matters Concerning and Affecting the Turkish Community in Cyprus* (Nicosia: 1949).

Part I. Legal Framework and Sources

Chapter 1. Constitutional Position of Religion

§1. The Constitutional Position of the Orthodox Church

I. Introduction

78. According to Article 110 §1 of the Constitution, the Autocephalous Greek Orthodox Church of Cyprus shall continue to have the exclusive right of regulating and administering its own internal affairs and property in accordance with the Holy Canons and its Charter in force for the time being. It is further provided that the Greek Communal Chamber shall not act inconsistently with such right of the Orthodox Church. Following the self-dissolution of the Greek Communal Chamber, it is implied that none of the state organs to which the competencies of the Greek Communal Chamber were transferred according to Law 12/1965 (namely the House of Representatives, the Council of Ministers, or the Ministry of Education, Sport and Youth), may act inconsistently with the exclusive right of the Orthodox Church to regulate and administer its internal affairs and property. Article 110 therefore confirms that the State may not interfere with the internal affairs of the Orthodox Church, similar to the existing legal position prior to independence.[113]

79. Moreover, Article 111 of the Constitution provides for certain privileges of the Orthodox Church with respect to the adjudication of issues relevant to the marriage and divorce of members of the Greek Orthodox Church. Prior to the First Amendment of the Constitution of 1989, Article 111 of the Constitution provided that family law matters would continue to be governed by the law of the Orthodox Church and to be cognizable by the ecclesiastical courts of such Church.[114] Following the First Amendment of 1989, however, all family law matters of members of the Orthodox Church came under the jurisdiction of the Family Courts; further, only

113. *See* A. Emilianides, 'The Constitutional Position of the Charter of the Church of Cyprus', *Nomokanonika* 2, 41–54 (2005), (in Greek).
114. *See* G. Serghides, *Internal and External Conflict of Laws in Regard to Family Relations in Cyprus* (Nicosia: 1988).

issues relating to betrothal or ecclesiastical marriage, or nullity of ecclesiastical marriage have continued to be governed by the Canon Law of the Orthodox Church even after 1989.[115]

II. The Constitutional Safeguard of Holy Canons

80. Article 110 §1, which establishes the right of the Orthodox Church to regulate and administer its own internal affairs and property, stipulates that this right shall be exercised *in accordance with the Holy Canons and its Charter in force for the time being*. The Holy Canons, whose force is safeguarded by Article 110 of the Constitution, are not primarily those which relate to Church doctrine; doctrinal rules of all religions are safeguarded by Article 18 of the Constitution, which provides for the free exercise of religious freedom and therefore, no special provision was needed. The aim of Article 110 is, rather, to safeguard the application of those Holy Canons, which refer to the administration of the Church's internal affairs and property. This constitutional safeguard includes both the strict observance of the doctrines (doctrinal unity) and the effect of those fundamental administrative institutions of Canon Law which give a Church its Orthodox character (Canonical unity).[116] While the Church is constitutionally called upon to respect its Holy Canons, the State has the constitutional obligation to abstain from any interference with such Holy Canons of the Orthodox Church.

81. In addition to the Holy Canons, the Constitution also makes reference to the Charter of the Church of Cyprus. However, the relevant provisions of the Charter in force are only safeguarded to the extent that they are not inconsistent with the Holy Canons. The Holy Canons are, thus, superior to the Charter in force under the Orthodox Church; a different interpretation would lead to the doctrinally unacceptable conclusion that a local Orthodox Church has the right to abolish or differentiate from Holy Canons accepted by Ecumenical or Major Synods; the Autocephaly of a Church does not justify any deviation from the Holy Canons.[117] This evident fact is acknowledged in Article 1 of the Charter of the Orthodox Church of 2010, which states that the Orthodox Church is governed by its Charter, which has been enacted on the basis of the Holy Scriptures, the Holy Canons and the Holy Traditions of the Orthodox Church. It is therefore accepted that any provisions of the Charter which are inconsistent with the Holy Canons are invalid.[118]

---

115. *See* A. Emilianides, *The Cypriot Law of Marriage and Divorce* (Thessaloniki: Sakkoulas, 2006, in Greek).
116. *See* C. Papastathis, 'The Legal Status of Religions in the Republic of Cyprus', in *The Status of Religious Confessions of the States Applying for Membership in the European Union* 208 (F. Messner ed., Strasbourg: 2000); A. Emilianides, 'State and Church in Cyprus', in *State and Church in the European Union* (G. Robbers ed., Baden-Baden: Nomos Verlagsgesellschaft 3rd ed. 2019).
117. N. Milas, *The Ecclesiastical Law of the Eastern Orthodox Church* 473, 674 (Athens: 1906, in Greek); P. Panayiotakos, *System of Ecclesiastical Law*, Vol. III, 272–273 (Athens: 1962, in Greek).
118. *See* A. Emilianides, *The Cypriot Law of Marriage and Divorce* 59 ff. (Thessaloniki: Sakkoulas, 2006, in Greek); A. Gavrielides, *Nomocanonical and Political Study on the Unfrocking of Bishops*

82. The above issue was raised during the ecclesiastical crisis of 1973. The Metropolitans of Paphos, Kition and Kyrenia, all members of the Holy Synod, demanded that the remaining member – and President – of the Holy Synod, Archbishop Makarios, resign from his office as President of the Republic of Cyprus. They argued that the exercise of political functions by a religious minister was contrary to the Holy Canons;[119] the Holy Canons explicitly stipulate that no bishop, priest, or deacon is allowed to undertake a secular position. Makarios refused to resign, arguing that he performed his duties as the spiritual leader of the Ethnarchy and not as a political leader. He further clarified that he had retained the presidential office only due to the abnormal situation prevailing in Cyprus; thus, Makarios argued that he had not undertaken a secular position since his functions as President were intrinsically linked to the struggle of the Greeks of Cyprus for national survival.[120]

83. The three Metropolitans, acting as the majority of the Holy Synod, defrocked Archbishop Makarios on 7 March 1973. However, Makarios reacted at once and convened a Major Synod, with the participation of Patriarchs and Archbishops of other Orthodox Churches; this Synod reversed the Canonical penalty imposed upon Makarios and defrocked the three Metropolitans, who refused to renounce their previous actions.[121] The Major Synod held that the decision to defrock Makarios, although consistent with the provisions of the then-in-force 1914 Charter of the Church of Cyprus, was contrary to the 12th Rule of the Synod of Carthage, which expressly stipulates that only an ecclesiastical court composed by a minimum of thirteen Bishops, may legally hold that another Bishop is defrocked. In view of the fact that the decision to defrock Makarios was reached by an ecclesiastical court composed only of three Metropolitans, such decision was invalid since it was inconsistent with the Holy Canons.[122]

---

in Cyprus in Conjunction to the Exercise of Their Ethnarchical Rights (Nicosia: 2nd ed. 1973, in Greek); G. Konidaris, *On the Problem of Canonical Courts for Bishops in the Church of Cyprus* (Athens: 1972–1974, in Greek).

119. Committee of Coordination of the Struggle for Union with Greece, *The Inconsistency of Being an Archbishop with Performing Secular Functions* (Nicosia: 1972, in Greek); P. Mpoumis, *The Unanimity of Holy Canons with Respect to the Inconsistency Between the Function of a Bishop and Secular Functions* (Athens: 1971, in Greek).
120. A. Gavrielides, *Nomocanonical and Political Study on the Defrocking of Bishops in Cyprus in Conjunction to the Exercise of their Ethnarchical Rights* (Nicosia: 2nd ed. 1973, in Greek); C. Tornaritis, 'The Occupation of Secular Power by a Religious Minister According to the Law of the Orthodox Church of Cyprus', *Cyprus Law Tribune* 2–3, 3–10 (1973), (in Greek).
121. *See* A. Mitsides, *The Major Synod of Nicosia* (Nicosia: 1973, in Greek); I. Panagopoulos, *The Major Holy Synod* (Athens: 1974, in Greek).
122. G. Konidaris, *On the Problem of Canonical Courts for Bishops in the Church of Cyprus* (Athens: 1972–1974, in Greek); C. Tornaritis, *The Ecclesiastical Courts, Especially in Cyprus* 30–31 (Nicosia: 1976); A. Gavrielides, *Nomocanonical and Political Study on the Defrocking of Bishops in Cyprus in Conjunction to the Exercise of Their Ethnarchical Rights* (Nicosia: 2nd ed. 1973, in Greek). *See*, however, the criticism of I. Theodoropoulos, *The Major Synod of Cyprus and Its Work* (Nicosia: Holy Synod of Cyprus Publications, 1973, in Greek).

III. The Legislative Power of the Church

84. A further question that arises is whether the Church of Cyprus possesses its own legislative power and has, therefore, the right to draft and enact a new Charter. Article 110 §1 provides that the exclusive right of regulating and administering the Church's own internal affairs and property should be in accordance with the Holy Canons and *its Charter in force for the time being*. It has been argued that the reference to *the Charter in force for the time being* implied that only the 1914 Charter, which was in force when the Constitution came into force, was constitutionally safeguarded; thus, according to such a view, only the 1914 Charter provides a framework for the regulation and administration of the internal affairs and property of the Orthodox Church. On the basis of such reasoning, it has been argued that the Church had no legislative power to enact a new Charter.[123]

85. The above view is incorrect. From the aspect of Canon Law, the Church is entitled to legislate freely, subject to the condition that its new statutes do not contravene the Holy Scriptures, the Holy Tradition and those Holy Canons that are accepted by all the Orthodox Churches. The same holds from the point of view of the Constitution. Article 110 §1 stipulates that the Church has the exclusive right to regulate and administer its internal affairs and property and that the State shall not act inconsistently with such right. Such right is exercised on the basis of the Holy Canons and the Charter, which is enacted from time to time. There is no constitutional restriction on the right of the Church to legislate freely with respect to its internal affairs by drafting and enacting a new Charter. Increased formal force is recognized by the Constitution for each Charter in force, so long as it has been drafted and enacted by the Church according to the Holy Canons. If the new Charter contains provisions for issues that were not regulated in the 1914 Charter, which was in force when the Constitution was enacted, such issues are not safeguarded by the Constitution.[124]

IV. The Ambit of the Charter

86. In the case of *The Holy Monastery of Mahairas*, the Supreme Court held *obiter*, that the Charter does not have 'the status of a Law and is not superior to the laws of the State, in such a manner so as to neutralize the effect of the Succession and Inheritance Law, Cap. 195'.[125] It is considered that in the aforementioned judgment, the Supreme Court was restricted in finding that the Charter is not superior to a law which does not concern the internal affairs or property of the Church, such as Cap. 195; however, the Charter of the Orthodox Church is superior to any legislation of the Republic of Cyprus in so far as it refers to matters which concern the

123. *See* Opinion in the newspaper 'Cyprus' of Nicosia, 28 Jan. 1980 (in Greek).

124. *See* C. Papastathis, *On the Administrative Organisation of the Church of Cyprus* 55–64 (Thessaloniki: 1981, in Greek); A. Emilianides, 'The Constitutional Framework of the Relations Between Church and State in the Republic of Cyprus', *Nomokanonika* 1, 61 ff. (2006), (in Greek).

125. *The Holy Monastery of Mahairas v. Papasavva*, [2007] 1 CLR 436 (in Greek).

internal affairs or the property of the Church. A state law which regulates matters which fall in the ambit of internal affairs or property of the Orthodox Church and which is inconsistent with the provisions of the Charter in force under the Church is therefore contrary to Article 110 of the Constitution.[126]

87. On the other hand, the State may freely legislate with regard to matters which would not properly be considered religious (and consequently as falling within the ambit of the competencies of the Greek Communal Chamber, prior to its self-dissolution), even if such matters are covered by the Charter in force. Thus, matters for which the House of Representatives would normally exercise its legislative competencies, even prior to the self-dissolution of the Greek Communal Chamber, may not be considered matters concerning the internal affairs or the property of the Orthodox Church. This explains why Article 110 §1 provides that the Greek Communal Chamber only – and not the House of Representatives – may not act inconsistently with such rights of the Orthodox Church; the notion of internal affairs of the Church, properly understood, refers only to religious matters which would otherwise fall under the legislative competence of the Greek Communal Chamber, according to Article 87 of the Constitution. The above view is consistent with the interpretation of the term prior to Independence.

88. Consequently, the House of Representatives may, in principle, legislate freely with respect to inheritance and succession of clergymen or monks, despite the fact that such matters are also covered in the Charter of the Orthodox Church.[127] This is due to the fact that succession and inheritance fall within the legislative ambit of the House of Representatives and not of the Greek Communal Chamber; therefore, succession and inheritance are not matters concerning the internal affairs or property of the Orthodox Church. Nonetheless, the House of Representatives may not legislate with respect to matters pertaining to the internal status of the Holy Synod, the election of Bishops, the ordination of clergymen, or the tonsure of monks, the rights and obligations of members of the clergy, the requirements of an electoral assembly for an Archbishop, the establishment of central and peripheral boards for the administration of the Church's property, or other relevant matters. In any event, the superior force of the Charter is only recognized with respect to the Charter in force and not with respect to matters regulated by other acts or resolutions of the Holy Synod.

§2. The Constitutional Position of the Three Religious Groups

I. Religious Groups in the Constitutional Sense

89. A '*Religious Group*', in the constitutional sense, is, according to Article 2 §3 of the Constitution, a group of persons, ordinarily resident in Cyprus, professing the

126. A. Emilianides, 'The Constitutional Position of the Charter of the Church of Cyprus', *Nomokanonika* 2, 41–54 (2005), (in Greek).
127. *See* A. Emilianides, 'The Matter of Hereditary Succession of Monks under Cypriot Law', *Cyprus and European Law Review* 5, 368–378 (2007), (in Greek).

same religion and either belonging to the same rite or being subject to the same jurisdiction thereof. The number of such a group on the date of the coming into operation of the Constitution must have exceeded one thousand persons, out of whom at least five hundred became, on that date, citizens of the Republic. Such difference in the number of persons ordinarily residing in Cyprus and the number of persons who became citizens of the Republic was due to the fact that a great number of Roman Catholics and Armenians had retained their British citizenship, even following 16 August 1960, when the Constitution came into force.

90. The constitutionally recognized Religious Groups are the Armenians,[128] Maronites[129] and Roman Catholics (Latins).[130] There is no possibility to constitutionally recognize in the future, a new Religious Group, even if such a group fulfils the numerical criteria provided for in Article 2 §3 of the Constitution; nor is it possible to remove the constitutional status of a Religious Group from any of the three aforementioned Religious Groups, even if the number of their members who reside in Cyprus, or who are citizens of the Republic, is diminished, so that the numerical criteria provided for, in Article 2 §3 of the Constitution may no longer be fulfilled. According to Article 2 §3 of the Constitution, Religious Groups would need to opt as groups whether they would belong to the Greek or the Turkish Community within three months of the coming into operation of the Constitution. It should be noted that the Armenian and Maronite Religious Groups have considered that their characterization as *Religious Groups* does not represent their position as ethnic or even national minorities. However, it is submitted that the recognition of the Armenians and the Maronites as Religious Groups does not necessarily entail a non-recognition of their ethnic characteristics. Indeed, the Republic of Cyprus has considered that both the Maronites and the Armenians constitute *National Minorities* within the context of the Framework Convention for the Protection of National Minorities (FCNM) of the Council of Europe.[131] In view of the above, the Maronites and the Armenians enjoy the constitutional protection of a religious minority, as well as the international protection of a national minority.

91. All three Religious Groups opted to belong to the Greek Community and now reside in the non-occupied territories, with the exception of about 100 Maronites residing in Kormakitis. In a referendum held on 13 November 1960,

128. *See* in general A. Emilianides, *The Status of the Armenian Church of Cyprus* (Nicosia: Cyprus Institute of Church and State Relations, 2006, in Greek); C. Tornaritis (ed.), 'The Legal Position of the Armenian Religious Group', in *Constitutional and Legal Problems of the Republic of Cyprus* 85–90 (Nicosia: 2nd ed. 1972); A.M., Hadjilyra, *The Armenians of Cyprus* (Larnaca: Kalaydjian Foundation, 2009).

129. A. Emilianides, 'Legal Opinion on the Legal Personality of the Karpasha Church Committee of the Maronite Church of Cyprus', *Cyprus and European Law Review* 11, 164–169 (2010); A. Haji Roussos, 'The Maronite Community of Cyprus', *Cyprus Today* 40 (2002).

130. *See* A. Emilianides, 'The Legal Status of the Latin Community of Cyprus', in *Minorities of Cyprus* 229–240 (A. Varnava, N. Coureas & M. Elia eds, Cambridge: Cambridge Scholars Publishing, 2009); N. Coureas, 'The Latins of Cyprus: The Genesis and Development of Cyprus' Modern Latin Community', *Cyprus Today* 40 (2002).

131. Report Submitted by Cyprus pursuant to Art. 25, para. 1 of the FCNM, 1 Mar. 1999, Part II, Art. 3.

1,077 Armenians, 1,046 Maronites and 322 Roman Catholics voted in favour of adhering to the Greek Community, while only five Armenians and one Roman Catholic voted in favour of adhering to the Turkish Community; thus, all members of the three Religious Groups became members of the Greek Community. The Constitution further provides that any individual member of a Religious Group may choose not to abide by the option of such group and, by a written and signed declaration, opt to belong to a Community other than that to which such group shall be deemed to belong. However, all individual members of the three Religious Groups abided by the choice of their respective group.

92. The Representative of the Latins in the House of Representatives had expressed the view that the term *Latins* does not properly reflect the essential element of their identity, namely the Roman Catholic rites they share in common. The Advisory Committee on the FCNM observed, in its Opinion on Cyprus adopted on 6 April 2001, that the Republic could address this matter without undue difficulties and modify the name of the Roman Catholic Religious Group to *Roman Catholics-Latins* since such modification does not require a change to the Constitution.[132] On 2 September 2004, the Attorney-General of the Republic also advised the Ministry of Interior that the intended modification in the name of the Latin Religious Group would not amount to an amendment of the Constitution of Cyprus and that the change could be implemented with an amendment of laws, where reference is made to the constitutionally recognized Religious Groups. Thus, in December 2004, a proposal to that effect was submitted to the Council of Ministers for approval.

93. However, the Council of Ministers, at its meeting of 20 January 2005, decided to postpone its decision because, as it stated, the above matter *had been associated by the Representative of the Latins with other issues that presented constitutional difficulties.*[133] Such issues included primarily the issue of who is to be considered members of the Roman Catholic Religious Group according to the Constitution of Cyprus. The issue has been pending since. It is submitted that it is not correct that the issue of modifying the name of the Latin Religious Group to the Roman Catholic Religious Group should be associated with any other issue presenting constitutional difficulties. Thus, the Government of the Republic of Cyprus should promptly proceed with the proposed change since it does not present any constitutional difficulties.[134]

II. Members of a Religious Group

94. Article 2 §3 of the Constitution does not provide for the criteria as to who may be considered to be a member of each specific Religious Group. There is,

132. Advisory Committee on the FCNM, *Opinion on Cyprus*, 6 Apr. 2001, para. 20.
133. Second Report submitted by Cyprus pursuant to Art. 25, para. 1 of the FCNM, 27 Oct. 2006, Part III, Art. 3.
134. *See* A. Emilianides, 'Who May Be Considered to Be Members of Religious Groups According to the Constitution of Cyprus', *Lysias* 26–31 (2006) (in Greek); Advisory Committee on the FCNM, *Third Opinion on Cyprus*, 19 Mar. 2010, paras 31 ff.

therefore, no provision which stipulates who the state should consider to be a member of the Roman Catholic Religious Group. This is due to the fact that according to a universally recognized legal principle, being a member of a church should depend upon the law of such a church and not upon a state's law. This was the position of the Supreme Court of Cyprus prior to Independence in the case of *Tsivitanides*, where it was held that *whether a church admits a person to its membership no doubt depends on the ecclesiastical law of that church.*[135] Thus, whether a person is a member of a specific Religious Group depends primarily upon the law of such a group and not upon any state legal provisions.[136]

95. The only criteria which the state law may apply, apart from ecclesiastical law, in order to specify whether a person should be considered as a member of a specific Religious Group are whether such person is a citizen of the Republic and whether he/she resides ordinarily in Cyprus.[137] Such criteria are contained in the definition of Religious Groups provided for in Article 2 §3 of the Constitution. Accordingly, it was held that a person may not belong to a Religious Group, defined as *a group of persons ordinarily resident in Cyprus*, if such person is not ordinarily resident in Cyprus.[138] Further, a person may not be considered to belong to the Greek Community unless such person is a citizen of the Republic since members of the Greek or the Turkish Community are, by definition, citizens of the Republic of Cyprus.

96. According to one view, initially supported by the Government, members of the three Religious Groups were fixed in 1960 and following such date, no new members may be added. The above view exempts only descendants of persons who were members of the three Religious Groups in 1960. The above view is not only misguided, but it is also not based upon any legal provisions. The drafters of the Constitution were perfectly aware that a great number of members of the three Religious Groups had not acquired citizenship to the Republic by the time of the coming into force of the Constitution. Such persons, ordinarily resident in Cyprus, could, of course, acquire citizenship to the Republic of Cyprus at any later stage and would, thus, become members of their respective Religious Group.

97. Nevertheless, any person has the right, at any given time, to opt to become a member of a religious community. Such a right is safeguarded by Article 18 of the Constitution, as well as by Article 9 of the ECHR. If a person considers that he/she belongs to one of the three Religious Groups of the Republic and, further, the respective Religious Group considers that such person is indeed a member of that Religious Group, it would be unconstitutional and in violation of fundamental

135. *Tsivitanides v. Tsivitanides* [1956] 21 CLR 111.

136. *See* G. Serghides, *Internal and External Conflict of Laws in Regard to Family Relations in Cyprus* 147 (Nicosia: 1988).

137. *See* A. Emilianides, *The Cypriot Law of Marriage and Divorce* 173 ff. (Thessaloniki: Sakkoulas, 2006, in Greek).

138. *Achcar v. Saad* [1979] 1 CLR 627.

human rights, should the state refuse to recognize such person as member of the relevant Religious Group, simply due to the fact that such person became a member of the Religious Group at a later stage.

98. Consequently, if a person belongs to the Orthodox Church or the Protestant Church, or indeed any other church, opts to change his/her religious beliefs, then the state must accept the change; otherwise, the right to religious freedom would be fettered.[139] Similarly, if Roman Catholics, Maronites or Armenians acquire Cypriot citizenship and ordinarily reside in Cyprus at any given time, they should properly be considered members of their respective Religious Groups; otherwise, not only would the constitutional provisions be inaccurately applied, but there would also be a violation of the right to non-discrimination, which is safeguarded by Article 28 of the Constitution and Article 14, as well as Protocol 12, of the ECHR.

III. The Constitutional Status of the Three Religious Groups

99. The documents presented to the British Parliament in July 1960 contained a statement by the British Government concerning the rights of the three smaller Religious Groups in Cyprus.[140] It was stated that the aim of the relevant constitutional provisions with respect to Religious Groups had been to secure for the minor Religious Groups in Cyprus the continued enjoyment of the liberties and status which those groups had under British rule, as well as to maintain the enjoyment of no less extensive rights in respect of religious matters than they had enjoyed by law before the Constitution came into force. It was further stated that the member of a Religious Group would enjoy the same benefits as the other members of the Community to which they had opted to belong.

100. According to Article 110 §3 of the Constitution, the three Religious Groups of the Republic shall continue to have every right with respect to religious matters that they had before the coming into force of the Constitution. Furthermore, prior to the First Amendment of the Constitution of 1989, Article 111 of the Constitution had provided that family law matters would be governed by the law of the respective Religious Group and would be cognizable by the ecclesiastical courts of that Religious Group. Following the First Amendment of the Constitution, family law matters of members of the three Religious Groups came under the jurisdiction of the Family Courts of Religious Groups; only issues relating to betrothal or ecclesiastical marriage, or nullity of ecclesiastical marriage have continued to be governed

139. *Tsivitanides v. Tsivitanides* [1956] 21 CLR 111.
140. *Cyprus: Presented to Parliament by the Secretary of State for the Colonies, the Secretary of State for Foreign Affairs and the Minister of Defence*, Cmnd. 1093, July 1960, App. E. *See also* A. Emilianides, 'The Negotiation of the Constitutional Rights of the Religious Minorities of the Republic of Cyprus'. *Nomokanonika* 1, 11–34 (2022).

by the Canon Law of the Religious Groups even after 1989.[141] A further amendment of Article 111 of the Constitution by Law 3(I)/2023 has abolished the Family Courts of Religious Groups.

101. The provisions of Articles 110 §3 and 111 of the Constitution, with respect to Religious Groups, correspond to the relevant provisions of Articles 110 §1 and 111 of the Constitution with regard to the Orthodox Church. While Article 110 §1 of the Constitution is more detailed compared to Article 110 §3, this is only due to the fact that the Orthodox Christian religion is the religion of the great majority of the population, and thus, it was considered necessary that the extent of its competencies be defined with greater clarity; however, this does not signify any difference in treatment between the Orthodox Church on the one hand, and the three Religious Groups on the other.[142] Article 110 §3 of the Constitution provides for the maintenance of the rights that the Religious Groups had enjoyed prior to independence. Such rights correspond to those of the Orthodox Church and relate to the Religious Groups' internal affairs and the administration of their property.

102. While Article 110 §3 of the Constitution does not provide, contrary to Article 110 §1 of the Constitution, that the Greek Communal Chamber shall not interfere with the rights of the three Religious Groups, it is suggested that this is heavily implied.[143] Thus, the Greek Communal Chamber, and following its self-dissolution, the House of Representatives may not interfere with issues relating to the internal affairs of the Religious Groups or the administration of their property. It is further stressed that Article 110 §3 of the Constitution safeguards the rules of the three Religious Groups, which refer to the administration of their respective Church's internal affairs and property since Canons related to Church doctrine are already safeguarded by Article 18 of the Constitution, which safeguards religious freedom.

103. It is observed that since 1935, the smaller religious communities had no longer held jurisdiction to adjudicate the family disputes of their members; section 50 of Law 38/1935 provided that the state courts would enjoy jurisdiction to adjudicate over the relevant disputes.[144] Consequently, the three Religious Groups would have enjoyed less protection in this respect, compared to the Orthodox Church, had it not been for the specific provisions of Article 111 of the Constitution. Article 111 of the Constitution, therefore, confirmed that the three Religious Groups would enjoy similar rights with respect to the adjudication of family law disputes as the Orthodox Church.

---

141. *See* A. Emilianides, *The Cypriot Law of Marriage and Divorce* (Thessaloniki: Sakkoulas, 2006, in Greek).
142. A. Emilianides, 'The Constitutional Framework of the Relations Between Church and State in the Republic of Cyprus', *Nomokanonika* 1, 46–47 (2006), (in Greek).
143. *See also* C. Tornaritis (ed.), 'The Legal Position of the Armenian Religious Group', in *Constitutional and Legal Problems in the Republic of Cyprus* 90 (Nicosia: 2nd ed., 1972).
144. *See* G. Serghides, *Internal and External Conflict of Laws in Regard to Family Relations in Cyprus* 61–62 (Nicosia: 1988).

IV. The Right to Elect Representatives of the Religious Groups

104. According to Article 109 of the Constitution, each Religious Group had the right to elect member(s) to that group into the communal chamber of the Community to which such group has opted to belong, as provided by relevant communal law. Such was the Greek Communal Chamber Law 8/1960 regarding the Composition of the Greek Communal Chamber, which provided that the Religious Groups of the Armenians and of the Roman Catholics would elect one member each in Nicosia, while the Religious Group of the Maronites would elect one member in Kyrenia.[145] This specific right of the three Religious Groups was in addition to the right of electing and being elected into the House of Representatives. A Maronite, Joseph Yiamakis, was elected as a member of the House of Representatives on behalf of the Greek Community in the first parliamentary elections of 1960.[146]

105. Following the self-dissolution of the Greek Communal Chamber, section 10 of Law 12/1965 provided that the elected members of the three Religious Groups would continue to represent their groups and would have the right to present their views before the House of Representatives; the House of Representatives would have to request for these views of the elected members of the Religious Groups before legislating upon specific matters concerning the relevant Religious Group. Law 12/1965 was held to be constitutional on the basis of the doctrine of necessity and in view of the abnormal situation prevailing in Cyprus.[147] The relevant provisions of Law 12/1965 were repeated in the Religious Groups (Representation) Law 58/1970.

106. The Religious Groups (Representation) Law 38/1976, which is currently in force, provides that the members of the three Religious Groups of the Republic, in addition to the right of electing and being elected in parliamentary elections, elect, in their capacity as members of their respective Religious Groups, one representative of each Religious Group who represents their group in the House of Representatives. These representatives have the right to address the House of Representatives with regard to all matters which concern the relevant Religious Group but do not have the right to vote; their status, concerning remuneration and other benefits, is equivalent to that of a regular member of the House of Representatives.

107. It has been suggested that the presence of representatives from the three Religious Groups in the House of Representatives is unconstitutional and

145. It is interesting to note that this was also provided in the Colonial Law 6/1960, despite the fact that such a law was enacted before the referendum of 13 Nov. 1960, when the three religious groups opted to belong to the Greek Community.

146. Another Maronite, Avraam Antoniou, was elected as member of the House of Representatives in both the 1991 and 1996 elections, while an Armenian, Marios Karoyian, was elected as a member of the House of Representatives in 2006 and as the President of the House of Representatives in 2008.

147. *Cypiom Ltd v. The Police* [2003] 2 CLR 459 (in Greek).

unjustified.[148] According to the above view, such participation of the members of the three Religious Groups in the House of Representatives violates the principle of equality, which is safeguarded by Article 28 of the Constitution; this is due to the fact that all the remaining members of the Greek Communal Chamber were forced to quit their positions in 1965 when the Greek Communal Chamber was self-dissolved. It has been further argued that Article 79 of the Constitution provides that only members of the Council of Ministers may participate in the House of Representatives with regard to matters falling within their competencies.

108. It is submitted that the above view is not correct.[149] The presence of representatives of the three Religious Groups in the House of Representatives was the direct result of the self-dissolution of the Greek Communal Chamber with Law 12/65 and the transfer of its legislative competencies to the House of Representatives. The Constitution provided for the participation of representatives of the three Religious Groups in the Greek Communal Chamber in order to safeguard their rights. Thus, the participation of the representatives of the three Religious Groups in the House of Representatives, far from being discriminatory, is consistent with the need to protect the rights of the minority groups of the Republic in a proportionate manner, pursuant to the obligations of the Republic according to the FCNM.

109. It is further observed that Article 79 of the Constitution does not impede the participation of officials other than members of the Council of Ministers in the House of Representatives with regard to matters falling within their competencies. There could be no specific provision in the Constitution with respect to the representatives of the Religious Groups, similar to that of Article 79 since the constitutional legislator could not be expected to predict that the Greek Communal Chamber would have been self-dissolved. It is thus submitted that the participation of the representatives of the three Religious Groups in the House of Representatives is entirely justified.

110. If anything, the participation of the three representatives to the House of Representatives, without the right to vote, even with regard to matters which concern the relevant Religious Group, provides less minority protection compared to that afforded by the Constitution since the representatives of the three Religious Groups would have had the right to vote on such matters in the Greek Communal Chamber, should such Communal Chamber not have been self-dissolved. In view of the above, methods should be explored in order to further improve the effective participation of the representatives of the Religious Groups by providing for a right to vote or initiate legislation in matters within their competence.[150]

---

148. *See* L. Papaphilippou, 'Constitutional Problems from the Participation of the Armenian, Maronite and Latin Religious Groups in the House of Representatives', *Cyprus Law Tribune* 4, 626–638 (1991), (in Greek).
149. A. Emilianides, 'The Constitutional Framework of the Relations Between Church and State in the Republic of Cyprus', *Nomokanonika* 1, 70–71 (2006), (in Greek).
150. *See also* Advisory Committee on the FCNM, *Opinion on Cyprus*, 7 Jun. 2007, para. 143.

§3. The Constitutional Position of the Islamic Religion

111. Article 110 §2 of the Constitution provides that all matters relating to, or in any way affecting the institution or foundation of Vakf, or the Vakfs, or any Vakf properties, including properties belonging to Mosques and any other Muslim religious institution, shall be governed solely by, and under the Laws and Principles of Vakfs (ahkamul evkaf) and the Laws and Regulations enacted or made by the Turkish Communal Chamber. It is further provided that no legislative, executive or other act whatsoever shall contravene, override or interfere with such Laws or Principles of Vakfs and with such Laws and Regulations of the Turkish Communal Chamber.

112. The Vakf had a specific meaning at the time of the coming into operation of the Constitution. It denoted the tying up of a property and the imposition of an interdiction on its transfer in such a manner that its benefit is given to men on the condition that the property is to be regarded as the property of God. A Vakf was, thus, the equivalent of a 'dedication'. A Vakf further denotes, however, the object of the dedication and not only the act. Evkaf is the plural of Vakf, although Vakfs may also be used.[151] Article 110 §2 of the Constitution thus safeguarded that all matters relating to Muslim religious institutions, including Vakf properties or properties belonging to Mosques, would be governed by the Laws and Principles of Vakfs and the Laws and Regulations enacted by the Turkish Communal Chamber.

113. Therefore, the autonomy of the Islamic religion, with respect to its internal affairs and the administration of its property, was provided for, similar to the relevant provisions regarding the Orthodox Church and the three Religious Groups.[152] The provision that not only the Laws and Principles of Vakfs but also the Laws and Regulations enacted by the Turkish Community would govern matters relating to Vakfs or other Muslim religious institutions was consistent with the recommendations of the Interim Committee of Turkish Affairs; such Committee had observed in its Report in 1949 that the system of administration of Vakfs ought to be revised.[153] Thus, the Turkish Communal Chamber ought to enact specific laws in order to revise the system.

114. The State may not interfere with such matters pertaining to the administration of Vakfs, or Vakfs properties, or relating to other Muslim religious institutions. Thus, it is provided that neither the House of Representatives, the Council of Ministers, nor any other state organ have competencies with respect to such matters. Any interference with such Laws or Principles of Vakfs and with such Laws and Regulations of the Turkish Communal Chamber shall be invalid. The Constitution does not contain a similar provision as Article 111, stipulating to competence of

151. O. Effendi, *The Laws of Evqaf* (Nicosia: 2nd ed., 1922); K. Dizdar, 'The Origin and Administration of the Cyprus Evkaf', in *Proceedings of the First International Cyprological Conference*, Vol. II, 63–78 (Nicosia: Society for Cypriot Studies, 1973).
152. A. Emilianides, 'Islamic Faith as One of the Main Religions: The Case of Cyprus', in 'Institute for State – Church Relations', in *Islam in Europe* 220–228 (M. Moravcikova ed., Bratislava: 2005).
153. Cyprus Government Printing Office, *Interim Report of the Committee on Turkish Affairs: An Investigation into Matters Concerning and Affecting the Turkish Community in Cyprus* (Nicosia: 1949).

Muslim religious institutions concerning the family relations of Muslims due to the radical amendments of the Turkish Cypriot institutions following the acceptance of the Kemalic reforms.[154]

§4. The Constitutional Position of the Orthodox Christians Who Follow the Old Calendar

115. The New (Gregorian) Calendar was adopted in Cyprus during the early years of the British rule of the island; thus, the Gregorian Calendar was, and continues to be, the state calendar of Cyprus. However, the Orthodox Church of Cyprus, similar to the other Orthodox Churches, refused to adopt the Gregorian calendar and continued to apply the Old (Julian) Calendar. A New Revised Julian Calendar was proposed for adoption by the Orthodox Churches in a synod held in Constantinople in May 1923. According to the proposal, the synod would synchronize the Revised Julian Calendar with the Gregorian Calendar by specifying that the next 1 October of the Julian Calendar would be 14 October in the Revised Julian Calendar, thus dropping thirteen days.

116. The New (Revised) Julian Calendar was adopted by the Orthodox Patriarchates of Constantinople and the Orthodox Churches of Cyprus and Greece on 10/23 March 1924.[155] The Patriarchates of Alexandria and Antioch, Romania and Bulgaria, as well as the Church of Poland, have also adopted the New Julian Calendar, albeit at a later stage. On the contrary, the Orthodox Patriarchates of Jerusalem, Russia, Serbia and Georgia have not adopted the New Calendar. It should be noted that the leap year rule adopted in the Revised Julian Calendar differs from that of the Gregorian Calendar. In particular, while the Gregorian Calendar provides that years evenly divisible by 100 are considered to be leap years only if they are also divisible by 400, the Revised Julian Calendar provides that years evenly divisible by 100 are not leap years, unless they leave a remainder of 200 or 600 when divided by 900. This means that the two calendars will first diverge in 2,800, which will be a leap year in the Gregorian Calendar but a common year in the Revised Julian Calendar. Easter is celebrated in all Orthodox Churches according to the Old Calendar, irrespective of whether they follow the New Calendar or the Old Calendar.[156]

117. A number of Orthodox Christians have continued to adhere to the Old Julian Calendar in both Cyprus and Greece, despite the fact that the Orthodox Churches of Cyprus and Greece had adopted the New Julian Calendar. Such Old Calendarists have separated themselves from the traditional Orthodox Churches and

154. A. Emilianides, 'Private International Law in Cyprus', in *Symposium on Cypriot Legal Issues* 91 (Thessaloniki: Aristotle University, 1974, in Greek).

155. *Papasavvas v. The Republic* [1982] 3 CLR 547; *Hasapopoulos v. The Electricity Authority of Cyprus* [1983] 3 CLR 1196.

156. For a detailed account *see* A. Emilianides, *The Status of the Old-Calendar Church of Cyprus* (Nicosia: Cyprus Institute of Church and State Relations, 2008, in Greek); A. Emilianides, 'Legal Aspects of the Old-Calendar Church of Cyprus' in *Antipelargisis. Honourary Volume for I.M. Konidaris* 3–22 (Athens-Thessaloniki: Sakkoulas, 2018).

have formed their own Churches.[157] There are various divisions of Old Calendarists in Greece; however, in Cyprus, Christians who follow the Old Calendar are generally considered to be Matthewites (after Bishop Matthew of Bresthena). Bishop Spyridon of Trimithus was consecrated by Matthew, who was a Bishop of the Old Calendar Church of Greece and became the first Bishop of the Old Calendar Church of Cyprus in 1949. Spyridon was soon replaced by Bishop Epiphanius of Kition, who served from 1957 until his death in 2005.[158] Sevastianos was then elected as Bishop, and his position was initially confirmed despite lengthy legal procedures disputing his election.[159] However, the Supreme Court eventually declared his election as Bishop as inconsistent with the Church's Charter and, reversing the trial court's judgment, held that Sevastianos had not lawfully been elected as Bishop.[160] It should further be noted that there is also a distinct fraction of followers of the Old Calendar Church in Cyprus; however, such fraction does not have a Cypriot Bishop and is under the spiritual administration of the respective Greek Church. It should be observed that the Cypriot and Greek Old Calendarists are not in communion with those Orthodox Churches who follow the Old Calendar, such as the Patriarchates of Jerusalem or Russia; the latter Churches are in communion with the Orthodox Church of Cyprus and Greece, respectively.

118. There is no doubt that Articles 110 and 111 of the Constitution refer to the Autocephalous Orthodox Church of Cyprus, which is in communion with the Ecumenical Patriarchate and the other Orthodox Churches, irrespective of whether such Churches adhere to the New or the Old Calendar. The Church of the Orthodox Christians who follow the Old Calendar may not be considered part of the Autocephalous Orthodox Church of Cyprus, to which the great majority of the population adheres since it has its own separate administrative organization, its own Metropolises, Bishops and priests, as well as its own Charter which differs from the Charter of the Orthodox Church of Cyprus. Therefore, Orthodox Christians who follow the Old Calendar have opted to exercise their constitutionally safeguarded rights and to separate themselves from the Autocephalous Orthodox Church of Cyprus. In view of the above, the Church of the Orthodox Christians who follow the Old Calendar is not the Church provided for in Articles 110 and 111 of the Constitution, and its position is not safeguarded by express constitutional provisions, similar to the Autocephalous Orthodox, the Islamic, the Maronite, the Armenian and the Roman Catholic Churches.[161]

---

157. *See* C. Paraskevaides, *Historical and Canonical Analysis of the Old Calendarist Issue during Its Genesis and Evolution in Greece* (Athens: 1982, in Greek); K. Ware, 'Old Calendarists', in *Minorities in Greece: Aspects of a Plural Society* 5 ff. (R. Clogg ed., London: Hurst & Co., 2002). For an Old – Calendarist perspective *see* Bishops Chrysostomos, Auxentius & Ambrose, *The Old Calendar Orthodox Church of Greece* (California: Center for Traditionalist Orthodox Studies, 4th ed. 1994).
158. V. Moss, 'A Review of the Struggle Against Ecumenism', *Vertograd* 1, 25–27 (1998); The Holy Orthodox Church in North America, *The Struggle against Ecumenism* (Boston, MA: 1998).
159. *See* A. Emilianides, 'Comment on the Case of Holy Monastery of Metamorphosis', *Nomokanonika* 2, 199–212 (2014), (in Greek).
160. *Nun Markella a.o v. Sevastianos Stavrou*, Civil App. 9/2016, Judgment of 12 Oct. 2022 (in Greek).
161. A. Emilianides, *The Status of the Old-Calendar Church of Cyprus* (Nicosia: Cyprus Institute of Church and State Relations, 2008, in Greek).

Chapter 2. Other Legislation with Regard to Religion

§1. State Laws Concerning Religion

119. The most basic legal source for religions, in general, is the Constitution of Cyprus. In view of the fact that the Constitution of Cyprus provides for the autonomy of the various religions of the Republic in organizing and administering their internal affairs, state laws relating to religion are few; other state laws with respect to religion may be found scattered in various legal instruments, such as the Income Tax Law 118/2002, the Customs and Excise Regulations, the Regulations on Animal Protection at the Time of Slaughter or Killing, the Radio and Television Stations Law 7(I)/1998, the Family Courts (Religious Groups) Law 87(I)/1994, the Criminal Code Cap. 154, or the Law providing for the Marriage of Members of the Old Calendar 60(I)/1994. Of specific importance is the Religious Groups (Representation) Law 38/1976, which has already been mentioned while discussing the legal status of the representatives of the three Religious Groups.

120. With respect to the religious affairs of the Turkish Cypriot Muslims, there are three important laws which have remained in force in the Republic of Cyprus. Such Laws are the Turkish Religious Head (Mufti) Law (Cap. 340 of the Laws of Cyprus, 1959 Edition), the Vakfs and Evcaf Law (Cap. 337 of the Laws of Cyprus, 1959 Edition, as amended by Law 60/1972) and the Establishment of a Department of Vakfs and Religious Matters Law of the Turkish Communal Chamber 12/1960. Cap. 340 and Cap. 337 were enacted during the British rule of the Republic and have continued to be in force insofar as they are not inconsistent with the provisions of the Constitution. While the provisions of such Laws shall be analysed in this part, it should be stressed that due to the abnormal situation prevailing on the island, the application of such Laws is problematic since the great majority of the Turkish Cypriot Community currently resides in the occupied territories. In view of the provisions of Article 110 §2 of the Constitution, such Laws were to be applied in any event by the Turkish Cypriot Community of the island and not by the Central Government; the Turkish Communal Courts should, therefore, have jurisdiction to adjudicate such matters.

§2. The Turkish Religious Head (Mufti) Law

121. The Turkish Religious Head (Mufti) Law provides for the election of a religious head of the Turkish Community in Cyprus. Section 4 of Cap. 340 provides that no person shall be eligible for election or shall be elected as a Mufti unless he is a Muslim of Turkish race, who has attained the age of 40 and possesses an Ijazet diploma, or a degree in theology from the Istanbul, Ankara, or El Azhar Universities. An Ijazet diploma is a certificate of competence granted by an authoritative high school of religion functioning at the time (Medreseh) in the presence of religious dignitaries to those who had completed their studies therein on the subjects of Arabic language and literature, Sheri Law and jurisprudence of Islam, traditions of

Mohammed and commentaries thereon, interpretation and commentaries on the Quran, Theology, logic, philosophy and the Muslim sacred Law of inheritance.

122. For the purpose of electing a Mufti, a Muslim of Turkish race is appointed as Presiding Officer to supervise the election; the Presiding Officer may nominate, in turn, any other Muslim of Turkish race to act as his representative in respect of a particular place. Within thirty days from the date on which the office of Mufti becomes vacant, the Presiding Officer requests the Turkish Mukhtar of every quarter or village to prepare and post at a conspicuous place, no later than thirty days after such request, a list of all male Muslims of Turkish race within such quarter or village, who on the date of the request, have completed their eighteenth year and were ordinarily residents in the quarter or village during the twelve months immediately preceding such date. If the Mukhtar fails to prepare and post the aforementioned list within a period of thirty days after the request, then the Presiding Officer shall prepare the list himself or nominate another person to prepare such a list.

123. Objections to the lists may be made to the Presiding Officer in writing within ten days; the Presiding Officer, after considering the objections, may cause any alterations or additions to the lists that he deems necessary, and thereafter, such lists shall be considered as final and conclusive, specifying the persons entitled to vote for the election of special representatives. No later than ten days after the date on which the lists become final and conclusive, the Presiding Officer shall publish in the Official Gazette of the Republic and in no less than two Turkish-speaking Cypriot newspapers a notice providing for the nomination of candidates for election as Mufti of the Turkish Cypriot Community. Each nomination paper must be subscribed by ten persons, one of whom shall subscribe as proposer and another as seconder.

124. The Presiding Officer then publishes the list of nominated candidates in the Official Gazette and in no less than two Turkish-speaking Cypriot newspapers. Any person whose name appears in the final lists may object in writing to the Presiding Officer that a person nominated does not possess the required qualifications; such objections must be raised within eight days from the publication of the nomination in the Gazette. Objections are then examined by a Committee consisting of the three senior Turkish judges of the Muslim faith, who decide finally and conclusively on the matter. If there is only one candidate and there are no objections, or if such objections have been rejected by the Committee, such candidate is deemed to have been elected; otherwise, elections of special representatives are held.

125. A person is eligible for election as a special representative of a quarter or a village if his name appears in the final list of such quarter or village. The persons having the majority of the votes in each quarter or village shall be deemed to have been elected as special representatives. A quarter or village with a population of not less than 300 and no more than 500 Muslims of Turkish race shall elect one representative; with a population between 500 and 1,000, it shall elect two representatives; with a population between 1,000 and 2,000, it shall elect three representatives; and with a population exceeding 2,000 persons, it shall elect four representatives. If a quarter or village has a population of less than 300 persons, then it shall be grouped together with some other neighbouring quarter or village.

126. All elected special representatives, together with the Muderris and the Mussevit, if any, and with the Chairman of the High Council of Evkaf, any Turkish members of the Executive Council of Muslim faith and the Turkish councillors of every municipal corporation of Muslim faith, shall form the electoral assembly for the election of Mufti. The electoral assembly meets under the chairmanship of the Presiding Officer within twenty days from the election of the special representatives and elects a Mufti by open vote unless a secret ballot is demanded by two or more members of the assembly. The person who receives the greatest number of votes is elected as Mufti; if more than one candidate receives an equal number of votes, then the Presiding Officer shall draw a lot.

127. The Mufti is the religious head of the Turkish Cypriot Community and exercises several powers. In particular, he has the power to: (a) appoint Muderris, Mussevits, Imams, Muezzins, Preachers and other personnel as may be required to assist in religious functions and to prescribe their training and duties, exercising supervision over them, as may be necessary to secure proper compliance. He also has the power to suspend or dismiss any of them if they fail to carry out their respective duties in a satisfactory manner; (b) deliver sermons in the Mosques and advise members of the Turkish Community on religious matters; (c) issue fatwa, defining religious principles and prescribing religious holidays, time for prayers and fasting hours; (d) direct and supervise the distribution to the poor of alms and zekats contributed by Muslims; (e) authorize the erection of new Mosques and major repairs to existing Mosques and supervise the smooth function of Mosques, tekkes, shrines and Muslim cemeteries.

128. A Mufti retires upon attaining 75 years of age, or if by reason of physical or other disability, is unable to attend or perform the duties of his office, or if he has been guilty of conduct unbecoming to his function or of serious, persistent or continued negligence of duty. If, for any reason, the Mufti ceases to hold office, the senior Mudderis shall exercise all duties and powers of a Mufti until a Mufti is elected. The emoluments of the Mufti, the Muderris, the Mussevit, the Imams, the Muezzins, the Preachers and any other personnel appointed by the Mufti are paid by the revenue of the Evkaf Department.

§3. The Vakfs and Evcaf Law

129. Section 4 of the Vakfs and Evcaf Law, Cap. 337 provides that no dedication of a Vakf shall be valid unless made:

(a) by a person competent to dedicate; according to section 5 of Cap. 337, such a person is considered any person of a Muslim faith competent to contract;

(b) for an object which may be the object of a dedication according to section 6 of Cap. 337; no dedication shall be made for an object which is unlawful or prohibited by Islam, or is of a limited duration, or appears at the time of the dedication as if it will fail, or is subject to a contingency, or consists of the repair or upkeep of a private tomb, or is not defined with certainty;
(c) in respect of property capable under section 7 of Cap. 337 to be the subject of a Vakf, namely any immovable property, or any movable property held or enjoyed as an accessory of immovable property, or which is not consumed by use. The dedicator of the property must be the owner of such property at the time of the dedication;
(d) in a form provided by sections 8, 9 and 10 of Cap. 337. Section 8 provides that no dedication shall be valid unless the following requirements are fulfilled: (i) if the dedication is made *inter vivos*, its declaration must be made in writing in any appropriate words showing an intention to make a dedication by way of a Vakf; such written declaration must be signed by the dedicator in the presence of at least two witnesses, competent to contract or, where the dedicator is illiterate, in the presence of two such witnesses and a certifying officer serving the same function as the witnesses certifying the signature. The dedication must be registered, according to section 9 of Cap. 337, following a court's decision and after notice is given to the Director of Lands and Surveys, so that the latter may inform the court of any impediments; (ii) if the dedication is made by will, the dedicated property shall be valid, according to section 10 of Cap. 337, only so far as it does not exceed the portion that may be disposed of by will, unless the heirs consent, and it shall be registered according to the provisions of section 9.

130. A registered Vakf shall be considered to be irrevocable, and the dedicator shall have no power to rescind such Vakf; however, the dedicator may alter or amend the terms of any registration if he has reserved to himself such power therein, provided that any such alterations or amendments shall also be subject to registration. While the ultimate benefit must always be reserved for a charitable purpose, the dedicator may validly provide for the benefit of a succession of persons during their lives, or during specified periods, or for the maintenance and support, wholly or partially, of the family, children, or descendants of the dedicator, or the maintenance of the dedicator himself during his lifetime. In any event, no dedication of a Vakf shall be valid if made in circumstances as to defeat or delay the rights of creditors of the dedicator or if, at the time of the dedication, the dedicator was insolvent or bankrupt. An aggrieved person may apply to the court within one year from the registration of the Vakf for a declaration that the Vakf is void.

131. A dedication by way of a Vakf shall be in perpetuity, and thus, the subject of the Vakf cannot thereafter, be alienated or transferred either by the dedicator or by his heirs; where the subject of a Vakf is unlawfully alienated, any person may apply to the court to have the alienation set aside. The benefit or income or proceeds of the Vakf property shall be applied in the following order: (a) for the maintenance and repair of the subject of the Vakf; (b) for the specified object of the Vakf; (c) for that which is necessary for the general purpose of the specified objects; (d) for any other charitable object. If some of the objects for which a Vakf is purported to be made fail, or cannot be given effect, or are unlawful, or prohibited by Islam, effect shall be given to those purposes which are lawful or which can be given effect.

132. The dedicator may further provide for the appointment of a person or persons to act as the manager(s) or administrator(s) of the Vakf (Mutevelli) and of his successors and may also specify the conditions on which, the manner in which, the period for which, and the person by whom, the Mutevelli and his successors may be appointed. A Mutevelli shall have the power to do all acts which are reasonable and proper for the protection of the Vakf property and with respect to its management and administration; the Mutevelli has to prepare once every year and submit to the High Council a true statement of accounts of the Vakf property for which he is the administrator, supported with all relevant vouchers and receipts. Once appointed, a Mutevelli may not be removed by the dedicator unless there is a specific provision thereof in the written declaration; a Mutevelli may, however, be removed by a decision of the High Council if he is found incapable or unfit to administer the Vakf. It is not, however, possible to appoint a Mutevelli with respect to Vakf property, which is under the control of the Guardian of Turkish Cypriot properties by virtue of the Turkish Cypriot Properties (Administration and other Issues) (Temporary Provisions) Law 139/1991, a law which was enacted on the basis of the doctrine of necessity due to the abnormal situation currently prevailing in Cyprus as a result of the Turkish invasion of 1974. So far as the abnormal situation continues, such Vakf property shall remain under the control of the Guardian and the application of the relevant provisions of Cap. 337 shall be suspended.[162]

133. Where a person erects or designates a building for the purpose of dedicating it as a mosque, he shall divide such property from the rest of his property, provide a means of access thereto, transfer the property and deliver the possession thereof to the village mosque committee; where the object of a Vakf is a mosque, the dedicator cannot reserve any benefit to himself under such Vakf and any such reservations are invalid; however, there may exist provisions for the expenses connected with the use and upkeep of the mosque as a place of worship. Property may also be dedicated by way of a Vakf for the benefit of an existing mosque.

§4. The Establishment of a Department of Vakfs and Religious Matters Law

134. Cap. 337 and Cap. 340 were supplemented by the Establishment of a Department of Vakfs and Religious Matters Law of the Turkish Communal Chamber 12/1960. According to Law 12/60, the Department of Vakfs and Religious Matters shall comprise the Office of Evkaf and the Office of Mufti. The Office of Evkaf

162. *Balce and the Vakf of Siddika* [2010] 1 CLR 680 (in Greek); *Hakki v. Minister of Interior*, Case. 209/2011, Judgment of 31 Oct. 2012 (in Greek). *See also* A. Emilianides, 'Turkish Cypriot Properties and the Guardian: A Critical Review of the Case-Law', *Cyprus and European Law Review* 9, 457–501 (2009), (in Greek).

has competencies with respect to all matters concerning Vakfs or any other Muslim religious institutions or cemeteries, while the Office of the Mufti has competencies with respect to all religious matters concerning the Turkish Community of the island. It is provided that the Office of Evkaf shall have a Director, as well as other employees as its staff, while the Office of the Mufti shall have a secretary and religious ministers to assist the Mufti; all employees shall be remunerated by the Turkish Communal Chamber.

Chapter 3. The Typology of the System

135. It has been suggested that the constitutional protection of the Orthodox Church is wider than the respective constitutional protection of the three Religious Groups; it has further been suggested that the state and church relations between the Orthodox Church and the State in Cyprus are governed by the *State-law rule*, similarly to Greece, *even if the control of the Church on behalf of the State is limited.*[163] The above views are hardly convincing and have to be rejected. Despite the different terminology used, the aim of the Constitution is to treat the five major religions in an equal manner and not to differentiate among them. The Orthodox Church, the three Religious Groups and the Islamic religion all enjoy exclusive competence with respect to their internal affairs, as well as the administration of their property. Such autonomy derives from the pre-existing legal regime prior to independence since the Constitution has not created a new internal legal regime for the various religions in Cyprus but has essentially maintained, in effect, the provisions of Ottoman Law, especially Hatt-i-Humayun, albeit without affording a dominant position to the Islamic religion.

136. Such similarity in treatment is also evident in the provisions of Article 23 of the Constitution, which safeguards the right to property. Article 23 §9 stipulates that no deprivation, restriction or limitation on the right to acquire, own, possess, enjoy or dispose of any movable or immovable property belonging to any See, monastery, church or any other ecclesiastical corporation or any right over it or interest therein, shall be made, except with the written consent of the appropriate ecclesiastical authority being in control of such property. The same right is accorded to all Muslim religious institutions. According to Article 23 §10, no such deprivation, restriction or limitation may be imposed on the immovable or movable property of any Vakf, except with the approval of the Turkish Communal Chamber and subject to the Laws and Principles of Vakfs. Such property includes the objects and subjects of the Vakfs and the properties belonging to the Mosques or to any other Muslim religious institutions or any right thereon or interest therein.

137. It has already been noted that the Orthodox Christian and the Islamic religion constitute one of the criteria of the bi-communal character of the Republic of Cyprus since Article 2 of the Constitution provides that the Greek Community comprises, *inter alia*, all citizens of the Republic who are members of the Greek Orthodox Church, while the Turkish Community comprises, *inter alia*, all citizens of the Republic who are Muslims. This peculiarity does not, however, signify the recognition of a special status in favour of the Orthodox Church, nor the Muslim religion, at the expense of the other religions;[164] such was simply a method of

163. C. Tornaritis, 'The Constitutional Position of the Autocephalous Greek Orthodox Church in the Republic of Cyprus', *Cyprus Law Tribune* 4, 485–495 (1990), (in Greek); C. Tornaritis, 'The Relations Between Church and State According to Cypriot Law', *Review of Public and Private Law* 1, 14–15 (1967), (in Greek).

164. As suggested by C. Tornaritis, 'The Relations Between Church and State According to Cypriot Law', *Review of Public and Private Law* 1, 15 (1967), (in Greek).

distinguishing between members of the Greek and the Turkish Communities, without any further implications with respect to the status of either religion.[165]

138. From the aforementioned constitutional provisions, it emerges that no single religion or creed is established as the official religion. As a result, there is no prevailing, established or state religion in Cyprus. All the religions and creeds in Cyprus deal restrictively with their own affairs without in any way interfering in the affairs of the State. However, the five main religions of the Republic, namely the Orthodox Christian, the Islamic, the Maronite, the Armenian and the Roman Catholic, enjoy a special constitutional status. The State has recognized broad discretionary powers in their favour and does not have the right to intervene in their internal affairs or in the administration of their property. Whenever matters of common interest arise, such as religious education, the State and the religious corporations debate in order to reach a common solution;[166] if, however, this is not possible, the State may reach any decision, so long as it does not interfere with the internal affairs or the administration of the property of the constitutionally protected religions.[167]

139. It is further observed that the State is not confessional. Thus, when assuming their duties, state officials are not sworn in but affirm their faith in and respect for the Constitution and the laws made thereunder, the preservation of the independence and territorial integrity of the Republic of Cyprus, pursuant to Articles 42 §1, 59 §4, 69 and 100 of the Constitution (with respect to the President of the Republic, the Ministers, the Representatives and the members of the Communal Chambers, respectively). Accordingly, state officials do not have to believe in any particular religion or even that a God exists in order to be elected or appointed. Their only allegiance is towards the Constitution and the laws made thereunder, and not towards any religious beliefs.

140. In view of the above, it is suggested that the Constitution has introduced a system of coordination between the Republic of Cyprus and the major religions and Christian creeds.[168] Such a system differs substantially from the *State-law rule* system prevailing in Greece since it is based upon the autonomy of religious organizations, which are distinct from the State and deal restrictively with their own

---

165. *See* C. Papastathis, *On the Administrative Organisation of the Church of Cyprus* 36–37 (Thessaloniki: 1981, in Greek).
166. *See* A. Emilianides, 'The Mutual Role of Religion and the State in Cyprus', in *The Mutual Role of Religion and the State in Europe* 25–31 (B. Schanda ed., Trier: European Consortium for State and Church Research, 2014).
167. *See* A. Emilianides, 'State and Church in Cyprus', in *State and Church in the European Union* 281–296 (G. Robbers ed., Baden-Baden: Nomos Verlagsgesellschaft 3rd ed. 2019); A. Emilianides, 'Law and Religion in Cyprus', *Kanon* 20, 7–21 (2008), A. Emilianides, 'Kirche und Staat in Zypern'. In *Kirche und Staat in West-Süd – und Nordeuropa* 213–230 (S. Mückl und A. Uhle ed., Berlin: Duncker & Humblot, 2020).
168. A. Emilianides, 'The Constitutional Framework of the Relations Between Church and State in the Republic of Cyprus', *Nomokanonika* 1, 37 ff. (2006), (in Greek); C. Papastathis, *On the Administrative Organisation of the Church of Cyprus* 34 (Thessaloniki: 1981, in Greek); A. Gavrielides, *Nomocanonical and Political Study on the Defrocking of Bishops in Cyprus in Conjunction to the Exercise of Their Ethnarchical Rights* (Nicosia: 2nd ed. 1973, in Greek).

affairs. It further differs from the separation system since the State has recognized broad discretionary powers with regard to the main religions' internal affairs, administration of their property, and, in general, matters of communal character. The model prevailing in Cyprus is essentially a pluralistic model, which recognizes and embraces the public dimension of religion while at the same time attempting to cooperate with all religions. The significance of faith in people's lives is considered as worthy of protection by the state, and where the function of the state overlaps with religious concerns, the state seeks to accommodate religious views insofar as they are not inconsistent with the state's interests.

141. In consequence, pluralism is achieved through the recognition that the state and the various religions occupy, in principle, different societal structures; religious neutrality is not, however, achieved simply because there is religious autonomy but also through positive measures on behalf of the state, which aims at the protection of religions.[169] Other religious minorities, such as the Jews, the Jehovah's Witnesses, the Buddhists, the Protestants, or the Orthodox Christians who follow the Old Calendar, enjoy religious freedom according to Article 18 of the Constitution and are equal before the law so that no legislative, executive or administrative act could discriminate against them. However, such religions are not considered Religious Groups in the constitutional sense and, therefore, do not enjoy the special constitutional status of the five main religions of the island; the difference in treatment between the five constitutionally recognized religions and other religions of the island principally occur with respect to religious education, direct financing and family law matters.[170]

169. A. Emilianides, 'Secularism, Law and Religion Within the Cypriot Legal Order', in *Religion, Rights and Secular Society. European Perspectives* 169–188 (P. Cumper & T. Lewis eds, Cheltenham: Edward Elgar Publishing, 2012); A. Emilianides, 'Religious Jurisdiction and Pluralism of Legal Adjudication in Cyprus', in *Religious Adjudication and the State* 39–48 (R. Potz & W. Wieschaider eds, Granada: Comares, 2015).

170. *See also* A. Emilianides, 'Recognized, but not fully Appreciated: The Legal Status of Religious Minorities in Cyprus' in *The Legal Status of Old and New Religious Minorities in the European Union* 97–106 (M. Ventura ed., Granada: Comares, 2021).

Part II. Religious Freedom in General

Chapter 1. Individual Religious Freedom

§1. The Constitutional Right to Religious Freedom

I. Introduction

142. Article 18 of the Constitution of Cyprus safeguards the right to religious freedom, including the freedom of religious conscience and freedom of worship.[171] The aforementioned article corresponds in many ways to Article 9 of the ECHR, but it is more detailed, while its provisions cover sectors which are not recorded in Article 9. Article 18 § 1 provides that every person has the right to freedom of thought, conscience and religion. Such right is far-reaching and profound. Freedom of thought, conscience and religion is safeguarded for any person, either a believer or an atheist, a citizen or a non-citizen of the Republic of Cyprus. Conscience and religion are thus not confined to the belief in the relation between a human being and a Creator. Religion or conviction refers to theistic, non-theistic and atheistic convictions. It includes convictions such as agnosticism, free-thinking, pacifism, atheism and rationalism. It is, therefore, not limited in its application to traditional religions or to religions and beliefs with institutional characteristics or practices analogous to traditional religions.[172] Until a person attains the age of 16, the decision as to the religion to be professed by him/her shall be taken by the person having the lawful guardianship of such person on the basis of Article 18 §7 of the Constitution.

143. The Supreme Court has specified that Article 18 of the Constitution safeguards religious liberty, which is not to be confused with religious tolerance. It was held that:

> Tolerance as a legal concept is premised on the assumption that the State has ultimate control over religion and the churches, and whether and to what extent religious freedom will be granted and protected is a matter of state policy. The

171. *See* A. Emilianides (ed.), *Religious Freedom in the European Union* 89–98 (Leuven: Peeters, 2011); C. Tornaritis, *The State Law of the Republic of Cyprus* 145–148 (Nicosia: Cyprus Research Centre, 1982, in Greek).
172. *Pitsillides v. The Republic* [1983] 2 CLR 374.

> right of religious liberty is a fundamental right. The days that oppressive measures were adopted and cruelties and punishments inflicted by Governments in Europe and elsewhere for many ages, to compel parties to conform in their religious beliefs and modes of worship to the views of the most numerous sect, and the folly of attempting in that way to control the mental operations of persons and enforce an outward conformity to a prescribed standard, have gone. Mankind has advanced and the right to freedom of thought, conscience and religion is now a fundamental right.[173]

144. Indirectly related to religious freedom is the constitutional provision of Article 10 §3(b). Article 10 §3(b) states that the term *forced or compulsory labour*, which no person shall be required to perform, shall not include *any service of military character if imposed or, in the case of conscientious objectors, subject to their recognition by a law, service exacted instead of compulsory military service*. The said constitutional provision implements Article 4 §3 section b of the ECHR and empowers the legislative branch to relieve of their compulsory military service those who object to it for reasons of conscience and order them to provide services of another nature. There are also several other articles of the Constitution which might be indirectly related to religious freedom; in most cases, the aforementioned constitutional rights are wider and regulated in more detail compared to the provisions of the ECHR.

145. Other articles indirectly related to religious freedom include: (a) Article 15, which provides for the right to respect private and family life, similar to Article 8 of the ECHR; (b) Article 19, which safeguards the right to freedom of speech and expression, similarly to Article 10 of the ECHR; (c) Article 20 which safeguards the right to education corresponding to Article 2 of the First Protocol of the ECHR; (d) Article 21 which guarantees the right to assembly and the freedom of association similar to Article 11 of the ECHR; (e) Article 22 safeguarding the right to marry and found a family corresponding to Article 12 of the ECHR; (f) Article 23 which provides for the protection of property, safeguarding the right enshrined in Article 1 of the First Protocol of the ECHR; (g) Article 28 §2 of the Constitution providing for the right to non-discrimination, similar to Article 14 of the ECHR.

II. Manifestation of Religious Freedom

146. Article 18 §4 guarantees the more particular manifestations of an individual's religious freedom, stipulating that every person is free and has the right to profess his/her faith and to manifest his/her religion or belief, in worship, teaching, practice or observance, either individually or collectively, in private or in public, and to change his/her religion or belief. While religious freedom is primarily a matter of individual conscience, it also implies the freedom to manifest one's religion

173. *Ibid.*

since such freedom is intrinsically linked with the very existence of religious convictions.[174] The term *worship* embraces but is not confined to institutional forms of worship; it extends to ritual and ceremonial acts giving direct expression to belief, as well as practices integral to such acts, including the building of places of worship, the use of ritual objects, the display of symbols and the observance of holidays and days of rest. The observance and practice of religion may include such customs as the observance of dietary regulations, the wearing of distinctive clothing or headcovers, participation in rituals, and the use of a particular language customarily spoken by a group.

147. Freedom to manifest one's religion entails the right to exercise religious activities in public, as well as trying to convince others, through teaching, to change their religion or belief. A person may further establish and maintain communication with individuals and communities in matters of religion or belief at a national or international level. Any person may write, issue and disseminate texts or publications in order to manifest their religious beliefs and may teach such religious beliefs to others and train, appoint, elect or designate by succession appropriate leaders called for by the requirements and standards of their religion.

148. The constitutional right to religious freedom further includes the negative aspects of such right, namely the right not to disclose one's religion. This was accepted by the Supreme Court in an obiter dictum in the case of *Elia*, where it was held that revealing in official documents the religion of a candidate for a position in the public service should be avoided in view of Article 18 of the Constitution. Thus, it was held that the fact that the official documents referred to the applicant as a Maronite was strictly prohibited by the Constitution.[175] While the above comments of the Supreme Court were only *obiter*, it is considered that they accurately reflect the position under Article 18 of the Constitution; a person has, therefore, a constitutional right not to disclose one's religion.

149. In a subsequent case of the Supreme Court, the case of *Panayiotou*, it was held that while the simple fact that the candidate was referred to in an official document by the Public Service Commission as a Maronite did not constitute by itself discrimination on the grounds of religion; such references in official documents ought, in principle, to be avoided, because they might cause suspicion of religious discrimination, or inequality.[176] As a general rule, religion is not referred to in official Cypriot documents, such as passports or identity cards. Further, the application form for appointment or promotion in the civil service no longer requires information about the candidate's religion.[177]

174. *Kokkinakis v. Greece*, Judgment of 25 May 1993; (1994) 17 EHRR 397.
175. *Elia v. The Republic* [1985] 3 CLR 38.
176. *Panayiotou v. The Republic* [1991] 3 CLR 1837 (in Greek).
177. Second Report Submitted by Cyprus pursuant to Art. 25, para. 1 of the FCNM, 27 Oct. 2006, para. 39.

III. Right to Change One's Religion

150. Any person has the right to replace their current religion with another or to adopt atheistic views. The case of *Tsivitanides,* which was decided by the Supreme Court prior to Independence, referred to the right to change one's religion or belief.[178] The petitioner, born a Roman Catholic, was received into the Greek Orthodox Church the month before her marriage. The marriage was dissolved in 1946, and in 1951, the petitioner was readmitted to the Roman Catholic Church. Later that year, the parties performed a civil wedding ceremony under the (civil) Marriage Law. Both the petitioner in her petition and the respondent in his answer sued for divorce. The respondent also, in these proceedings, alleged that the civil marriage under Cap. 116 was a nullity since, at the date of the marriage, the parties were both members of the Greek Orthodox Church. It was argued for the respondent that the petitioner could only cease to be a member of the Greek Orthodox Church if excommunicated, according to the ecclesiastical law of that Church.

151. According to a universally recognized legal principle, being a member of a church should depend upon the law of such a church and not upon a state's law.[179] When making reference to membership of an ethnic group or of a religious community, the law should be taken to mean those persons who are members thereof in accordance with the rules of that community. In such an instance, the connecting principle cannot possibly be qualified under the State's law, which does not contain any rule on the matter. The aforementioned principle was readily accepted by the Supreme Court in the case of *Tsivitanides.*[180]

152. However, a person may not be considered to continue to belong to a religion if that person does not wish to. Thus, a person may cease being a member of a particular religion or creed, not only if excommunicated according to the ecclesiastical law of such Church, but also if he/she exercises his/her right to change religion or beliefs. As the Court held in Tsivitanides:

> Ordinary men and women of the free world to-day know that they have freedom of conscience to choose their own religion, and when making their declaration before a marriage officer they will consider their faith to be that to which they at the time of their marriage adhere. This essential freedom in religious matters would be fettered if, while adhering to one Church, a person was bound by the law of the State to be married in another.[181]

153. The Supreme Court thus held that the petitioner had voluntarily ceased to be a member of the Orthodox Church. It is submitted that such a view of the Supreme Court prior to Independence is now further enhanced by the wording of

---

178. *Tsivitanides v. Tsivitanides* [1956] 21 CLR 111.
179. *See* G. Serghides, *Internal and External Conflict of Laws in Regard to Family Relations in Cyprus* 147 (Nicosia: 1988).
180. *Tsivitanides v. Tsivitanides* [1956] 21 CLR 111.
181. *Ibid.*

Article 18 §4 of the Constitution, which expressly safeguards the right to change one's religion or belief.[182] It is immaterial why the person has chosen to change religion and whether such a choice was the result of that person acting in good faith or not, so long as it was the consequence of the exercise of the person's will and not, for instance, the result of duress, or psychological force; thus 'a person may renounce his faith for love or for avarice. He/she may do so to get rid of his present commitments or truly to seek salvation elsewhere'.[183] Therefore, secession from a church shall be valid, even if the motive was simply to be capable of not performing the obligations associated with the person's religion.[184]

154. The issue was indirectly considered in the case of *Houssain*.[185] The petitioner, a Greek Cypriot and a member of the Greek Orthodox Church had entered into a civil marriage in England with a Pakistani national of Muslim faith. The respondent insisted both before and after the marriage that his wife ought to change her religion and become a Muslim; due to his wife's refusal to change her religion, he refused to consummate their marriage and maintained that he would not consummate their marriage, so long as she remained a Greek Orthodox. Eventually, she left England and returned to Cyprus, where she filed a petition for nullity of marriage on the grounds of non-consummation due to the wilful refusal of her husband. The Court held that the wife's refusal to change religion could not justify the husband's refusal to her request for intercourse and granted a decree of nullity after finding the husband guilty of a wilful refusal to consummate the marriage.

IV. Restrictions to the Manifestation of Religious Freedom

155. Interference with the right to religious freedom is in principle prohibited, irrespective of whether such interference is direct or indirect. No limitations whatsoever are permitted with respect to the freedom of thought, conscience or the freedom to have or adopt a religion or belief of one's choice; such freedoms are protected unconditionally and are considered to be absolute. However, the freedom to manifest one's religion can be restricted by virtue of Article 18 §6, so long as such limitations are prescribed by law and are necessary in the interests of: (a) the security of the Republic; (b) constitutional order; (c) public safety; (d) public order; (e) public health; (f) public morals; (g) the protection of the rights and liberties guaranteed to every person by the Constitution. In view of the above, three general principles may be accepted: (i) There has to be a legal basis for the interference with the fundamental right to religious freedom; a restriction has to be prescribed by law and in accordance with the national law. Such a law must be adequately accessible and sufficiently precise and must have been enacted by the appropriate organ. (ii)

182. A. Emilianides, *The Cypriot Law of Marriage and Divorce* 168 (Thessaloniki: Sakkoulas, 2006, in Greek).
183. *Bibi v. Bakhsh* (1938) 19 Indian LR 277: 286.
184. *See* G. Serghides, *Internal and External Conflict of Laws in Regard to Family Relations in Cyprus* 152 (Nicosia: 1988).
185. *Houssain v. Houssain* [1979] 1 CLR 600.

The interference has to be necessary for one of the constitutionally specified legitimate aims; a limitation which has been prescribed by law in order to facilitate the interests of others than those explicitly referred to in Article 18 §6 of the Constitution shall not be considered to be legitimate. (iii) The restriction has to be absolutely necessary and hence proportional to the objective for which it was enacted.

156. Any limitations on the freedom to manifest one's religion must be considered to be necessary in a democratic society under the mandate of Article 9 §2 of the ECHR, and this has been readily accepted by the Cypriot courts. Establishing that the measure is necessary in a democratic society involves showing that the action taken is in response to a pressing social need and that the interference with the rights protected is no greater than is necessary to address such pressing social need; consequently, a test of proportionality should therefore be applied. Any restrictions should further not discriminate among religions. Thus, the manifestation of religious freedom may, in certain cases, be subject to certain limitations in order to preserve social rights, as well as the rights of others.

157. Clashes between positive law and religious practices are not unusual. If the law is based upon a particular system of values, such as Christian morality or secularism, there could be circumstances under which the law requires what the religion prohibits or, conversely, where the law prohibits what the religion requires. Certain religions permit polygamy, religious divorces, marriage under the legal age, some forms of animal slaughter or sacrifice, wearing a turban or a headscarf, or religious use of drugs, all of which are practices which are legally prohibited. Other religions prohibit blood transfusion, military service, compulsory animal sacrifice, or compulsory wearing of a crash helmet, contrary to what is legally required. Certain religions argue that the observance of some religious holy days of Christianity amounts to religious discrimination; others argue that the obligation of children to attend schools violates their religious beliefs. The question of how to resolve such clashes has not been answered in a uniform manner by the various European states or non-European states.

158. It could be argued that the general principle so far accepted in Cyprus with respect to clashes between law and religion is that religious freedom does not necessarily imply that religious practices which are contrary to what is prescribed by law shall be upheld; furthermore, despite the fact that all religions are considered equal before the law, Cyprus socially constitutes a European, and therefore a predominantly Christian-oriented, civilization. While there have been few cases concerning new religious movements, probably due to the fact that the number of adherents to such religious movements in Cyprus is extremely low, it is very far-fetched to expect that a court might recognize that there should be a religious exemption for drug use, or that members of a particular religion could be excluded from compulsory schooling due to their religious beliefs. State interests are normally expected to prevail over religious interests unless there is a justification for why religious interests ought to exclude the application of state legal provisions.[186]

§2. SPECIAL CASES

I. Illicit Proselytism

159. Article 18 §5 of the Constitution prohibits illicit proselytism in favour of or against any religion. It prohibits, in particular, *the use of physical or moral compulsion for the purpose of making a person change or preventing him from changing his religion.* This constitutional prohibition, though, has never been supplemented by law. Consequently, there can be no prosecutions which concern illicit proselytism since, according to Article 12 §1 of the Constitution, which corresponds to Article 7 of the ECHR, there can be no crime, no offence and no punishment without law. Unlike Greece[187] – where the great majority of the population also adheres to the Orthodox doctrine – in Cyprus, there have not been any prosecutions of Jehovah's Witnesses with respect to proselytism since it has always been accepted that Jehovah's Witnesses is a free religion within the meaning of Article 18 §2 of the Constitution.[188] Therefore, illicit proselytism does not constitute a criminal offence; Article 18 §5 should be interpreted as setting out a constitutional principle which supplements the principle of religious freedom and not aiming at the oppression of religious minorities.

160. If the use of physical or moral compulsion constituted another criminal offence, irrespective of the fact that religion is concerned, then such compulsion could, of course, be prosecuted, though only as part of such other criminal offence. This would be the case, for instance, if the compulsion used in order to make a person change or prevent him/her from changing his/her religion was the direct result of a threat of injury to the person, reputation or property of the interested person. Such behaviour would amount to a violation of section 91 of the Criminal Code, Cap. 154 and would constitute the offence of *threatening violence*. However, in the aforementioned circumstances, it is the unlawful compulsion by threats and not the act of proselytizing which would constitute the offence. In practice, there has been, so far, no misapplication of section 91 of the Criminal Code; thus, no cases of religious proselytism have been included within its ambit when there were no threats of violence.[189]

186. *See also* A. Emilianides, 'Individual Rights and Internal Law of the Church', *Nomokanonika* 2, 21–29 (2015), (in Greek).
187. I. Konidaris, *Legal Theory and Practice on Jehovah's Witnesses* (Athens: A. Sakkoulas 4th ed. 2005, in Greek).
188. *The Minister of Interior v. The Jehovah's Witnesses Congregation (Cyprus) Ltd* [1995] 3 CLR 78 (in Greek). *See* C. Tornaritis, 'Is Chiliasm a Religion? Is It allowed by the Constitution and What Measures Are Provided against It?', *Cyprus Law Tribune* 1–2, 3–5 (1981), (in Greek).
189. *See* A. Emilianides, 'Religion in the Criminal Law in Cyprus', in *Religion and Criminal Law* 35–40 (M. Kottiranta & N. Doe eds, Leuven: Peeters, 2013).

II. Conscientious Objection

161. In the leading case of *Pitsillides*, there arose a question concerning the interpretation of Article 18 of the Constitution and of Article 9 of the ECHR with respect to conscientious objectors.[190] The two appellants were convicted and sentenced by the Military Court to twelve months and ten months imprisonment, respectively, for the offence of not joining the National Guard of the Republic, that is, the national army, when called up, contrary to the National Guard Law 20/1964 as amended. On being formally charged in respect of the offence, the appellants had replied that the reason for not enlisting was due to their being Jehovah's witnesses and that their conscience did not allow them to take up arms. The appellants argued that their religious belief and conscience constituted a reasonable cause that absolved them from any criminal liability and that compulsory military service ran contrary to Article 18 of the Constitution, violating their freedom of religion and conscience.

162. The Supreme Court held that *reasonable* is a relative term and for the cause to be reasonable, it must be objectively fair, with good faith and not contrary to, or incompatible with, the Law. It was, thus, held that the religious beliefs and grounds of conscience of the appellants do not by themselves constitute a reasonable cause, so long as the Law does not otherwise absolve them from criminal liability due to such beliefs. In declaring whether the limitation of religious freedom prescribed by the Law was deemed to be necessary in the interests of the security of the Republic, the Supreme Court considered that due to the Turkish military occupation of about 37% of the area of the Republic of Cyprus, the very existence of the State continues to be under express danger and that these circumstances justify the limitation of the right to freedom of religion and conscience by the imposition of compulsory military service.

163. The Court concluded that:

> so long as the National Guard is used for the defence and security of the country, the Law imposing the obligation for military service on the citizens of Cyprus, irrespectively of whether the right to religion and conscience is restricted, is not unconstitutional.[191]

However, the Court noted that the appropriate authorities of the Republic ought to consider, in the future, the exemption of conscientious objectors from compulsory military service and/or the imposition of alternative service. Law 2/1992 amended the National Guard Law 20/1964 so that the right of conscientious objectors to choose civilian service has been since recognized.[192] Law 2/1992 afforded

190. *Pitsillides v. The Republic* [1983] 2 CLR 374. *See also Christou v. The Republic* [1982] 2 CLR 365.

191. *Pitsillides v. The Republic* [1983] 2 CLR 374.

192. *See* T. Christodoulidou, 'Religious Conscientious Objection in Cyprus', *Cyprus and European Law Review* 2 324–330 (2006).

the possibility for conscientious objectors to be exempted from armed military service and instead to serve an alternative military service. Alternative service constituted either serving with a uniform for thirty-six months within the army precincts or serving without a uniform for forty-two months outside army precincts.

164. The length of the unarmed military service outside the armed precincts was twice as long as compulsory military service and was thus characterized as *a disproportionate restriction on the right of workers to earn their living in an occupation freely entered upon*, hence a violation of Article 1 §2 of the European Social Charter which stipulates the right of the worker to earn his/her living in an occupation freely entered upon by the European Committee of Social Rights.[193] Further, Alvaro Gil-Robles, the Council of Europe Commissioner for Human Rights, observed that: *these regulations do not correspond to the standards of the Council of Europe. Legislative measures are being contemplated to make Cypriot legislation compatible with the Recommendations on the subject by the Committee of Ministers.*[194]

165. The National Guard Law was recently further amended by Laws 88(I)/2007 and 61(I)/2008, which replaced the provisions of Law 2/1992. In 2011, a new National Guard Law was enacted (19(I)/2011). The new Law essentially reiterates the provisions of the previous legislation on conscientious objectors. It is further provided that in case of war or other necessity, the Minister may decide that conscientious objectors serving alternative social service have to serve an alternative military service. The Minister may further issue directions for the proper application of the Law. The new legal framework with respect to conscientious objectors is now more detailed and provides a higher degree of protection to conscientious objectors when compared to the previous legislation. In particular, section 47 of Law 19(I)/2011 provides that a person who refuses to perform his military service on grounds of his religious or ideological beliefs may be granted the status of conscientious objector by a decision of the Minister of Defence. The grounds of conscience must arise from a general approach towards life, which is the result of religious, moral or philosophical convictions which the person strictly applies in his life; as a result, persons who have a licence to carry a gun or for hunting, or are members of associations of hunting or shooting or of related activities, or who have been convicted, or are being prosecuted for an offence related to illegal use of guns, arms or violence, or who have served in military forces, carrying arms, after they adhered to their beliefs, may not be considered as conscientious objectors.

166. Moreover, a conscientious objector may cease to be recognized as such at any time, in which case he must serve regular military service for the remainder of his service if he: (a) submits a relevant petition and such petition is accepted by the Minister of Defence; (b) acquires a licence to carry a gun, or for hunting, or is a

193. European Committee of Social Rights, European Social Charter (Revised), Conclusions 2004 (Cyprus).
194. Report by Alvaro Gil-Robles on his visit to Cyprus, 25–29 Jun. 2003, CommDH (2004) 2, 12 Feb. 2004, para. 4.

member of associations of hunting or shooting or of related activities, or is convicted, or is being prosecuted for an offence related to illegal use of guns, arms, or violence, or it becomes known that he had previously served military service carrying arms; (c) participates in trade union activities, or a strike. It should be observed that certain requisites for the recognition of a conscientious objector seem to be quite problematic. To begin with, Article 12 §4 of the Constitution provides that *every person charged with an offence shall be presumed innocent until proven guilty according to law* since it is a fundamental constitutional principle that each person is considered to be innocent until proven guilty by a competent court, the provision that a person may not be considered as a conscientious objector simply due to the fact that he has been prosecuted – but not yet convicted – for an offence related to illegal use of guns, arms or violence, is in our view, unconstitutional. Further, in view of the fact that a person may opt to change his religion at any time, the fact that he had been convicted of an offence related to the illegal use of guns, arms, or violence at a time prior to changing his religion and thus becoming a conscientious objector, should be irrelevant. It is further unclear why participation in a trade union or a strike might be considered a valid ground for deciding that the conscientious objector should lose his status and why this is not a violation of the constitutional right to form and be part of trade unions and to participate in a strike as safeguarded by Articles 21 and 27 of the Constitution, respectively.

167. A person who is granted exemption from military service as a result of being a conscientious objector will have a duty to complete either an unarmed military service (special service) or alternative civil service. The unarmed military service is served in the National Guard; however, the conscientious objector does not carry guns and does not perform any activities relating to guns. The conscientious objector will have a duty to complete an unarmed military service for the period of time that he would have to serve in military service, plus an additional five months if he was to serve a military service of eighteen months or more, or four months if he was to serve a military service of more than twelve but less than eighteen months, or three months if he was to serve a military service of less than twelve months.

168. The alternative civil service is served in the public sector; the conscientious objector has to provide services which are for the benefit of the public in general, such as for the protection of the environment or the social sector. The conscientious objector will have a duty to complete an alternative civil service for the period of time that he would have to serve in military service, plus an addition of nine months if he was to serve a military service of eighteen months or more, or eight months if he was to serve a military service of more than twelve but less than eighteen months, or seven months if he was to serve a military service of less than twelve months. In practice, the alternative civil service has not been organized yet, and so far, no conscientious objectors have been called up for it. Instead, as a matter of practice, they are granted an indefinite exemption.

169. In order for a person to be recognized as a conscientious objector, the following procedure has to be followed: Each military office examines the applications of the alleged conscientious objectors, so long as such applications have been submitted within the relevant time frame. Within five days of the submission of the application by the alleged conscientious objector, such a person is examined by a medical committee in order to specify whether he is medically capable of serving in the National Guard. A Special Committee then examines whether the applicant should be properly considered to be a conscientious objector and provides a relevant opinion to the Minister of Defence. There are two types of special committees: the Committee for the Examination of Psychical Ability and the Committee for the Examination of Mental Ability. The Committee for the Examination of Psychical Ability consists of three military medical doctors appointed by the Minister, whereas the Committee for the Examination of Mental Ability consists of three psychiatrists from either the public or private sector who are also appointed by the Minister. The Committees may examine all relevant data and may request additional evidence or call for experts. The Minister of Defence decides finally on the issue within one month after having received the opinion of the Special Committee; if the Minister's decision is different from the opinion of the Special Committee, he should provide the grounds for his decision. An applicant who has not been recognized as a conscientious objector may have recourse to the Supreme Court against the relevant decision of the Minister of Defence.

170. Reservist obligation is served after the military service has been completed. Law 2/1992 did not provide for an exception for reserve duty where a conscientious objector had already completed the normal armed military service. As a result, a person would not be allowed to use his status as a conscientious objector in order to serve his reserve duty unarmed if he had completed his military service armed, either due to the fact that he had served in the army before 1992 when there had been no provisions for conscientious objectors, or because he became one later.[195] Until 2002, several Jehovah's Witnesses who had performed their armed military service and decided to claim their right for conscientious objection by failing to appear for reserve duty had been convicted and sentenced either to imprisonment of up to two years or to a fine of up to GBP 1,500.[196] However, since November 2002, the Government, as a matter of policy, has decided not to prosecute those Jehovah's Witnesses who refuse to do an armed reserve duty, pending a revision of the National Guard Law.

171. Law 88(I)/2007, which amended the National Guard Law, provided that reservist obligation is served for the period of time which the conscientious objector would have normally had to serve, irrespectively of whether such reservist obligation is served as an unarmed military service or alternative civil service; furthermore, reservists are afforded the right to opt for an alternative unarmed service, even if they had completed the regular military service. Therefore, the new Law safeguarded the rights of conscientious objectors in Cyprus, also in so far as reserve duty is concerned. This was reiterated in Law 19(I)/2011.

---

195. *Petrou v. The Republic*, Case 527/2000, Judgment of 31 Oct. 2002 (in Greek).
196. *Andreou v. The Republic* [1998] 2 CLR 300 (in Greek).

III. Religious Beliefs and Obligation to Serve in the Army

172. In the case of *Daniel Sarieddine*, the petitioner, an adherent of a Muslim sect, argued that he should not have an obligation to serve in the National Guard since such a National Guard has a Christian Orthodox character.[197] The Supreme Court rejected the petitioner's arguments and held that the obligation to serve in the National Guard refers to the citizens of the Republic and not to the adherents of any particular religion or creed; the National Guard is not considered to be of Christian Orthodox character, or of any other religious character. Indeed, the Ministry of Defence had provided that non-Christians ought to be facilitated in the exercise of their religious beliefs. In view of the above, it was held that there was no violation of Article 18 of the Constitution or of Article 9 of the ECHR.

173. According to a Decision of the Council of Ministers, Turkish Cypriots were excluded from the obligation to serve in the National Guard in view of the abnormal situation prevailing on the island. Furthermore, the military service of those belonging to the three constitutionally recognized Religious Groups was voluntary, and such persons were exempted from the obligation to serve in the National Guard.[198] In 2006, the Cypriot Ombudsman held that the decision of the Council of Ministers to exclude the members of the three Religious Groups of the Republic, namely the Maronites, the Roman Catholics and the Armenians, from the obligation to serve in the National Guard, violated the principle of equal treatment and constituted discrimination on the grounds of religion. Following the Ombudsman's decision, the Council of Ministers decided that members of the three Religious Groups now have an obligation to serve in the National Guard.[199]

174. It should further be noted that members of the clergy, religious ministers, or monks of any known religion are exempted from the obligation to serve in the army according to section 24 §1(i) of Law 19(I)/2011. This provision was examined in the case of *Andreou*;[200] the Apostolic Church of Jesus Christ had requested the exception of the obligation to serve in the National Guard of one of its members, who was the main deacon of ecclesiastical music of the Church. The Minister of Defence did not grant the exception, arguing that a deacon of music might not be considered a member of the clergy. The Court observed that the applicant had been consecrated as a member of the clergy of the Apostolic Church and that he had been authorized to perform sermons, take care of the religious needs of his community, attend religious ceremonies and represent the Church, and in general to perform willingly all services that the Church requires him to render. In view of the above, the Court held that the applicant was a member of the clergy since such a term ought to be examined in light of the specific circumstances of each individual Church and

197. *Sarieddine v. The Republic* [2004] 3 CLR 572 (in Greek).
198. Council of Ministers Decision 41/296 of 29 Jun. 1994.
199. Council of Ministers Decision 65.732 of 19 Jun. 2007.
200. *Andreou v. The Republic*, Case 50/2006, Judgment of 4 Jun. 2007, (in Greek).

in order to comply in the best possible way with the principle of religious freedom. Undoubtedly, the Court's interpretation is consistent with the principle of non-discrimination between religions.

IV. Work Permits of Religious Ministers

175. In the case of *Levantis*, the applicant was a Greek national married to a Greek Cypriot and resident in Cyprus. He impugned, by means of recourse before the Supreme Court of Cyprus, the decision whereby his application for a permit to work as a Religious Officer of the Church of God of Prophecy was rejected.[201] It was argued by the applicant that he was prevented from exercising and expressing his religious duties as a Religious Officer of the Church of God of Prophecy in Cyprus, that there was discrimination and unequal treatment against the applicant as a religious officer of the said Church, that the freedom of worship was violated, as well as that the applicant was compelled, in a manner tantamount to the exercise of moral pressure, to change his religion.

176. The Supreme Court rejected the application and held that Article 18 of the Constitution safeguards freedom of religion and not entitlement to work permit, a matter which is regulated specially by the Laws of Cyprus. The applicant was free to profess any religion he wished, while the refusal of a work permit did not prevent him from attending his Church or otherwise manifesting his religion or belief. Thus, it was held that there was no violation of Article 18 of the Constitution. While it can be generally accepted that granting work permits to aliens falls within the discretionary powers of the State and that religious freedom does not entail a right to be granted a work permit, it is suggested, on the other hand, that the aforementioned decision of the Supreme Court presents certain problems. The said alien was a resident of Cyprus who had married a Cypriot and who intended to work as a religious minister of a Church; rejecting his application for a work permit should not be arbitrary so as to cause concerns that this was due to his religious beliefs and to the fact that he wanted to work as a religious officer of that particular Church. There seemed to be no justification for why the application for a work permit was rejected in the case of *Levantis*, and this raises serious concerns about religious discrimination.

201. *Levantis v. The Republic* [1988] 3 CLR 2483.

Chapter 2. Collective Religious Freedom

177. Article 18 §2 of the Constitution provides that all religions whose doctrines or rites are not secret are free. For a religion to be constitutionally protected, it need not register with the authorities; the only requirement is that its doctrines or rites are not secret. There has been so far no court decision or any other attempt to define religion in Cypriot Law; in principle, however, not only mainstream religions, such as Christian denominations of many kinds, Jehovah's Witnesses, Judaism, Islam, Hinduism, Buddhism and Sikhism, but also less known religions, or new religious movements, have been held to constitute a religion in the sense of Article 18 §2 of the Constitution, so long as their doctrines or rites were free. A sect, or a specific religious creed, may well be considered a religion in the constitutional sense. The assessment of whether a particular creed forms a religion excludes an assessment by the State of the legitimacy of religious beliefs or the ways in which such beliefs are expressed.[202]

178. With respect to the recognition of a Religious Group as a separate 'religion', the case of the Orthodox Christians who follow the Old Calendar should be examined. As already stated, the Church of the Orthodox Christians following the Old Calendar may not be considered part of the Autocephalous Orthodox Church of Cyprus, for which Articles 110 and 111 of the Constitution apply. In Greece, however, the Old Calendarists are not, in general, recognized as a separate religion since it is considered that they may not unilaterally distinguish themselves from the Orthodox Church.[203] Such a view, prevailing in Greece, was not accepted in Cyprus. The Family Court, in the case of *Onisiphorou*, correctly observed that the Church of the Orthodox Christians following the Old Calendar has its own administrative organization, Charter, clergy and temples and does not consider itself bound by the provisions of the Charter of the Orthodox Church of Cyprus.

179. The Family Court thus held that:

> Since a person belonging to the Church of the Orthodox Christians who follow the Old Calendar does not consider himself as a member of the Orthodox Church who follows the New Calendar, it may not be considered that such a person belongs to the latter Church. A person who resides in Cyprus, and yet has not been baptised, nor celebrate marriage, nor participated in any ecclesiastical ceremonies, in temples belonging to the Greek Orthodox Church of Cyprus, but rather he/she has been baptised and participated in ecclesiastical ceremonies in temples belonging to the Church of the Orthodox Christians who

202. *Metropolitan Church of Bessarabia v. Moldova*, Judgment of 14 Dec. 2001; (2002) 35 EHRR 306.
203. *See* C. Papageorgiou, 'The Constitutional Status of the Religious Communities of the Old-Calendarists or Genuine Orthodox Christians in the Greek Legal Order', in *State, Orthodox Church and Religions in Greece* 131–137 (C. Papastathis & G. Papathomas eds, Katerini: Epektasis, 2006, in Greek).

follow the Old Calendar, may not, even presumably, be considered as belonging to the Greek Orthodox Church of Cyprus, or any other Church which follows the New Calendar. A different result would be contrary to the principles of religious freedom, as well as the right to liberty, and the right to marry and found a family, which are all fundamental freedoms safeguarded by Articles 18, 11 and 22 of the Constitution respectively.[204]

180. In view of the above, it is considered that the Church of the Orthodox Christians, who follow the Old Calendar, is a religion in the sense of Article 18 of the Constitution, which may be properly distinguished from the Orthodox Church referred to in Article 110 of the Constitution.[205] The aforementioned approach is consistent with the Judgment of the ECtHR in the case of *Serif v. Greece.*[206] The applicant, in the case of Serif, enjoyed the support of part of the Muslim Community in Thrace and was elected Mufti, despite the fact that another Mufti had already been appointed by the Greek Government. The applicant was subsequently convicted of the criminal offence of having usurped the functions of a minister without having the right to do so. The ECtHR, finding a violation of Article 9 of the ECHR, noted that tension between competing Religious Groups is an unavoidable consequence of pluralism; the role of the authorities in such a situation is not to remove the cause of the tension, thereby eliminating pluralism, but instead to ensure tolerance between the rival factions. In a democratic society, there is no need for the State to take measures to ensure that religious communities remain, or are brought under, a unified leadership.

181. What is more, Article 18 §3 provides that all religions are equal before the law, and no legislative, executive or administrative act of the Republic shall discriminate against any religious institution or religion. There should, in principle, be no discrimination between newly established religions or religions which represent religious minorities. The leading case with respect to discrimination between religions is the case of *The Jehovah's Witnesses Congregation (Cyprus) Ltd.*[207] The Minister of Interior had decided to omit marriage officers of the Jehovah's Witnesses Congregation from the annual list of officers authorized to conclude marriages on the ground that such officers had ceased to be considered as such following the enactment of Civil Marriage Law 21/90. The Supreme Court held that according to Article 18 of the Constitution, freedom of religion should not be violated, either directly or indirectly, and that all religions whose rites are known are equal before the law. It further held that Law 21/90 should not have been interpreted in the manner in which the Minister of Interior had. Thus, it was held that the marriage officers of the Jehovah's Witnesses Congregation should not have been omitted from the relevant list of officers authorized to conclude marriages.

---

204. *Onisiphorou v. Onisiphorou Cyprus Law Review* 49–50 (1995): 7439 (in Greek).
205. This view was confirmed in Action 2046/11, *Nun Markella and Others v. Archimandrite Sevastianos Stavrou and Others*. Decision of 30 Nov. 2015 (District Court Larnaca, in Greek).
206. *Serif v. Greece*, Judgment of 4 Dec. 1999; (2001) 31 EHRR 561. *See also Agga v. Greece*, Judgment of the ECtHR of 17 Oct. 2002.
207. *The Minister of Interior v. The Jehovah's Witnesses Congregation (Cyprus) Ltd* [1995] 3 CLR 78 (in Greek).

Chapter 3. Organizational Religious Freedom

182. Were the organizational life of a religious community not protected by Article 18 of the Constitution, all other aspects of the individual's freedom of religion would become vulnerable.[208] A legal person who constitutes a religious organization is capable of having or exercising the rights mentioned in Article 18 of the Constitution. While a religious association is not capable of exercising the right of freedom of conscience since this would be a metaphysical impossibility, such a religious association is capable of exercising the right to manifest its religion. The right of a religious community to religious freedom complements the individual right to religious freedom of the members of such community so that non-discrimination of religious communities may be effected; equality of religions necessarily implies that a religious community enjoys certain rights as such, in addition to the rights of its members.

183. With respect to legal persons, Article 18 should be read in conjunction with Article 21 of the Constitution. Article 21 provides, *inter alia*, that every person has the right to freedom of association with others, including the right to form and join trade unions for the protection of his/her interests. No restrictions shall be placed on the exercise of these rights other than such as are prescribed by law and are only absolutely necessary in the *interests of the security of the Republic or the constitutional order or the public safety or the public order or the public health or the public morals or for the protection of the rights and liberties guaranteed by this Constitution to any person*, whether or not such person participates in such assembly or is a member of such association. Notwithstanding any restriction imposed as above, no person shall be compelled to join any association or to continue to be a member thereof. Any association, the object or activities of which are contrary to the constitutional order, is prohibited.

184. Article 21 of the Constitution corresponds to Article 11 of the ECHR, which provides, *inter alia*, that everyone has the right to freedom of association with others, including the right to form and join trade unions for the protection of his/her interests. No restrictions shall be placed on the exercise of these rights other than such as are prescribed by law and are necessary in a democratic society in the interests of national security or public safety, for the prevention of disorder or crime, for the protection of health or morals, or for the protection of the rights and freedoms of others. The ECtHR held that:

> Where the organisation of the religious community is at issue, Article 9 must be interpreted in the light of Article 11 of the ECHR which safeguards associative life against unjustified State interference. Seen in this perspective, the believer's right to freedom of religion encompasses the expectation that the community will be allowed to function peacefully, free from arbitrary State intervention. Indeed, the autonomous existence of religious communities is

208. *Hasan and Chaush v. Bulgaria*, Judgment of 26 Oct. 2000; (2002) 34 EHRR 1339.

indispensable for pluralism in democratic society and is thus an issue at the very heart of the protection which Article 9 affords.[209]

185. As already stated, the administrative organization of the five main religions of the island is explicitly safeguarded in Article 110 of the Constitution. This should not mean that other religions do not enjoy, to their full extent, all the freedoms safeguarded by Article 18 of the Constitution. In the case of *Ktimatiki Eteria Neas Taxeos*, the members of the applicant company were Jehovah's Witnesses.[210] The applicants applied for a building permit to erect at the quarter of Zakaki, a two-storey building. The respondents refused the permit without disclosing the real reasons for doing so. The applicants impugned the decision whereby the permit was refused. During the proceedings in the recourse, it was made apparent that the real reason was public order or safety because of the opposition of the Orthodox Church and the inhabitants of the Zakaki area to have a building belonging to the said religion erected in their area.

186. The Supreme Court annulled the *sub judice* decision and held that reasons for denying the right of a person or group of public safety or public order to manifest his/her or their religion or belief can only be limited by law, according to Article 18 of the Constitution and Article 9 of the ECHR; an administrative organ cannot, by itself, refuse on such grounds an application submitted to it. Thus, the right to manifest one's religion refers not only to individuals but also to Churches and other religious communities; any restriction of such right should be in accordance with the law, should meet one of the specified legitimate aims and should be necessary in a democratic society; any interference will be unconstitutional if it is not proportionate to the pressing social need that it addresses.[211]

187. However, only activities of a religious organization which refer to the exercise of their religious freedom are safeguarded by Article 18 of the Constitution; other activities are not safeguarded by this Article. In the case of *Church of Nazarene International Ltd*, the petitioners argued that the State should not have refused to grant them a permit to buy offices in Cyprus because that ran contrary to the freedom of religious liberty enshrined in Article 18 of the Constitution and Article 9 of the ECHR.[212] The Court acknowledged that the administration cannot hinder, directly or indirectly, the exercise of religious freedom but held that in the circumstances of that particular case, there had been no violation of Article 18 of the Constitution. This was due to the fact that the petitioners had asked for a permit to buy offices in Cyprus for residence purposes or vacation purposes and not for any purpose directly or indirectly related to the exercise of religious freedom. Thus, Article 18 of the Constitution was not deemed to be applicable in the aforementioned case.

209. *Ibid.*, para. 36.
210. *Ktimatiki Eteria Neas Taxeos v. The Chairman and Members of the Municipal Committee of Limassol* [1989] 3 CLR 461.
211. A. Emilianides, C. Adamides & E. Eftychiou, 'Allocation of Religious Space in Cyprus', *The Cyprus Review* 23, 97–121 (2011).
212. *Church of the Nazarene International Ltd v. Minister of Interior* [1996] 3 CLR 3091 (in Greek).

Part III. Legal Status of Religious Communities

Chapter 1. Formal Status of Religious Communities

§1. The Legal Status of the Five Constitutionally Recognized Religions

I. The Legal Status of the Orthodox Church

188. According to Article 94 of the 1914 Charter, the Church of Cyprus was established as a legal entity. Neither the 1980 Charter nor the current Charter of the Orthodox Church contains a provision similar to Article 94 of the 1914 Charter with regard to the Orthodox Church per se; however, the current Charter contains a similar provision with regard to particular ecclesiastical corporations, namely metropolises (Article 31), parish churches (Article 45), monasteries (Article 65 §11), and a number of Church-run charitable foundations (Article 71). Similar provisions were included in the 1980 Charter. It is indisputable that the Orthodox Church has remained a legal entity since the 1914 Charter maintained its force twenty years after the coming into operation of the Constitution, while the institutional status of the Orthodox Church is determined by Article 110, §1 of the Constitution, which provides that the Autocephalous Greek Orthodox Church of Cyprus shall continue to have the exclusive right of regulating and administering its own internal affairs and property in accordance with the Holy Canons and its Charter in force for the time being.[213]

189. A more complex question was whether the Orthodox Church should be properly viewed as a legal person under private law or under public law. According to one view, the Orthodox Church ought to be viewed as a legal person under private law and specifically as an association.[214] However, according to a different view, the Orthodox Church should be considered a legal person under public law due to the fact that the Constitution has conferred upon it powers which appertain to the state, especially with regard to the implementation of its religious law on

213. C. Papastathis, *On the Administrative Organisation of the Church of Cyprus* 37 (Thessaloniki: 1981, in Greek).
214. K. Chrysostomides, 'Cyprus Ecclesiastical Law in Force', in *Tribute to the Parish of Agion Panton of London* 131 (London: 1968, in Greek).

institutions of family law and to the adjudication of the relevant disputes by the appropriate religious tribunals, prior to the First Amendment of the Constitution in 1989.[215] According to Cypriot Law, a legal person is considered to be a legal person under public law if it has been established by law, is endowed with decisive public law competencies and is under the control of the State.[216] The Orthodox Church of Cyprus does not fulfil the requirements of the aforementioned definition since it is not under the control of the State.

190. It is suggested that it would be more accurate to characterize the Orthodox Church as a legal person of a unique and peculiar nature, to which the Constitution has explicitly conferred powers which appertain to the state. This was the view of Artemides J. in his dissenting opinion in the case of the *Orthodox Church of Cyprus*, where it was held that:

> It would be inaccurate to classify the Orthodox Church of Cyprus as any given legal person, known to our legal system … Churches in general are religious organisations, which exist independently of state boundaries and their spiritual functions do not alter with the various civic changes. The religious status of the Church of Cyprus is considered to be a legal fact, since it has existed for centuries without any alterations, even though Cyprus had been conquered by several rulers until the establishment of the Republic of Cyprus in 1960. Article 111 of the Constitution has ensured for the Church of Cyprus and the other Religious Groups their competencies and powers with respect to matters of personal status. Such constitutional provision safeguards that the Church enjoys the same civic competencies it always had. Therefore, the legal status of the Church of Cyprus does not fall within any of the known definitions of legal persons but is described in accordance with the provisions of the Constitution concerning its internal administration, powers and rights.[217]

191. It was, therefore, suggested that the Orthodox Church should be considered to be an *authority* of the Republic in the sense of Article 139 of the Constitution.[218] *Organs* or *authorities* in the sense of Article 139 mean specific juridical creations, bearing the features of individual and concrete organic institutions of the Government and functioning for, and on behalf of, a primary legal entity, such as the Republic of Cyprus.[219] However, the majority of the Supreme Court of Cyprus, in the case of the *Orthodox Church of Cyprus*, held that the Orthodox Church was not an authority of the Republic of Cyprus in the sense of Article 139 of the Constitution and, consequently, did not have the right to apply before the Supreme Court

215. C. Papastathis, *On the Administrative Organisation of the Church of Cyprus* 38 (Thessaloniki: 1981, in Greek).
216. *Petrou and Others v. The New Co-operative Society of Karpashia* 3 RSCC 58.
217. *Autocephalous Orthodox Church of Cyprus v. The House of Representatives* [1990] 3 CLR 338 (in Greek), Judgment of Artemides J.
218. C. Papastathis, 'The Power of the Church to Have Recourse in the Supreme Court under Article 139', *Review of Public Law and Administrative Law* 34, 321–325 (1990), (in Greek).
219. *Celaleddin and Others v. The Council of Ministers* 5 RSCC 102; *Muderrisoglou and Others v. The Council of Ministers* 5 RSCC 59.

in order to challenge the constitutionality of Law 95/1989 in advance, which amended Article 111 of the Constitution (The First Amendment).[220]

192. The opinion of the majority of the Supreme Court in the above case was based on the following five arguments: (a) the Orthodox Church of Cyprus is not constituted and does not function on the basis of the Constitution; (b) its competencies with regard to the family matters of its members according to Article 111 of the Constitution, may not be considered to denote the exercise of state powers; (c) the execution of any judgments or orders of the ecclesiastical courts is carried out through the public authorities of the Republic and not through ecclesiastical organs; (d) the Church is not a public authority according to Article 29 of the Constitution which safeguards the right of an individual to petition the authorities; (e) the decisions of the Church are not considered to be administrative decisions of public law and are not subject to the judicial control of the Supreme Court, or to the issue of prerogative orders, such as certiorari or prohibition. Thus, it was held that the Orthodox Church of Cyprus is a sui generis legal person of private law, which may not be considered an organ or authority of the Republic.[221]

193. The above judgment of the majority of the Supreme Court seems to be problematic with regard to the period prior to the First Amendment of the Constitution in 1989.[222] With respect to the first of the aforementioned arguments, it should be noted that the existence of the Orthodox Church as a religious institution is provided for in Article 110 of the Constitution. Similarly, Article 110 of the Constitution provides for the existence of the institution of Vakf and the three Religious Groups of the Republic. The Constitution does not provide for the existence of other religious organizations. It is therefore inaccurate to argue that the Orthodox Church is not constituted and does not function according to the constitutional provisions. Article 110 §1 expressly provides that the Church shall regulate and administer its own internal affairs and property in accordance with the Holy Canons and its Charter in force for the time being. Thus, the supreme law of the State provides for the competencies and powers of the Orthodox Church of Cyprus; the Orthodox Church functions on the basis of explicit constitutional provisions.

194. With regard to the second argument of the majority of the Supreme Court, it has to be noted that Article 111 of the Constitution, prior to its amendment in 1989, had provided for exclusive competencies of the Orthodox Church regarding the family law matters of their members. Thus, prior to the 1989 amendment, the Orthodox Church had the exclusive competence to legislate on the family law matters of its members and to adjudicate the relevant family law disputes. It had further

---

220. *Autocephalous Orthodox Church of Cyprus v. The House of Representatives* [1990] 3 CLR 338 (in Greek).

221. *Ibid.*, Judgment of Stylianides, Malachtos, Demetriades, Kourris, Papadopoulos, Boyiadjis and Chrysostomis J.

222. *See* A. Emilianides, 'Religious Entities as Legal Persons: Cyprus', in *Churches and Other Religious Organisations as Legal Persons* 51 (Leuven: Peeters, 2007); A. Emilianides, 'The Constitutional Position of the Charter of the Church of Cyprus', *Nomokanonika* 2, 50 ff. (2005), (in Greek).

been provided that the Greek Communal Chamber would not act inconsistently with the provisions of ecclesiastical law; thus, the Orthodox Church – and the three Religious Groups of the Republic – had exercised its powers as a state organ, 'subject to the provisions of the Constitution'.[223]

195. Similarly, the fact that the execution of the judgments of the ecclesiastical courts is carried out through the public authorities of the Republic – which was the third argument of the majority of the Supreme Court – is an argument in favour of the view that the Orthodox Church exercises functions which appertain to the State. There would be no need to provide that the execution of the judgments of the ecclesiastical courts must be carried out by the public authorities unless the competencies of the ecclesiastical courts are considered to be *public* in nature.[224] The ecclesiastical courts were provided for by Article 111 of the Constitution in order to function as state courts with respect to the family law matters of their members, and this is the reason why the execution of their judgments and orders by the public authorities of the State was provided for.[225]

196. As already mentioned, the competencies provided for in Article 111 of the Constitution had been exercised prior to the First Amendment of 1989, subject to the provisions of the Constitution and, thus, subject to Article 35 of the Constitution, which provides that the legislative, executive and judicial authorities of the Republic shall be bound to secure, within the limits of their respective competence, the efficient application of the provisions of Part II of the Constitution. The protection of human rights in the Republic is safeguarded by Part II of the Constitution; moreover, the right to petition the authorities, provided for in Article 29, forms an integral part of Part II of the Constitution. Therefore, the Orthodox Church, insofar as it functions as a legislative or judicial authority on the basis of Article 111 of the Constitution, is subject to Part II of the Republic;[226] as a result, it could be argued, contrary to the majority opinion of the Supreme Court, that the Church is a public authority according to Article 29 of the Constitution and that the decisions of the Church under Article 111 of the Constitution are properly considered to be subject to the judicial control of the Supreme Court.

197. It has been correctly suggested that the Supreme Court has the competence to issue prerogative orders according to Article 155 §4 of the Constitution in order to safeguard the constitutional order and prohibit the usurpation of competencies by the ecclesiastical courts;[227] the ecclesiastical courts might not exercise powers which were not provided for in Article 111 of the Constitution. In England, prior to

223. *Autocephalous Orthodox Church of Cyprus v. The House of Representatives* [1990] 3 CLR 338 (in Greek), Judgments of Loizou J, Artemides J and Pikis J.
224. *Ibid.*, Judgment of Nikitas J.
225. C. Tornaritis, *The Ecclesiastical Courts Especially in Cyprus* 41–42 (Nicosia: 1976).
226. A. Emilianides, 'The Constitutional Position of the Charter of the Church of Cyprus', *Nomokanonika* 2, 58 (2005), (in Greek). *See also Pellegrini v. Italy*, Judgment of the ECtHR of 20 Jul. 2001.
227. G. Serghides, *Internal and External Conflict of Laws in Regard to Family Relations in Cyprus* 346 ff. (Nicosia: 1988).

1857, prohibition orders might be issued against the orders of the ecclesiastical courts, even though such courts were not subject to state courts. Thus, the fact that the ecclesiastical courts enjoyed exclusive jurisdiction with respect to matters within their competence, according to Article 111 of the Constitution, did not imply that the Supreme Court might not exercise judicial control in cases of acts of the ecclesiastical courts which were *ultra vires* and thus, invalid due to lack of jurisdiction.

198. In view of the above, it is suggested that the Orthodox Church ought to have been considered a public authority in the sense of Article 139 of the Constitution when the case of the *Orthodox Church of Cyprus* was adjudicated. It would have been highly paradoxical if the Constitution had conferred certain competencies on the Orthodox Church without simultaneously providing for the means by which such competencies could have properly been applied.[228] Since the relevant competencies of the Orthodox Church would have otherwise belonged to the Greek Communal Chamber, which should properly be considered a state organ,[229] classifying the Orthodox Church as a legal person of private law seems particularly peculiar. However, the legislative and judicial competencies with regard to family matters of members of the Orthodox Church are presently exercised by the House of Representatives (with the exception of laws regarding the validity of marriages celebrated in the Greek Orthodox Church) and the Family Courts, respectively, it is suggested that there is no actual possibility, or necessity, that the Supreme Court should change its view in the future with regard to the legal status of the Orthodox Church. Thus, the Orthodox Church of Cyprus should be properly considered a peculiar legal person of private law; such legal person is a non-profit association.

II. The Legal Status of the Three Religious Groups of the Republic

199. Although the Supreme Court's aforementioned judgment concerned only the legal status of the Orthodox Church of Cyprus, it is undisputed that its principles also apply with regard to the three constitutionally recognized Religious Groups of the Republic, namely the Maronites, the Armenians and the Roman Catholics. This is due to the fact that all the aforementioned rights of the Orthodox Church are also granted to the three Religious Groups, according to Articles 110 §3 and 111 §1 of the Constitution. The view suggested above is in line with the principles of the system of coordination, as applied in the Republic of Cyprus.[230] Therefore, the three Religious Groups of the Republic should also be properly considered peculiar legal persons of private law.

228. *Autocephalous Orthodox Church of Cyprus v. The House of Representatives* [1990] 3 CLR 338 (in Greek), Judgment of Pikis J.
229. *See also Turkish Communal Chamber v. The Council of Ministers* 5 RSCC 59.
230. A. Emilianides, 'Religious Entities as Legal Persons: Cyprus', in *Churches and Other Religious Organisations as Legal Persons* 52 (L. Friedner ed., Leuven: Peeters, 2007).

200. It should be noted, however, that in the Statement by the Government of the United Kingdom concerning the rights of the smaller Religious Groups of the Republic in 1960, it was provided that:

> it will also be possible under the Constitution for any Religious Group, in common with other bodies, to have recourse as a group to the Supreme Constitutional Court to complain of any breach of the Constitution or abuse of power directly affecting the group as a body.[231]

In view of the fact that the legal status of the Orthodox Church is the same as the legal status of the three Religious Groups of the Republic, it would be inconceivable to categorize the three Religious Groups as legal persons under public law so long as the Orthodox Church is considered to be a legal person under private law. Therefore, the aforementioned judgment of the Supreme Court in the case of the *Orthodox Church of Cyprus* also deprives the right of the three Religious Groups to petition the Supreme Court as authorities of the Republic on the basis of Article 139 of the Constitution, contrary to what the Statement by the Government of the United Kingdom had provided.[232]

III. The Legal Status of the Islamic Community

201. It is further suggested that the same legal status should also be accorded to the Islamic religion since Article 110 §2 of the Constitution recognizes the institution of Vakf and the Principles and Laws of Vakfs and stipulates that all matters relating to, or in any way affecting the institution or foundation of Vakfs or any Vakf properties, including properties belonging to Mosques and any other Muslim religious institution, shall be governed solely by the Laws and Principles of Vakfs and the Laws and Regulations enacted or made by the Turkish Communal Chamber.[233] Therefore, the Vakfs should be properly considered legal persons of private law.[234]

§2. The Legal Status of Other Religions

202. Religions other than the five constitutionally recognized religions are not required to register with the authorities. Their members enjoy religious freedom according to the constitutional provisions, even if such religious organizations have

---

231. Cmnd. 1093, *Cyprus, Presented to Parliament by the Secretary of State for the Colonies, the Secretary of State for Foreign Affairs and the Minister of Defence by Command of her Majesty*, Appendix E: Statement by Her Majesty's Government, para. 5.
232. *See* further *Autocephalous Orthodox Church of Cyprus v. The House of Representatives* [1990] 3 CLR 338 (in Greek), Judgment of Artemides J.
233. *See* in general A. Emilianides, *Annotated Legal Documents on Islam in Europe: Cyprus* (Leiden: Brill, 2014).
234. *See* A. Emilianides, 'Islamic Faith as a One of the Main Religions: The Case of Cyprus', in *Islam in Europe* 220–229 (Institute for State-Church Relations & M. Moravcikova eds, Bratislava: 2005).

not registered with the authorities. However, if these religious organizations desire to engage in financial transactions, such as maintaining a bank account, they must register as a non-profit company. In order to register, a religious organization must submit an application stating the purpose of the non-profit organization and providing the names of the organization's directors. So far, applications by religious organizations have been accepted by the authorities of the Republic of Cyprus without any particular problems. However, the State has disputed whether a non-profit religious organization registered by the Coptic Church, i.e., a foundation entitled St Mark Coptic Orthodox Church, fulfilled the criteria for exercising religious freedom under Article 18 of the Constitution, claiming that the Foundation was not registered as a church per se. It is submitted that this is an incorrect interpretation of Article 18 of the Constitution.

203. It should be noted that there is no difference concerning the provisions of registering between emerging religious entities and historical majority churches, with the exception of the five constitutionally recognized religions. However, it is suggested that the authorities would refuse to register any religion whose doctrines or rites are secret in order to comply with the provisions of Article 18 §2 of the Constitution, which stipulates that all religions whose doctrines or rites are not secret are free.

204. Moreover, a religion could also register as a charitable foundation; such charitable foundations are, for instance, the *Charitable Foundation of the Church of the Grace of Jesus Christ* and the *Charitable Foundation of the Church of the God of Prophecy*. Religions could also register as private associations or clubs. Upon approval, non-profit organizations are tax-exempt and are required to provide annual reports of their activities. Registered religious entities may conclude contracts, own real property, or act as employers, without any restrictions other than those provided by law, for all legal persons that engage in financial transactions.[235]

235. *See* A. Emilianides, 'Religious Entities as Legal Persons: Cyprus', in *Churches and Other Religious Organisations as Legal Persons* 52–53 (L. Friedner ed., Leuven: Peeters, 2007).

Chapter 2. Autonomy of Religious Communities

§1. Introduction

205. As already mentioned, the Orthodox Church, the three Religious Groups and the Islamic religion all enjoy exclusive competence with respect to their internal affairs, as well as the administration of their property. In addition, other religions and creeds enjoy organizational religious freedom with respect to the administration of their internal affairs and property. Thus, religious communities enjoy a considerable extent of religious autonomy according to Cypriot Law and are regulated not by state laws but by their own internal Canon Law provisions. The only exception is the Turkish Islamic religion, since due to the Kemalic reforms, the administration of Vakfs and the election of Mufti had been regulated by state laws appertaining only to the Turkish Community of the island. Most religions and creeds in Cyprus do not follow specific 'Cypriot' Canon Law provisions contained in charters or internal regulations; thus, the Roman Catholics and the Maronites adhere to the Canon Law provisions followed generally by the Roman Catholic Church and the Maronite Church, respectively. However, the Orthodox Church, the Church of the Orthodox Christians who follow the Old Calendar and the Armenian Church, have enacted specific Cypriot Canon Law instruments which regulate their internal affairs; such legal instruments shall be specifically analysed.

§2. The Charter of the Orthodox Church of Cyprus

I. General Characteristics

206. The current Charter of the Orthodox Church of Cyprus was enacted by the Holy Synod on 13 September 2010.[236] The previous Charter was in operation from 1980–2010.[237] The 2010 Charter consists of ninety-two Articles, divided into nine chapters, namely (a) organization and administration (Articles 1–18); (b) election of bishops (Articles 19–30); (c) organization of the ecclesiastical districts (Articles 31–44); (d) organization of parishes (Articles 45–64); (e) monasteries (Articles 65–70); (f) ecclesiastical foundations (Articles 71–77); (g) administration of ecclesiastical justice (Articles 78–82); (h) family law institutions (Articles 83–90); and (i) final provisions (Articles 91–92). The Charter further contains three lengthy Annexes (Annex A: Table of parishes, communities and monasteries of parishes,

---

236. *See* in detail A. Emilianides & C. Katsaros (eds), *The New Charter of the Church of Cyprus* (Nicosia: Hippasus, 2013, in Greek); I. Konidaris & A. Emilianides, *Elements of Greek and Cypriot Ecclesiastical Law* (Athens-Thessaloniki: Sakkoulas, 2016, in Greek).

237. *See* Chrysostomos, Archbishop of Cyprus, 'Introductory Report to the New Charter of the Church of Cyprus', *Apostolos Varnavas* 40, 375–404 (1979), (in Greek); C. Papastathis, *On the Administrative Organisation of the Church of Cyprus* (Thessaloniki: 1981, in Greek); C. Papastathis, 'The New Charter of the Church of Cyprus' *Hydor ek Petras* 4–5, 5–17 (1980), (in Greek); E. Mantzouneas, *Ecclesiastical Law of the Apostolic, Autocephalous Orthodox Church of Cyprus* (Evrichou: 1988, in Greek).

Annex B: Ecclesiastical criminal law, Annex C: Administration of Church property). The main novelties of the 2010 Charter are the following: (a) the establishment of new Metropolises and Dioceses, (b) the amendment of the manner in which the Archbishop and the Bishops are elected, (c) the introduction of more detailed provisions governing the administration of ecclesiastical justice and ecclesiastical criminal law, (d) the introduction of the spiritual dissolution of the marriage and (e) the establishment of the central Fund for the Wages of the Clergy.[238]

II. Central Administration

207. The administration of the Orthodox Church is divided into central and local institutions. The central institutions are: (a) the Holy Synod and (b) the Archbishop, while the local institutions are: (i) the archdiocese and the metropolises, (ii) the parishes, and (iii) the monasteries. The Holy Synod, which is constituted by the serving Archbishop and the serving Metropolitans and Bishops, constitutes the highest authority of the Cypriot Church (Article 3 of the 2010 Charter). The Archbishop chairs the Holy Synod (Article 4). If he is impeded from presiding or if the See is vacant, a ranking metropolitan assumes the chair. The Chairman of the Holy Synod normally convenes it four times a year. The Synod is also convened for special sessions when the chairman deems it necessary or when the majority of the Holy Synod makes such a request (Article 9). The Holy Synod is in quorum when more than half of its members are present, including the Chairman (Article 5).

208. The decisions of the Synod are reached by an absolute majority of all members present unless an increased majority or unanimity is required by specific provisions of the Charter. The Holy Synod supervises the clergy and the overall ecclesiastical corporation and exercises legislative, judicial and administrative power. It also has the 'presumption of jurisdiction', which is the jurisdiction over any matter that does not fall within the jurisdiction of another body. Furthermore, it is the highest court for the Canonical offences of clergy, monks and laypersons. When it is called upon to try a prelate who is charged with an offence which, under Canon Law, is punishable with defrocking, then the Synod assembles as a Superior Court. This court, thirteen in number including the chairman, comprises the members of the Synod (Article 79).

209. The Archbishop is a central instrument of administration, as well as a Bishop in his local Archdiocese (Article 12).[239] He presides over the Holy Synod and represents the Church before the Republic, other states and churches. According to the privilege granted to him by the Byzantine Emperor Zeno in the fifth century, the Archbishop of Cyprus signs in cinnabar (red ink), is clad in imperial purple

238. A. Emilianides, 'The New Charter of the Orthodox Church of Cyprus: A First Approach', *Nomokanonika* 2, 19–36 (2011), (in Greek).

239. C. Papastathis, *On the Administrative Organisation of the Church of Cyprus* 114 ff. (Thessaloniki, 1981, in Greek).

and holds an imperial sceptre. Pursuant to the Charter of the Orthodox Church, laypersons participate in the elections of a new Archbishop. However, their participation in accordance with the 2010 Charter is more limited when compared to the previous one. The 1980 Charter provided that the Electoral Assembly would be composed of two separate bodies; the first body comprised one hundred General Representatives, out of which sixty-six were laypersons and thirty-four were clergymen, while the second body comprised a small number of ex officio members, which included, *inter alia*, members of the Holy Synod and Abbots of the royal monasteries; during the 2006 elections, there were thirty ex officio members. In order to be elected as Archbishop, a candidate should be supported by the majority of representatives in both bodies of the Electoral Assembly; namely, he should be supported by the majority of General Representatives, as well as by the majority of ex officio members. If no candidate was supported by the majority of voters in the first or second round of the elections, then the candidate who was supported by the majority of the General Representatives and the candidate who was supported by the majority of the ex officio members proceed to the third round of the elections; if the same candidate had the majority of voters in both bodies, then he proceeded in the third round of the elections together with the candidate who received the second highest number of total votes. During the third round, both bodies were united as one, and the candidate who received the majority of total votes was elected as the new Archbishop.[240]

210. It was considered that the electoral system established in the previous Charter was a complicated one and that its practical application in the 2006 elections led to intense and unnecessary debates between the laypersons who supported the candidates and among the candidates themselves. The new system provides that the election takes place in two distinct stages. During the first stage, all Orthodox Christians having the right to vote (either laypersons or clergy) shall vote for the candidate of their choice. The three candidates securing the highest number of votes shall proceed to the next stage, where only members of the Holy Synod have the right to vote. The candidate to be elected as Archbishop shall be the one who secures an absolute majority of the votes. If this is not possible, then the two persons securing the highest number of votes shall proceed to a second round, and the person receiving the highest number of votes shall be elected.[241] The first elections for an Archbishop, pursuant to the new system of elections, took place on 18 December 2022. In the first stage, the Metropolitan of Limassol (35.68%), the Metropolitan of Paphos (18.39%) and the Metropolitan of Tamasou and Oreinis (18.10%) secured the highest number of votes and proceeded to the next stage; the three remaining candidates, the Metropolitans of Constantias and Famagusta, Morphou, and Kyrenia did not advance to the second stage. In the second stage of elections, the Metropolitan of Paphos was elected as the new Archbishop Georgios after securing

240. *See* A. Emilianides, 'The Procedure for Electing an Archbishop in the Orthodox Church of Cyprus', *Nomokanonika* 2, 45–72 (2006), (in Greek).

241. A. Emilianides, 'The Procedure for Electing an Archbishop in the Orthodox Church of Cyprus', in *The New Charter of the Church of Cyprus* 57–70 (A. Emilianides & C. Katsaros eds, Nicosia: Hippasus, 2013, in Greek).

eleven votes out of sixteen; four members of the Holy Synod voted in favour of the Metropolitan of Limassol, while the remaining members cast a blank vote.

III. Peripheral Administration

211. In addition to the Archdiocese, whose prelate is the Archbishop (with his seat in Nicosia), there used to be, until recently, five metropolises, each administered by a Metropolitan (Paphos, Kition, Kyrenia, Limassol and Morphou). Following, however, a decision of the Holy Synod in 2007, four additional metropolises were established (Constantias-Famagousta, Kykkou and Tillyrias, Tamasou and Oreinis, Trimythountos and Lefkaron). This status has been retained in the Charter (Article 2). In addition to the above metropolises, there are also suffragan – Bishops, who are elected in order to aid the Archbishop or the Metropolitans in the performance of their duties; such suffragan – Bishops are the Bishops of Karpasia, Neapoleos and Mesaorias who reside in the Archdiocese,[242] Arsinoes who resides in Paphos and Amathus who resides in Limassol (Article 13). It should be further noted that the Abbots of the Royal Monasteries of Mahaira and St Neophytos have been elevated as Bishops of Ledras and Hytron, respectively.[243] The metropolitan holds the hieratic rank of a Bishop and exercises judicial, legislative and administrative authority within his area. He controls and supervises the administration and management of the parishes and monasteries of his province and is generally charged with all competencies conferred by the Holy Canons and the Charter. Metropolitans are elected in the same manner as the Archbishop. However, an existing Metropolitan may not be a candidate for the elections of Metropolitan in a different metropolis, nor is transfer among metropolises allowed.[244] The Archbishop and Metropolitans are elected for life unless they resign or are discharged on account of an illness or a conviction for a Canonical offence (Article 14).

212. A parish is a particular area whose Orthodox inhabitants meet for their religious needs in a specific church (Article 45). In order to establish a new parish, there need to be 2,500 inhabitants in cities and 1,500 in small towns and villages. Any special conditions of the region may, however, be taken into consideration if the number of the faithful is smaller. The head of the parish is the parish priest, who must be a married clergyman (Article 47). The staff of the parishes also comprises cantors and sacristans (Article 49).[245]

---

242. However, the Bishop of Neapoleos used to be the Director of the Representation of the Orthodox Church of Cyprus to the EU, until 2021 when the office of the Church of Cyprus in Brussels shut down.

243. *See* A. Emilianides, 'The Episcopal Territories of the Church of Cyprus', *Nomokanonika* 1, 29–42 (2008), (in Greek); C. Katsaros, 'Practical Issues Arising from the Application of the New Charter of the Church of Cyprus', *Nomokanonika* 2, 37–58 (2011), (in Greek).

244. A. Emilianides, 'The Possibility to Transfer a Metropolitan in the Church of Cyprus' *Nomokanonika* 1, 67–73 (2023), (in Greek).

245. *See* C. Papastathis, *On the Administrative Organisation of the Church of Cyprus* 159 ff. (Thessaloniki: 1981, in Greek).

213. Monasteries are centres of monastic life. From an administrative point of view, they are divided into royal monasteries, parochial monasteries and monasteries of the See (Article 65). The royal monasteries enjoy complete autonomy in their internal administration and management and are spiritually (but not administratively) subject to the Archbishop. Parochial monasteries enjoy self-administration and are spiritually subject to the local Metropolitan. Monasteries that have been abandoned are called monasteries of the See and belong to the local metropolis. The administration of the monasteries is carried out by the Abbot, the Abbatial Council and the brotherhood of the monks.[246]

IV. The Legal Status of Clergy, Monks and Lay Persons

214. Becoming an Orthodox Christian is effected by baptism and unction, which, in the Eastern Church, are administered simultaneously. Members of the Church of Cyprus are: all Orthodox Christians who reside on the island, regardless of citizenship, sex or age (Article 1). The previous Charter further provided that all persons of Cypriot origin who were baptized in Cyprus but live abroad were also members of the Church of Cyprus. This latter provision was problematic as, according to the views of the Greek Orthodox Churches (the Ecumenical Patriarchate, the Patriarchates of Alexandria and Jerusalem and the Archdioceses of Cyprus and Greece), the greater Diaspora is subject to the Ecumenical Patriarchate of Constantinople. Understandably, the Church of Cyprus had not established any parishes abroad, despite the existence of such provision.[247] The 2010 Charter has abolished the aforementioned problematic provision. However, by a decision of the Holy Synod, Orthodox Christians who resided in Cyprus but were not registered in the electoral registry of the Republic were not given the right to vote in the 2022 elections for an Archbishop; the justification given was that it would be practically impossible to verify the identity of such persons in the limited time between the announcement of the elections and the popular vote. The status of Orthodox Christians is forfeited with death, excommunication or voluntary secession from the Church.

215. As in every Orthodox Church, members of the Cypriot Church are divided into: (a) clergy, (b) monks, and (c) laity.[248] Clergy are composed of Deacons, Presbyters and Bishops. They hold ceremonial, administrative and teaching authority. The ordination of a Deacon or a Presbyter is performed by at least one Bishop. The ordination of a Bishop is performed by the Archbishop or, by order of the latter, by the most senior Metropolitan. If the See of a Metropolitan is vacant, the Archbishop

246. *See* E. Mantzouneas, *Ecclesiastical Law of the Apostolic, Autocephalous Orthodox Church of Cyprus* 184 ff. (Evrichou: 1988, in Greek); C. Papastathis, *On the Administrative Organisation of the Church of Cyprus* 171 ff. (Thessaloniki: 1981, in Greek).

247. C. Papastathis, *On the Administrative Organisation of the Church of Cyprus* 66 (Thessaloniki: 1981, in Greek).

248. A. Emilianides, 'Law and Religion in Cyprus', *Kanon* 20, 7–21 (2008).

acts as Vicar of the See. A candidate for the position of the Archbishop or a Metropolitan is expected to be unmarried, to be over 35 years old, to be a graduate of a Theology school and to have completed ecclesiastical service of at least ten years as a clergyman.

216. The Law of the Republic of Cyprus contains no provisions as to the legal status of the clergy. The succession of married clergy is governed by the rules of succession contained in the statutes of civil law. Under Canon Law, clergy are prohibited from practising certain professions: profitable activities which are inconsistent with their Presbyteral function, the assumption of state offices and, more generally, of secular concerns. The status of clergymen is forfeited when a clergyman is defrocked. The penalty of defrocking is imposed by the Holy Synod, convened as a Tribunal (Article 79). In a highly publicized case, the Holy Synod decided on 18 April 2018 to defrock Stylianos Savva, a priest who had been convicted by the courts in imprisonment for sexually harassing his foster daughter.[249] In the case of Prelates, the penalty of defrocking is imposed by a superior Synodical Court. The 2010 Charter provides, however, that a convicted Bishop may request that his case be examined by the Ecumenical Patriarch (Article 81), a provision which is an innovation as it did not exist in the previous Charter.[250]

217. The status of a monk is acquired by tonsure (Article 66). The minimum age for tonsure is 18, after the candidate has completed a three-year term as a novice. Tonsure is performed by the Abbot, a Bishop or a Presbyter with the permission of the local Bishop; otherwise, it is null and void. The Law of the Republic of Cyprus contains no provision as to the legal status of monks. The provisions of Canon Law apply, together with the internal regulations of monasteries.

218. Laypersons participate in all aspects of the work done by the Church. The participation of laity in the Church of Cyprus is probably the strongest in the entire Orthodox world, both in the extent of its competencies and its elevation to the status of an organ of Church administration.[251] Lay people participate in most of the central and peripheral organs of administration of the Church, as well as in the management of property and in the election of the Archbishop and the Metropolitans on the island. In carrying out their functions, laypersons are not appointed but are elected by secret and universal ballot by the congregation of the Church, with no discrimination between men and women. However, the participation of the laity in the election of the Archbishop and Bishops has decreased compared to the previous Charter. A case of excommunication of a layperson was decided in 2015, for the first time in decades. In particular, on 2 October 2015, a five-member committee of the Holy Synod, composed of the Bishops of Paphos, Tamasos, Trimythous, Karsapias

249. *See* e.g., 'Church Defrocks Priest Convicted of Sexual Assault', *Kathimerini* 18 Apr. 2018, available in http://knews.kathimerini.com.cy/en/news/church-deposes-priest-convicted-of-sexual-assault.
250. *See* in detail I. Kastanas, *The Right to Appeal (Ekkliton) before the Ecumenical Patriarch in the Church of Cyprus*, (Athens-Nicosia: Hippasus, 2021, in Greek).
251. *See* C. Papastathis, *On the Administrative Organisation of the Church of Cyprus* 84 (Thessaloniki: 1981, in Greek).

and Arsinoes, held that former Member of European Parliament (MEP) and celebrity theologian Andreas Pitsillides had intentionally misinterpreted the holy canons and had behaved in a manner provocative and unethical towards the Holy Synod. Pitsillides' views were considered in light of his status as a theologian as a serious affront towards the Orthodox faith, and he was called to renounce his falsehoods and misbeliefs and beg for God's mercy.[252] Following an expression of remorse, the Holy Synod eventually decided to revoke the decision of Pitsillides' excommunication on 13 July 2023.[253]

§3. The Regulations of the Armenian Diocese of Cyprus

219. The National Constitution of the Armenians was held to apply in Cyprus during the period of British rule.[254] The Constitution of the Armenians was, however, replaced on 13 March 1950 by the Regulations of the Armenian Diocese of Cyprus.[255] Such Regulations, consisting of 104 articles, were ratified by Catholicos Karekin of Cilicia and continue to be in effect today. Certain minor amendments were approved by Zareh I, Catholicos of Cilicia, on 7 November 1960. When the Armenian Religious Group submitted such Regulations to the then-British Governor of Cyprus for approval, he replied that there was no need to approve the Regulations since they referred to matters within the exclusive internal jurisdiction of the Armenian Religious Group, a view which is consistent with the current constitutional position of the Armenian Religious Group.

220. The Armenian Diocese of Cyprus is constituted by the members of the Armenian Church residing in Cyprus; it is subject to the supreme authority of the Catholicos of Cilicia and is substantially and morally accountable to it. Every individual belonging to the Diocese has obligations towards it. An Armenian has the duties to participate in the diocesan expenses to the extent of his/her ability, to perform willingly and conscientiously the services he/she may be required to render, to obey with pleasure the arrangements made by the diocesan bodies, to take care of the religious, moral, intellectual and educational needs of the community, to be vigilant over the regularity and decency of the religious ecclesiastical life and on the religious instruction at the Armenian schools, to keep in good order the Armenian Church and the schools and to safeguard that children of both sexes of the community receive at least a proper elementary education. The duties of an Armenian also include the wise administration of the Church-owned properties, endeavouring to increase their revenue and to provide for the necessary expenses, protecting the

252. *See* e.g., 'Theologian Excommunicated Must Beg for God's Mercy to Return', *Cyprus Mail* 2 Oct. 2015.

253. 'Holy Synod Welcomes Pitsillides back to the Church after Eight-Year Banishment', *Cyprus Mail* 13 Jul. 2023, available in https://cyprus-mail.com/2023/07/13/holy-synod-welcomes-pitsillides-back-to-the-church-after-eight-year-banishment/.

254. *See* C. Tornaritis (ed.), 'The Legal Position of the Armenian Religious Group', in *Constitutional and Legal Problems in the Republic of Cyprus* 89 (Nicosia: 2nd ed. 1972).

255. *See* in detail A. Emilianides, *The Status of the Armenian Church of Cyprus* 38 ff. (Nicosia: Cyprus Institute of Church and State Relations, 2006, in Greek).

needy and the poor, securing and improving the financial position of the teachers, clergymen and the church employees of the Diocese, the peaceful settling and, in general, the devoted contribution to the welfare and progress of the community.

221. The supreme organ of the Diocese is the Diocesan Council, which is elected by the Armenian Community and which itself elects the Prelate, the Administrative Council and the Religious Council. Each member of the Armenian Church has the right to vote for the election of the Diocesan Council, so long as he/she has resided in the electoral area for at least six months prior to the elections and he/she has been a permanent resident in Cyprus for at least one year before the elections, has attained the age of 21, has not been convicted of a criminal offence, has not been deprived of his/her civil rights by a judgment of the court, is not mentally deranged, has not been condemned for fraud or expelled from public services by the Diocesan or the Administrative Council, and has regularly paid the Church-Tax.

222. The Diocesan Council consists of fourteen persons, two of which are members of the clergy, while twelve are lay members; such members are elected for a term of office for four years, with the members being eligible for re-election. The lay members are elected with the participation of at least 30% of the persons entitled to vote in the Armenian Community of Cyprus, while the clergy members are elected by the assembly of clergymen in Cyprus. The election of the members of the Diocesan Council is supervised by an Electoral Committee, consisting of five to seven members and appointed by the Administrative Council two months prior to the elections. The election is by secret ballot by the voters.

223. The Diocesan Council is approved by the Catholicos of Cilicia and has jurisdiction to elect the Prelate, the Religious and Administrative Councils, the member who is to represent the Armenian Diocese of Cyprus in the General Council of the Catholicossate, as well as the delegates who will represent the Armenian Diocese in the conclave convened for the election of the Catholicos. It also has jurisdiction to be vigilant over the activities of the Prelate, the Religious and the Administrative Council, to settle any disagreements which may have arisen among them and to examine any serious complaints made against them. Every year, the Diocesan Council draws up the budget of the Church-owned institutions and properties of the Diocese and may impose a Church-tax to members of the Church with a view to meeting the expenses of the Diocese.

224. The Prelate is the Religious Head and the representative of the Armenian Diocese of Cyprus, as well as the President of the Diocesan, Religious, Administrative and other councils. The Prelate should be vigilant over the execution of the religious and administrative rules and rites of the Armenian Church, the development of the Community's spiritual life, the embellishment of the churches and the maintenance in good order of the schools, as well as the proper functioning of the Diocesan organizations. For the election of the Prelate, the Catholicos of Cilicia present a list of three candidates to the Diocesan Council. The Diocesan Council then elects the Prelate, by secret ballot, either from that list or from outside, by a majority of two-thirds of the votes. The election is then ratified by the Catholicos of

Cilicia. The Prelate is responsible to the Administrative Council and must execute the latter's decisions; in case of a disagreement between them, the Diocesan Council attempts to reconcile the different views. With respect to purely religious matters, however, the Prelate is solely responsible to the Catholicos of Cilicia.

225. The Administrative Council consists of five to seven members who should have attained 30 years of age and should enjoy the right to elect and be elected. The Administrative Council is elected by the Diocesan Council for a term of two years; however, only three out of five members or five out of seven members can be re-elected for the next term. The members of the Diocesan Council may also be elected as members of the Administrative Council. The Administrative Council is the highest executive organ of the Diocese and, as such, manages the educational, moral and material interests of the Diocese as well as the general administration of the national-ecclesiastical chattels and properties, elects the Church Committees and the Poor Boards as well as any other committees (and supervises their activities), lets the church-owned properties and executes the annual budget as approved by the Diocesan Council. On the other hand, the Administrative Council has no right to sell any church-owned properties, buildings or land, or purchase or exchange any property, or borrow money without previously obtaining the permission of the Diocesan Council.

226. The Religious Council consists of three or five members who are elected by the Diocesan Council for a term of office for two years; these elections are held simultaneously with the election of the members of the Administrative Council. The Religious Council supervises the Community's religious affairs; it has a duty to preserve the creed and traditions of the Armenian Church and to examine and solve all religious disputes which may arise within the Community. The Administrative and Religious Councils together constitute the Mixed Council which deals with problems which have both an administrative and a religious character. Other organs of the Armenian Church include the Church Committee and the Poor Board. The Church Committee is responsible for the substantial and moral splendour of the church, for the security of its employees, for the preservation of the ecclesiastical chattels and the proper recording in a special register of births, marriages and deaths which occur in each parish. The parish pastor of the village or town where the Church Committee is established functions as the President of the Church Committee. The Poor Board distributes the grants and takes care of the poor, widows and orphans under the presidency of the local senior priest.

§4. The Charter of the Church of the Orthodox Christians Who Follow the Old Calendar

227. The current Charter of the Church of the Orthodox Christians who follow the Old Calendar was enacted on 12 May 1961 by the Metropolitan of Kition

Epiphanius; the Charter consists of ninety-five articles.[256] The Orthodox Church of the Old Calendar considers that the Autocephalous Orthodox Church of Cyprus, as well as the other Orthodox Churches, are guilty of the heresy of Ecumenism and thus, only the Church of the Orthodox Christians who follow the Old Calendar may be held to be 'true Orthodox Christians'. While the congregation constitutes the highest authority of the Old Calendar Church of Cyprus, such authority is exercised by the Holy Synod. Article 16 of the Charter provides for two Episcopal territories; however, it is provided that the number of Episcopal territories may increase should there be such need. In view of the fact that there is no Archbishop of the Old Calendar Church of Cyprus or an adequate number of Bishops in order for the Holy Synod to be convened, the Bishop of Cyprus participates in the Holy Synod of the Matthewites Orthodox Christians of Greece, who were so-called after Bishop Matthew of Bresthena; the Archbishop of Athens of the Old Calendar Church of Greece presides over the Holy Synod.

228. Consequently, the Bishop or Bishops of Cyprus are responsible for the administration of the Old Calendar Church of Cyprus, subject to the decisions of the Holy Synod convened in Greece; a Bishop is the ecclesiastical and spiritual authority and has jurisdiction with respect to all affairs of the church, observance of Holy Traditions and Canon Law, discipline, as well as supervision over parishes and monasteries. A new Bishop is elected by an electoral assembly composed of both members of the clergy and lay persons, similar to the electoral system of the Autocephalous Orthodox Church of Cyprus. In order to establish a new parish, the prior written consent of the Bishop is required. The head of the parish is the parish priest, who must be a married clergyman. The administration of the monasteries is carried out by the Abbot.

256. *See* in detail A. Emilianides, *The Status of the Old-Calendar Church of Cyprus* 76 ff. (Nicosia: Cyprus Institute of Church and State Relations, 2008, in Greek).

Chapter 3. Fundamental Rights and Religious Communities

§1. The Incompatibility of Canon Law Provisions with Fundamental Rights

229. While it is provided that the competencies of the Orthodox Church and of the three Religious Groups with respect to family matters are subject, according to Article 111 §1 of the Constitution, *to the provisions of this Constitution*, it is not similarly provided in Article 110 of the Constitution that the exclusive right of the Orthodox Church and of the three Religious Groups of the Republic to regulate and administer their own internal affairs and property is also subject to the provisions of the Constitution; it could thus be argued that the Orthodox Church and the three Religious Groups shall regulate and administer their internal affairs and property on the basis of their Canon Law, without the provisions of such Canon Law being subject to the provisions of the Constitution.

230. Hence, it could be argued that the Orthodox Church and the three Religious Groups should be subject to the provisions of Part II of the Constitution, safeguarding the protection of human rights in the Republic of Cyprus, in so far as they functioned as legislative or judicial authorities on the basis of Article 111 of the Constitution. On the other hand, it would seem that the five constitutionally recognized religions are not subject to the provisions of the Constitution, including Part II of the Constitution, with respect to the regulation of their internal affairs and the administration of their property. Such an interpretation seems to be in line with the fact that the five major religions of the Republic do not constitute legal persons of public law, but instead, legal persons of private law; it is well established that the provisions concerning the protection of fundamental rights primarily refer to obligations of the State and legal persons of public law, and only under specific circumstances do they also refer to obligations of legal persons of private law.

231. The argument that the Canon Law provisions of a church do not necessarily have to be compatible with fundamental rights is not restricted to the five constitutionally recognized religions of the island; indeed, Article 18 of the Constitution safeguards the organizational religious freedom of religions other than the five constitutionally recognized religions, including the right to regulate their internal affairs. Therefore, the right to organize a religion on the basis of its Canon Law is, in principle, a constitutionally guaranteed fundamental right as well, and thus, the enjoyment of any other right should only be understood in conjunction with the right to religious freedom. Restricting the ambit of other fundamental rights when it comes to Canon Law provisions is not unusual; churches, for example, have always maintained that only men may become priests or bishops without this being considered a violation of gender equality.[257] However, the ECtHR has recently stressed that the function of a clergy and the claim of an 'internal autonomy' of a religious organization does not suffice in order to preclude the application of the

257. *See also* A. Emilianides, 'Individual Rights and Internal Law of the Church', *Nomokanonika* 2, 21–29 (2015), (in Greek).

ECHR; thus, with respect to their internal affairs, religions and churches enjoy a certain amount of autonomy, this autonomy is by no means absolute and may not justify, as a matter of principle, violations of fundamental rights.[258] The right to religious freedom would thus need to be balanced with other fundamental rights; this applies to both the five major and the minority religions.

§2. Hereditary Succession and Fundamental Rights

232. Difference of religion or creed does not constitute a ground incapacitating a person, otherwise qualified, from succeeding to an inheritance. In the case of *Christophi*, which had been decided prior to Independence and prior to the enactment of the Wills and Succession Law, Cap. 195, a daughter of Orthodox Christian parents married a Muslim and lived with him for twenty years under a Muslim name, without attending the religious rites of her original religious creed; it was held that even assuming that a formal renunciation of Christianity and acceptance of Islam could be presumed, such a change of religion would still not disqualify her from succeeding to the estate of her deceased father.[259] Cap. 195 did not include any provision stipulating that change of religion or difference of religion is a ground of incapacity to succeed, and in any view, it is suggested that following the coming into force of the Constitution, the findings of the Court in the case of *Christophi* have been consistent with the principle of religious freedom which is safeguarded in Article 18 of the Constitution.

233. With respect to legacies to religious corporations, section 33 of Cap. 195 provides that no person having any relationships within the third degree of kinship shall have the power to bequeath a legacy to any religious corporation, save by a will executed at least three months before his/her death; a religious corporation shall include, according to section 2 of Cap. 195, any religious establishment or religious institution belonging to any denomination and any throne, church, chapel, monastery, mosque, tekke, shrine, or synagogue, a definition which should essentially be considered as including any religion whose rites or doctrines are not secret and which is therefore free in accordance with Article 18 of the Constitution. Where, however, the testator is a Muslim, a legacy shall be deemed to constitute a valid dedication and shall be governed by the law in force for the time being relating to valid deeds of dedication.

234. In the 2007 case of the *Monastery of Mahairas*, the Supreme Court examined the issue of the hereditary succession of monks in Cyprus.[260] The deceased had been a monk of the Monastery of Mahairas from 1949 to 2000 when he passed away. According to the Charter of the Orthodox Church of Cyprus and the internal

---

258. *Syndicatul Pastorum cel Bun v. Romania*, Judgment of 9 Jul. 2013. *See also* C. Katsaros, 'The Right to Association and to Form Trade Unions Within the Orthodox Church', *Nomokanonika* 1, 75 (2014), (in Greek).
259. *Christophi v. Christophi* (1910) 9 CLR 65.
260. *Holy Monastery of Mahairas v. Papasavva*, [2007] 1 CLR 436 (in Greek).

regulation of the Monastery, the property of all monks belongs to the monastery and not personally to them. The relatives of the deceased monk argued that such property should belong to the relatives of the deceased monk and not to the monastery and that all contrary articles of the Charter of the Orthodox Church violated Article 23 of the Constitution safeguarding the right of property.

235. The Supreme Court acknowledged that according to Article 110 §1 of the Constitution, the Autocephalous Greek Orthodox Church of Cyprus shall continue to have the exclusive right of regulating and administering its own internal affairs and property in accordance with the Holy Canons and its Charter in force for the time being. However, it did not accept that the exclusive right of the Orthodox Church to regulate and administer its property extends also to the property of its monks, or that the property of its monks could be considered to be the property of the Church. In view of the above, it was held that each monk continues to have a right to his own property, as safeguarded by the Constitution and that the monastery does not have any right to such property. Thus, the relatives of the deceased monk were considered to be the heirs of the deceased monk. A similar interpretation might, in the future, be followed also with respect to members of the clergy.

236. The case of the *Monastery of Mahairas* could be criticized due to the fact that it failed to examine the application of Article 18 with respect to religious freedom. The monk had exercised his religious freedom by acquiring the capacity of a monk and by accepting the provisions of Canon Law and the internal regulation of the monastery, where he had been a monk for fifty years. The right to individual property cannot be examined in isolation and without examining whether, in the circumstances of the particular case, the monk had exercised his religious freedom, which is also safeguarded by the Constitution.[261] In any event, however, it is correct that hereditary succession does not fall within the ambit of the Charter of the Orthodox Church since it is the House of Representatives and not the Greek Communal Chamber, which has competencies with regard to laws relating to hereditary succession; Article 110 may not safeguard the competence of the Orthodox Church concerning matters which would not fall within the exclusive competencies of the Greek Communal Chamber.

237. Nevertheless, the Court failed to examine the application of section 53 of the Succession Law, Cap. 195, which stipulates that the recognized rights of religious organizations should be safeguarded.[262] The notion of a religious organization undoubtedly includes the Orthodox Church of Cyprus. Furthermore, the right of the Orthodox Church to acquire the property of a monk was safeguarded by the Charter of 1914, as well as by the Charter of 1980, and was, therefore, an established and well-recognized right of a religious organization at the time of the entry

261. *See* A. Emilianides, 'The Constitutional Position of the Charter of the Orthodox Church of Cyprus', *Nomokanonika* 1, 41–54 (2005), (in Greek).
262. *See* A. Emilianides, 'Hereditary Succession of Monks in Cyprus: New Developments', *Cyprus and European Law Review* 5, 368–378 (2007), (in Greek).

into force of the Succession Law, Cap. 195.[263] The property of a monk might not become the subject of hereditary succession within the meaning of Cap. 195, precisely due to the fact that a monk does not own any property which could legally become the subject of hereditary succession, and this is the reason for including the specific exception of section 53 of Cap. 195. There was, therefore, no incompatibility between Cap. 195 and the Charter of the Orthodox Church that needed to be resolved since section 53 of Cap. 195 explicitly safeguarded all recognized rights of religious organizations, which were based on their Canon Law.[264]

§3. Religion-Based Claims for Refugee Status

238. Section 3 §1 of the Refugee Law 6(I)/2000, as amended, provides that a person may acquire the status of a refugee so long as he/she is outside his/her country due to a well-founded fear of persecution, and cannot, or is not willing, due to such well-founded fear of persecution, to be protected by his/her country. Persecution may relate to racial, political, or religious grounds or to the fact that the refugee is part of a specific social group. A refugee may be persecuted by the State, groups or organizations controlling the State or a substantial part of the State, or even non-state actors, so long as the state actors – including international organizations – may not, or are not willing, to provide protection from persecution or harm.

239. Religious grounds of persecution include, *inter alia*, according to section 3D of Law 6(I)/2000, as amended by Law 112(I)/2007, the adoption of theistic, non-theistic or atheistic convictions or the manifestation of such convictions, either individually or collectively, in private or in public, or abstention from such manifestation, or other religious acts or expression of beliefs or other types of individual or collective behaviour based upon religious convictions. When examining a petition on the basis of Law 6(I)/2000, the authorities may not discriminate on the grounds of religion.[265] The above principles have been applied by the Supreme Court of Cyprus, *inter alia*, in the cases of *Sarmadi*,[266] *Faramarzian*[267] and *Gad*.[268]

240. The applicant in the case of *Sarmadi* was of Iranian origin. While his initial application for being recognized as a refugee within the meaning of Law 6(I)/00 had been rejected, the applicant requested that his application be reconsidered in

263. *See* C. Tornaritis, 'The Property of Monks and Whether It Is Subject to Estate Duty Tax', *Cyprus Law Review* 1, 177 (1983).
264. A. Emilianides, 'Hereditary Succession of Monks in Cyprus: New Developments', *Cyprus and European Law Review* 5, 368–378 (2007), (in Greek). *See also* A. Emilianides, *Cypriot Succession Law* (Nicosia: Hippasus 3rd ed. 2015, in Greek).
265. A. Emilianides, 'Immigration and Religion in Cyprus', in *Immigration, National and Regional Laws and Freedom of Religion* 27–34 (A. Motilla ed., Leuven: Peeters, 2012).
266. *Sarmadi v. The Republic*, Judgment of 3 Apr. 2007 (in Greek). Also *Sarmadi v. The Republic*, Judgment of 17 Dec. 2009 (in Greek).
267. *Faramarzian and Hayati v. The Republic*, Judgment of 22 May 2008 (in Greek).
268. *Gad v. Revisional Authority for Refugees*, Judgment of 14 Oct. 2015 (in Greek).

light of the fact that he had subsequently been baptized as a Christian. The applicant maintained that he had abandoned his country due to his political and religious beliefs and that he had been imprisoned for sixteen months for refusing to cooperate with Iranian authorities; he argued that when he was in Iran, he had some Christian friends and during his meetings with them he read the Bible and was fascinated; he was then baptized as a Christian and attended religious classes. He further maintained that his life was in danger should he ever return to Iran due to the fact that he had been baptized as a member of the Christian Community Church; in particular, the applicant argued that the Iranian authorities would kill him because of the fact that he had converted to Christianity.

241. The Asylum Authority maintained that the applicant had not proved genuine Christian convictions or knowledge. It was further maintained by the authorities that there was no well-founded fear of persecution should the applicant return to Iran since the Iranian authorities had not been aware of his conversion to Christianity prior to his leaving Iran. The Supreme Court rejected the arguments of the Government and held that the conclusion of the Government that the applicant had not proven a well-founded fear of persecution or genuine Christian convictions was fundamentally flawed. It held that the fact that the applicant had not answered correctly certain specific questions with respect to Christianity was immaterial since the applicant had correctly answered most of the questions and had, in general, provided sufficient evidence of his conversion to Christianity; genuine religious feelings are associated not only with theoretical knowledge but also with the way one has chosen to live, while the evidence showed that the applicant had chosen to live as a Christian. Furthermore, the Court observed that while the authorities had essentially acknowledged that the Christian minority of Iran is persecuted, they incorrectly held that the fact that the Iranian authorities might not be aware of the applicant's conversion meant that his life was not in danger should he ever return to Iran.

242. The Court also held that each claim requires examination on its merits on the basis of the individual's situation. In this context, the well-founded fear need not necessarily be based on the applicant's own personal experience. What happened to similarly situated individuals, such as the claimant's friends and relatives or other members of the same Religious Group, may well show that his fear that he also will become a victim of persecution is well-founded. While mere membership of a particular religious community will not normally be enough to substantiate a claim to refugee status, there may be, however, special circumstances where even mere membership suffices, particularly when taking into account the overall political and religious situation in the country of origin, which may indicate a climate of genuine insecurity for the members of the religious community concerned.[269] The principles

269. *Sarmadi v. The Republic*, Judgment of 3 Apr. 2007 (in Greek). Also *Sarmadi v. The Republic*, Judgment of 17 Dec. 2009 (in Greek).

of *Sarmadi* were further applied in *Gad*, with regards to an Egyptian who had fled Egypt, allegedly because of pressures and threats she suffered after having been baptized as Christian.[270]

243. In the case of *Faramarzian*, the applicants – also Iranian citizens – were husband and wife, whose application to be recognized as refugees had been rejected by the authorities. It was maintained on behalf of the applicants that their conversion to Christianity had put their lives and fundamental freedoms in danger should they ever return to Iran. The authorities concluded that the applicants had not been baptized and had not proven that they had genuine Christian convictions since their knowledge concerning Christianity was inadequate. The Supreme Court held that the decision of the authorities was flawed; it held that the applicants had, in general, answered correctly many questions about Christianity, and they could not be expected to know all details about their new religion when they were still in the process of being religiously educated by their church. In addition, the questions concerned the Orthodox Church, while the applicants had adhered to the Protestant Church; thus, many of the questions asked by the authorities did not prove that the applicants' knowledge of Christianity was inadequate, as maintained by the authorities.

§4. Religious Slaughter of Animals

244. Both the Muslim and Jewish faiths have specific requirements for the religiously acceptable slaughter of animals. The major difference from the general practices in most countries is that the animals are not stunned prior to slaughter. Religious slaughtering is not a common practice in the Republic of Cyprus. In order to perform religious slaughtering, the competent religious authorities apply to the Veterinary Services for a special derogation; the Veterinary Service examines the application, and, in case of a positive answer, religious slaughtering can be carried out. The religious authority on whose behalf the slaughter is carried out is competent in the application and monitoring of the relevant religious provisions during the slaughter. Section 32 of the Protection and Well-Being of Animals Law 46(I)/1994 provides that the Council of Ministers of the Republic may enact Regulations in order to specify, *inter alia*, matters relating to the stunning, killing or slaughter of animals. By virtue of section 32 of Law 46(I)/94, the Council of Ministers enacted the Regulations on the Protection of Animals at the Time of Slaughter or Killing of 2 May 2002.[271]

245. Regulation 5 of the 2002 Regulations provided that in the case of animals subject to particular methods of slaughter required by certain religious rites, the requirement that the animals should be stunned before slaughter or killed instantaneously shall not apply. It was further provided that the religious authority on behalf of which the slaughter is being carried out shall be competent for the application of

270. *Gad v. Revisional Authority for Refugees*, Judgment of 14 Oct. 2015 (in Greek).
271. Official Gazette 2002 Annex III(I) 1891.

such religious rite; as regards other issues, the religious authority has to apply the Regulations under the responsibility of a veterinarian. However, the religious exception was effectively abolished by amending Regulation 347/2014, and the Regulations of 2002, as amended, were abolished altogether with Regulation 616/2020. Whereas the Council of Ministers initiated a bill pursuant to which the religious kosher exception would be reintroduced, following protests by organizations supporting animal rights, the bill was withdrawn.[272]

246. The Republic has further ratified the European Convention for the Protection of Animals for Slaughter of 10 May 1979, with Law 27(III)/2004. Article 17 of the Convention provides that each Contracting Party may authorize derogations from the provisions concerning prior stunning of animals in the case of slaughtering, in accordance with religious rituals; each Contracting Party shall ensure in such cases, when it does not itself issue the necessary authorizations, that animal sacrificers are duly authorized by the religious bodies concerned. The Convention is superior to municipal laws, with the exception of laws having constitutional status, according to Article 169 of the Constitution. Moreover, since 1 January 2013, Cyprus applies Regulation 1099/2099, which, as a Community instrument, has a superior force to municipal legislation.[273] Article 4 §4 of the Regulation expressly provides that in the case of animals subject to particular methods of slaughter prescribed by religious rites, the requirement that animals should be killed only after stunning in accordance with the specifically provided methods and requirements shall not apply, provided that the slaughter takes place in a slaughterhouse. Accordingly, the religious exception was, in principle, maintained at an EU level.[274] However, there are no regulations currently in effect in Cyprus implementing the possibility for such a religious exception.

---

272. *See also* A. Emilianides, 'Meat Slaughtering via Kosher', *dikaiosyni* 13 Apr. 2020, available in https://dikaiosyni.com/katigories/arthra/sfagi-kreatwn-me-ti-methodo-koser/.
273. Council Regulation (EC) No. 1099/2009 of 24 Sep. 2009 on the protection of animals at the time of killing.
274. Case C-426/16, *Liga van Moskeeën en Islamitische Organisaties Provincie Antwerpen, VZW and Others v. Vlaams Gewest* EU:C:2018:335. *See also* S. Ferrari & R. Bottoni, *Legislation regarding Religious Slaughter of Animals in the EU Member States and Associated Countries* (Milan, 2010).

Chapter 4. Contractual Religious Freedom

247. There are no concordats in Cyprus. The dialogue and cooperation of the state and the various religions take place within the framework of the Constitution, which provides for a system of coordination between the Republic of Cyprus and the various religions and creeds. While it could be considered that such a system of coordination might present some similarities to the various concordant systems, there is an essential difference; any agreements between the church and the state are unilateral on behalf of the state and have the form of constitutional and other legal provisions. As such, these provisions could be amended by another unilateral decision of the state, and are scrutinized by the courts in the same manner as any other law of the Republic.

Part IV. International, Transnational and Regional Effects on Religious Communities

Chapter 1. International Law Effects on Religious Communities

§1. The International Covenant on Civil and Political Rights

248. Article 18 of the Universal Declaration on Human Rights provides that everyone has the right to freedom of thought, conscience and religion; this right includes freedom to change one's religion or belief and freedom, either alone or in community with others and in public or private, to manifest one's religion or belief in teaching, practice, worship and observance.[275] Article 18 §1 of the International Covenant on Civil and Political Rights is identical to Article 18 of the Universal Declaration on Human Rights.[276] Article 18 §1 of the International Covenant and Article 18 of the Universal Declaration correspond to paragraphs 1 and 4 of Article 18 of the Constitution of Cyprus and, therefore, essentially enjoy Constitutional status. Article 18 §2 of the International Covenant further provides that no one shall be subject to coercion which would impair his/her freedom to have or to adopt a religion or belief of his choice; this Article essentially corresponds to Article 18 §5 of the Constitution which prohibits the use of physical or moral compulsion for the purpose of making a person change or preventing him/her from changing his/her religion.

249. Article 18 §3 of the International Covenant further corresponds to Article 18 §6 of the Constitution; Article 18 §3 provides that freedom to manifest one's religion or beliefs may be subject only to such limitations as are prescribed by law and are necessary to protect public safety, order, health, or morals or the fundamental rights and freedoms of others. The only difference between Article 18 §6 of the Constitution and Article 18 §3 of the International Covenant is the fact that the former refers to the security and constitutional order of the Republic while the latter refers

275. *See* N. Robinson, *Universal Declaration of Human Rights: Its Origins, Significance, Application and Interpretation* (New York: Institute of Jewish Affairs, 1958).
276. *See* K.J. Partsch, 'Freedom of Conscience and Expression and Political Freedoms', in *The International Bill of Rights. The Covenant on Civil and Political Rights* 209–245 (L. Henkin ed., New York: Columbia University Press, 1981).

to public order as a legitimate aim; it is suggested that such a difference is, rather, a variation in drafting, rather than an essential one.

250. Article 18 §4 of the International Covenant on Civil and Political Rights further provides that the States undertake to have respect for the liberty of parents and, when applicable, legal guardians to ensure the religious and moral education of their children in conformity with their own convictions. As already mentioned, Article 18 §7 of the Constitution provides that until a person attains the age of 16, the decision as to the religion to be professed by him/her shall be taken by the person having the lawful guardianship of such person; thus, there is, in principle, no inconsistency between Article 18 §4 of the International Covenant and Article 18 of the Constitution, since the parents, or legal guardians, as the case may be, may decide as to the religion to be professed by their children and consequently ensure the religious and moral education of their children in conformity with their own convictions until their children attain the age of 16.

251. The International Covenant on Civil and Political Rights was ratified by the Republic of Cyprus with Law 14/1969; in view of the fact, however, that the Constitution was based, *inter alia*, on the provisions of Article 18 of the International Covenant on Civil and Political Rights, it is suggested that in practice, the application of the International Covenant in Cyprus is superseded by the existence of the more detailed constitutional provisions. Thus, the United Nations instruments of international law in Cyprus provide general guidance with respect to the interpretation of the constitutional provisions rather than being applied by the courts as a separate legal instrument.

252. The body charged with the monitoring of the implementation of the International Covenant on Civil and Political Rights is the Human Rights Committee.[277] In 1979, the Committee asked Cyprus whether the provision with respect to the prohibition of the use of physical or moral compulsion for the purpose of making a person change or preventing him/her from changing his/her religion was compatible with the Covenant; the Committee noted that in certain religions such as Islam, it is possible to resort to persuasion to prevent someone from changing his/her religion.[278] It is noted that Article 18 §5 of the Constitution has never been implemented by Law and does not, in any event, refer to persuasion but rather to illegal proselytism, namely, to compulsion, which is the result of a threat of injury to the person, reputation, or property of the person concerned. Thus, such constitutional provision is indeed compatible with Article 18 of the Covenant and, as already noted, it essentially corresponds to Article 18 §2 of the Covenant.

277. *See* in general P. Taylor, *Freedom of Religion* (Cambridge: Cambridge University Press, 2005).
278. UN Doc. A/34/40 (1979): 92, para. 388.

§2. The 1981 Declaration of the General Assembly

253. In 1981, the General Assembly of the United Nations further endorsed a Declaration on the Elimination of All Forms of Intolerance and Discrimination based on Religion or Belief. Article I of the Declaration is identical to paragraphs 1–3 of Article 18 of the International Covenant on Civil and Political Rights. Article 6 of the Declaration specifies that the freedom of thought, conscience, religion or belief shall include, *inter alia*, the freedom: (a) to worship, or assemble in connection with a religion or belief and to establish and maintain places for these purposes; (b) to make, acquire, and use to an adequate extent the necessary articles and materials related to the rites or customs of a religion or belief; (c) to write, issue and disseminate relevant publications in these areas; (d) to teach a religion or belief in places suitable for these purposes; (e) to solicit and receive voluntary financial and other contributions from individuals and institutions; (f) to train, appoint, elect or designate by succession appropriate leaders called for by the requirements and standards of any religion or belief; (g) to observe days of rest and to celebrate holidays and ceremonies in accordance with the precepts of one's religion or belief; and (h) to establish and maintain communications with individuals and communities in matters of religion and belief, at the national and international level.

254. Article 2 of the Declaration stipulates that no one shall be subject to discrimination by any State, institution, group of persons, or person, on the grounds of religion or other beliefs, namely any distinction, exclusion, restriction or preference based on religion or belief and having as its purpose or as its effect, nullification or impairment of the recognition, enjoyment or exercise of human rights and fundamental freedoms on an equal basis. By virtue of Article 3 of the Declaration, discrimination between human beings on the grounds of religion or belief constitutes an affront to human dignity and a disavowal of the principles of the Charter of the United Nations and shall be condemned as a violation of the human rights and fundamental freedoms proclaimed in the Universal Declaration on Human Rights and enunciated in detail in the International Covenants on Human Rights. All States therefore engage, according to Article 4 of the Declaration, to take effective measures in order to prevent and eliminate discrimination on the grounds of religion or belief in the recognition, exercise and enjoyment of human rights and fundamental freedoms in all fields of civil, economic, political, social and cultural life. All States further undertake to enact or rescind legislation, where necessary, to prohibit any such discrimination and to take all appropriate measures to combat intolerance on the grounds of religion or other beliefs.

255. With respect to religious education, Article 5 of the Declaration further provides that the parents, or as the case may be, the legal guardians of the child, have the right to organize life within the family in accordance with their religion or belief and that every child shall enjoy the right to have access to education in the matter of religion or belief in accordance with the wishes of his/her parents, or as the case may be, legal guardians, and shall not be compelled to receive teaching on religion or belief against such wishes; the best interests of the child being the guiding principle. In addition, it is provided that the child shall be protected from any form of discrimination on the grounds of religion or belief and shall be brought up in a spirit of understanding, tolerance, friendship among peoples, peace and universal brotherhood, and respect for freedom of religion or the beliefs of others. However, Article 5 §5 sets limitations to the principle that the parents or the legal guardians, as the case may be, decide as to the religion to be professed by their child since it is provided that the practices of a religion or belief in which a child is brought up must not be injurious to his/her physical or mental health or to his/her full development.

256. It has been suggested by the United Nations that the 1981 Declaration might serve as a guide in measuring compliance with Article 18 of the International Covenant on Civil and Political Rights. The Special Rapporteur is an organ appointed by the Commission on Human Rights, which examines incidents and governmental actions which are inconsistent with the provisions of the Declaration and recommends remedial measures in such a situation. In 1999, the Special Rapporteur reported that the desecration of non-Muslim cemeteries in the occupied area of Cyprus violates the provisions of the Declaration.[279]

279. UN Doc. E/CN.4/1999/58 (1999), para. 49.

Chapter 2. Transnational Law Effects on Religious Communities

257. The Republic of Cyprus concluded an Association Agreement with the European Economic Community (EEC) on 19 December 1972. This Agreement provided for two stages: during the first stage, which was due to expire in 1977, a reduction on tariffs of industrial goods and agricultural products was envisaged, while in the second stage, Cyprus would sign the customs union with the Community.[280] The first stage was eventually extended until 1987 due to the Turkish invasion; the Protocol for transition to the second stage of the Agreement was signed on 19 October 1987 and entered into force on 1 January 1988.[281] On 4 July 1990, the Republic of Cyprus submitted an application to become a member of the Community.[282] Cyprus became a full member of the EU on 1 May 2004.[283] However, while EU Law was superior to municipal law on the basis of Article 169 of the Constitution, its provisions would be invalidated if they were contrary to the Constitution.[284]

258. The Constitution was accordingly modified with Law 127(I)/2006, which aimed at facilitating the exercise of the rights and obligations of the Republic of Cyprus as a Member State of the EU; Article 1A of the Constitution now provides that no constitutional provision may invalidate any laws, acts or measures which arise from the obligations of the Republic of Cyprus as a Member State of the EU, or impede the legal effect and application of Regulations, Directives or other EU, or European Communities' legal instruments in the Republic. As a result, EU Law now has an intra-constitutional effect, in the sense that it is considered to be an integral part of the Constitution, and no constitutional provision may invalidate any provision of EU Law.[285]

280. *See* N. Antonopoulos, *Cyprus and the European Economic Community* (Nicosia: 1977, in Greek); C. Tornaritis, *The Common Market and Cyprus* (Nicosia: 1973, in Greek); C. Tornaritis, *The Association Agreements and the Association Between Cyprus and the European Economic Community* (Nicosia: 1977, in Greek).
281. C. Tornaritis, 'The Customs Union of Cyprus with the European Economic Community', *Cyprus Law Tribune* 1, 137–141 (1991); A. Antoniou, 'L' Union Douanière entre la CEE et la Chypre: Une Nouvelle Expérience en Vue', *Revue du Marché Commun* 311, 607–613 (1987); V. Philippou, 'Cyprus and the European Community', *Cyprus Law Tribune* 2, 369–375 (1991).
282. *See* K. Chrysostomides, *The Republic of Cyprus. A Study in International Law* 443–477 (The Hague: Martinus Nijhoff Publishers, 2000); P. Ifestos & C. Tsardanides, *The Relations of Cyprus and the EEC 1972–1990* (Athens: Papazisis, 1991, in Greek).
283. C. Ioannides, *The European Union and Cyprus: The Capacity to Assume the Obligations of Membership. The Accession Negotiations* (London, 2003).
284. *Attorney-General v. Costantinou* [2005] 1 CLR 1356 (in Greek).
285. A. Emilianides, *Beyond the Constitution of Cyprus* 218 ff. (Thessaloniki: Sakkoulas, 2006, in Greek); A. Emilianides, *Constitutional Law in Cyprus* 35 ff. (The Hague: Kluwer 2nd ed. 2019). *See also* C. Lycourgos, 'Cyprus Public Law as Affected by Accession to the European Union', in *Studies in European Public Law* 101 ff. (C. Kombos ed., Thessaloniki: Sakkoulas, 2010); C. Lycourgos, 'The Application of EU Law in Cyprus: Selected Aspects', *The Cyprus Yearbook of International Law* 43 ff. (2012); S. Laulhe-Shaelou, 'Back to Reality: The Implications of EU Membership in the Constitutional Legal Order of Cyprus', in *Brave New World. Application of EU Law in the New Member States* 471–502 (A. Lazowski ed., The Hague: TMC Asser Press, 2010); C. Kombos, *The Impact of EU Law on Cypriot Public Law* (Thessaloniki: Sakkoulas, 2015).

259. The Treaty establishing the EU does not contain provisions with respect to religious organizations;[286] the only reference to 'religion' is contained in Article 13 of the Treaty, which provides that the Council may take appropriate action to combat discrimination based on sex, race or ethnic origin, religion or belief, disability, age or sexual orientation. There are various other provisions of EU Law, in Directives and Regulations, providing for non-discrimination on grounds, *inter alia*, of religion, or providing that religious factors should be taken into account.[287] Further, the Declaration on the status of churches and non-confessional organizations, which was annexed to the Treaty of Amsterdam establishing the EU on 2 October 1997, provides that the EU respects and does not prejudice the status which churches and religious associations or communities enjoy in the Member States according to national law. Therefore, EU Law does not prejudice the system of coordination between the state and the various religions prevailing in Cyprus.[288]

260. The Charter of Fundamental Rights of the EU was a non-binding legal document containing human rights provisions solemnly proclaimed by the European Parliament, the Council of the EU and the European Commission on 7 December 2000. The Treaty of Lisbon, amending the Treaty of the EU, contains an adapted version of the Charter so as to enable the Charter to become legally binding in all EU countries, with the exception of the United Kingdom and Poland. Article 10 of the Charter provides that everyone has the right to freedom of thought, conscience and religion, including the freedom to change religion or belief, as well as freedom – either alone or in community with others and in public or private – to manifest religion or belief, in worship, teaching, practice and observance. The right to conscientious objection is also recognized in accordance with the national laws governing the exercise of the right. Article 14 §3 of the Charter further provides that the freedom to found educational establishments with due respect for democratic principles and the right of parents to ensure the education and teaching of their children in conformity with their religious, philosophical and pedagogical convictions shall be respected, in accordance with the national laws governing the exercise of such freedom and right.[289]

261. Religious slaughter enjoys some protection within the Community legal framework. Protocol 33 on the Protection and Welfare of Animals, which was annexed to the Treaty of Amsterdam, provides that in formulating and implementing the Community's agriculture, transport, internal market and research policies,

---

286. *See also* R. McCrea, *Religion and the Public Order of the European Union* (Oxford: OUP, 2010).
287. *See* M. Hill, *Religion and Discrimination Law in the European Union* (Trier: European Consortium for State and Church Research, 2012).
288. For the general European landscape of law and religion *see* N. Doe, *Law and Religion in Europe: A Comparative Introduction* (Oxford: OUP, 2011); S. Ferrari & R. Cristofori (eds), *Law and Religion in the 21st Century* (London: Ashgate, 2010); G. Robbers (ed.), *State and Church in the European Union* (Baden-Baden: Nomos 3rd ed. 2019); R. Puza & N. Doe (eds), *Religion and Law in Dialogue* (Leuven: Peeters, 2006).
289. *See* in general S. Peers et al. (eds), *The EU Charter of Fundamental Rights. A Commentary* (Oxford: Hart, 2014); G. Di Federico (ed.), *The EU Charter of Fundamental Rights* (Berlin: Springer, 2011).

the Community and the Member States shall pay full regard to the welfare requirements of animals while respecting the legislative or administrative provisions and customs of the Member States relating in particular to religious rites, cultural traditions and regional heritage. Specific provisions with regard to religious slaughter may be found in various Community instruments, such as Regulation 1099/2009[290] and formerly Directive 93/119/EC.[291] Furthermore, the Republic of Cyprus has ratified the 1979 European Convention for the Protection of Animals for Slaughter with Law 27(III)/2004 in order to conform to its obligations as a Member State of the EU. Further, community law influence may be traced in other provisions of Community law as well, for instance, in laws relating to customs and excise, such as Council Regulation (EC) 1186/2009,[292] as well as in laws relating to employment, such as Council Directive 2000/78/EC.[293]

290. Council Regulation (EC) No. 1099/2009 of 24 Sep. 2009 on the protection of animals at the time of killing.
291. Of 22 Dec. 1993 on the protection of animals at the time of slaughter or killing.
292. Of 16 Nov. 2009 setting up a Community system of reliefs from customs duty.
293. Establishing a general framework for equal treatment in employment and occupation.

Chapter 3. Regional Law Effects on Religious Communities

§1. The European Convention on Human Rights

I. The Status of the ECHR in the Cypriot Legal Order

262. The ECHR first became applicable to Cyprus during the British rule of the island. The United Kingdom, by its Declaration 61/48/53 of 23 October 1953, made under Article 63 of the ECHR, extended it to various territories for the international relations of which it was held to be responsible, including the then colony of Cyprus.[294] Following the declaration of independence of the Republic of Cyprus, the application of the ECHR in Cyprus ceased.[295] On 24 May 1961, the Republic of Cyprus became a member of the Council of Europe,[296] and on 16 December 1961, it acceded to the ECHR. The ECHR was ratified in the internal legal order by the European Convention for the Protection of Human Rights (Ratification) Law 39/1962. The instrument of ratification was deposited with the Secretary of the Council of Europe on 6 October 1962. Part II of the constitution of Cyprus, which guarantees fundamental rights and liberties, is modelled on the ECHR; however, the provisions of the ECHR have been extended and enlarged, in some respects, with a number of social and economic rights added, in order to meet the basic requirements of modern society.[297]

263. Consequently, to the extent that it has been incorporated in constitutional provisions and to the degree that its provisions have not been altered during incorporation, the ECHR enjoys limited Constitutional status.[298] Legislation which is contrary to the provisions of the Constitution safeguarding individual human rights may be declared unconstitutional by the trial court. Moreover, the ECHR and its Protocols have, on the basis of Article 169 §3 of the Constitution, superior force to

294. *See* for its application to the island during the turbulent years of 1955–1959 the first interstate application of *Greece v. United Kingdom*, Case 176/1956, as well as the second interstate application of *Greece v. United Kingdom*, 299/1957, *Human Rights Law Journal* 18 (1997): 348 ff.; A. Emilianides (ed.), *The Reports of the European Commission of Human Rights with Respect to Cyprus. App. 176/1956 & 299/1957* (Nicosia: Ministry of Education and Culture, 2008, in Greek). Also E. Lauterpacht, 'European Convention on Human Rights: Suspension of Its Application to Cyprus', *International and Comparative Law Quarterly* 6, 432–434 (1956).

295. *See also* C. Tornaritis, *The European Convention on Human Rights in the Legal Order of the Republic of Cyprus* 6 (Nicosia: 1975).

296. *See* C. Tornaritis, *Council of Europe and the Republic of Cyprus* 42 (Nicosia: 1978); A. Loizou, 'Cyprus', in *Fundamental Rights in Europe: The European Convention on Human Rights and Its Member States, 1950–2000* 219 (R. Blackburn & J. Polakiewicz eds, Oxford: Oxford University Press, 2001).

297. Acknowledged in several judgments of the Supreme Court of Cyprus, such as *Attorney-General v. Ibrahim* [1964] CLR 195: 225, *Attorney-General v. Afamis* 1 RSCC 121: 125–126. *See* further C. Tornaritis, *The Human Rights as Recognized and Protected by Law, with Special Reference to the Law of Cyprus* (Nicosia: 1967); C. Tornaritis, 'The Social and Economic Rights under the Law of the Republic of Cyprus', in *Melanges Bridel* 533–556 (Lausanne: Imprimeries Réunies, 1968).

298. *See* A. Emilianides, *Beyond the Constitution of Cyprus* (Athens: Sakkoulas, 2006, in Greek).

any municipal law, either antecedent or subsequent to their ratification by law. However, the ECHR is not superior to the Constitution; thus, the Constitutional provisions shall prevail in case of any inconsistency between them and the provisions of the ECHR.[299] It should be further observed that the Cypriot courts are invoking the case law of the ECtHR, not only with respect to the interpretation of the ECHR but also with respect to the interpretation of the corresponding Constitutional articles. Therefore, the courts will try, wherever possible, to interpret the relevant Constitutional provisions in a manner which is consistent with the interpretation adopted by the ECtHR.[300]

II. The Application of Article 9 of the ECHR

264. Article 9 §1 of the ECHR provides that everyone has the right to freedom of thought, conscience and religion; this right includes freedom to change one's religion or belief and freedom, either alone or in community with others and in public or in private, to manifest one's religion or belief in worship, teaching, practice and observance. The freedom to manifest one's religion or belief shall be subject, according to Article 9 §2 of the ECHR, only to such limitations as are prescribed by law and are necessary in a democratic society, in the interests of public safety, for the protection of public order, health or morals, or for the protection of the rights and freedoms of others.[301]

265. In essence, Article 9 §1 of the ECHR corresponds to paragraphs 1 and 4 of Article 18, which safeguard the freedom of thought, conscience and religion, as well as the right to manifest one's religion, respectively, while Article 9 §2 of the ECHR corresponds to paragraph 6 of Article 18, which provides for the potential restrictions of the freedom to manifest one's religion. It should be noted that while Article 18 §6 of the Constitution refers to the security and constitutional order of the Republic, Article 9 §2 of the ECHR refers, similar to Article 18 §3 of the International Covenant on Civil and Political Rights, to public order as a legitimate aim; it is suggested, however, that this does not signify any difference in the essence of the legitimate aims concerned, since such aims have in any event been interpreted in a rather vague manner by the courts. The case law of the ECtHR provides guidance to the courts of Cyprus with regard to the interpretation of Article 18 of the Constitution.

299. *See* T. Hadjanastassiou, 'The European Convention on Human Rights Applicable in Cyprus', *Cyprus Law Tribune* 3, 97–113 (1976).
300. *See* further A. Loizou, *Cyprus and the European Convention on Human Rights* (Athens: Sakkoulas, 2003, in Greek); C. Tornaritis, 'The Operation of the European Convention for the Protection of Human Rights in the Republic of Cyprus', *Cyprus Law Review* 3, 455–464 (1983); C. Clerides, 'The Operation of the European Convention on Human Rights in the Civil Courts of Cyprus', *Cyprus Law Review* 39–40, 6029–6043 (1992), (in Greek).
301. *See* in general A. Emilianides (ed.), *Religious Freedom in the European Union* (Leuven: Peeters, 2011); C. Evans, *Freedom of Religion under the European Convention on Human Rights* (Oxford: Oxford University Press, 2001); M. Evans, *Religious Liberty and International Law in Europe* (Cambridge: Cambridge University Press, 1997).

266. The ECtHR has underlined the importance of the rights protected by Article 9 of the ECHR; it stressed that freedom of thought, conscience and religion is one of the foundations of a democratic society and that pluralism depends upon this freedom.[302] The Court has accepted that the protection afforded by Article 9 extends to a wide range of convictions and philosophies, not limited to religious belief; however, for the Article to apply, a belief must attain a certain level of cogency, seriousness, cohesion and importance.[303] The ECtHR, as well as the European Commission of Human Rights, have adopted a broad approach to the recognition of religions; less mainstream religions, such as Druidism,[304] the Divine Light Zentrum[305] and the Church of Scientology,[306] have therefore been recognized as religions within the meaning of Article 9 of the ECHR. In the case of the *Metropolitan Church of Bessarabia*, the ECtHR considered a refusal by the State to recognize a particular group as a religion.[307] In Moldova, only religions recognized by the Government may be practised; the Government of Moldova, however, had refused to recognize the Metropolitan Church of Bessarabia. The Court held that there was a violation of Article 9 of the ECHR since the refusal to recognize the aforesaid religion was arbitrary and contrary to the need to safeguard pluralism.[308]

267. The first case to come before the Court was the case of *Kokkinakis*.[309] The applicants, who were Jehovah's Witnesses, engaged in evangelical activity, including calling at houses to persuade other people to join their religion; a priest of the Orthodox Church of Greece reported them to the police, and they were arrested and convicted for the criminal offence of proselytism. The ECtHR concluded that the applicants had been convicted on the basis of a law which pursued the legitimate aim of protecting the rights and freedoms of others; however, there was no evidence that the applicants had attempted to convince other people by improper means. Thus, the conviction could not be justified in a democratic society. In the case of *Larissis*, however, the Court accepted that the means employed by the applicants had been improper.[310] The applicants were officers in the Greek Air Force and were convicted of proselytism following complaints from soldiers under their command that they had attempted to persuade such soldiers to become Jehovah's Witnesses. The Court held that the Greek authorities had been justified in taking measures to protect the junior airmen from the applicants in view of the fact that a subordinate in the armed forces might not easily rebuff the approaches of a superior officer or withdraw from a conversation with him.

302. *Kokkinakis v. Greece*, Judgment of 25 May 1993; (1994) 17 EHRR 397.
303. *Campbell and Cosans v. United Kingdom*, Judgment of 25 Feb. 1982; (1982) 4 EHRR 293.
304. *Chappell v. United Kingdom*, Decision of 14 Jul. 1987; (1987) 53 DR 241.
305. *Omkarananda and the Divine Light Zentrum v. Switzerland*, Decision of 19 Mar. 1981; (1981) 25 DR 105.
306. *Pastor X and the Church of Scientology v. Sweden*, Decision of 5 May 1979; *Yearbook of the European Convention on Human Rights* 22 (1979): 244.
307. *Metropolitan Church of Bessarabia v. Moldova*, Judgment of 14 Dec. 2001; (2002) 35 EHRR 306. *See also Jehovah's Witnesses of Moscow v. Russia*, Judgment of 10 Jun. 2010, *Bektashi Community and Others v. The Former Yugoslav Republic of Macedonia*, Judgment of 12 Apr. 2018.
308. *See also Serif v. Greece*, Judgment of 4 Dec. 1999; (2001) 31 EHRR 561.
309. *Kokkinakis v. Greece*, Judgment of 25 May 1993; (1994) 17 EHRR 397.
310. *Larissis and Others v. Greece*, Judgment of 24 Feb. 1998; (1999) 27 EHRR 329.

268. Manifesting religious beliefs in the professional sphere may sometimes be limited if there is no indication that the applicants could not manifest their religious beliefs without interference outside that sphere. Thus, the ECtHR held that the prosecution of pharmacists for refusing to supply contraceptives did not violate their rights under Article 9 of the ECHR.[311] Similarly, schools are hierarchical structures, and teachers are in a position to influence their students. The Court considered that the Swiss authorities were justified in forbidding a teacher in a Swiss State school to wear the Islamic headscarf at work since such action might have a proselytizing effect on children at a young and impressionable age, contrary to the Swiss policy of maintaining religious neutrality in schools.[312] Similarly, in the case of *Leyla Šahin*, the Court held that the prohibition on wearing the Islamic headscarf in Turkish universities did not violate Article 9 of the ECHR; the Court recognized the significance of secularism in Turkey and observed that in states where several religions coexist, it may be necessary to place restrictions on the manifestation of religious beliefs in order to reconcile the interests of different groups and to ensure that everyone's beliefs are respected.[313]

269. Article 9 of the ECHR prevents the State from imposing obligations which offend one's religious beliefs unless such obligations are necessary in a democratic society.[314] The obligation to disclose religious convictions in official identity documents might thus amount to a violation of Article 9.[315] In the case of *Buscarini*, the applicants, who had been elected as members of the San Marino Parliament, were required to swear an oath on the Holy Gospels before taking office; the ECtHR held that the requirement for elected representatives to swear allegiance to a particular religion was not compatible with Article 9.[316] In the case of *Manoussakis*, the applicants, who were Jehovah's Witnesses, had rented a room for the purpose of conducting activities connected with their religious beliefs. The applicants were prosecuted and convicted for having established and operated a place of worship without the authorizations required by law, including the authorization of the established Orthodox Church; it was held that the conviction could not be regarded as proportionate to the aim pursued and was thus, not necessary in a democratic society.[317]

270. In the *Thlimmenos* case, the applicant, a Greek Jehovah's Witness, had been convicted of the criminal offence of insubordination as a result of his refusal to wear a military uniform.[318] He was subsequently refused permission to practice as an

311. *Pichon and Sajous v. France*, Admissibility Decision of 2 Oct. 2001.
312. *Dahlab v. Switzerland*, Admissibility Decision of 15 Feb. 2001.
313. *Šahin v. Turkey*, Judgment of 10 Nov. 2005.
314. *Hamidovic v. Bosnia and Herzegovina*, Judgment of 5 Dec. 2017.
315. *Isik v. Turkey*, Judgment of 2 Feb. 2010.
316. *Buscarini and Others v. San Marino*, Judgment of 18 Feb. 1999; (2000) 30 EHRR 208. *See also Dimitras and Others v. Greece*, Judgment of 3 Jun. 2013.
317. *Manoussakis and Others v. Greece*, Judgment of 26 Sep. 1996; (1997) 23 EHRR 387. *See also Association for Solidarity with Jehovah Witnesses and Others v. Turkey*, Judgment of 24 May 2016.
318. *Thlimmenos v. Greece*, Judgment of 6 Apr. 2000; (2001) 31 EHRR 411.

accountant, in accordance with a law providing that anyone with a criminal record is excluded from the profession. The Court held that the refusal amounted to a violation of Article 9, taken in conjunction with Article 14 of the ECHR, since a conviction for refusing on religious and philosophical grounds to wear the military uniform cannot, in principle, imply any dishonesty or moral turpitude likely to undermine the offender's ability to exercise the profession of an accountant.

271. There have been, so far, no cases against Cyprus before the ECtHR concerning alleged violations of Article 9; certain cases, however, which will be discussed in subsequent chapters, are related to religion, such as the *Modinos* case[319] or the *Selim* case.[320] Of particular importance with respect to Article 9 is a case where the Republic of Cyprus was not the respondent, but rather the applicant state, namely the Fourth Inter-State Application of *Cyprus v. Turkey*; the Court accepted that Turkey had violated Article 9 in respect of Greek Cypriots living in the occupied areas.[321] The Court observed that the existence of a number of measures limited the religious life of the enclaved Greek Cypriot population and noted that restrictions were placed on their access to the Apostolos Andreas Monastery, as well as on their ability to travel outside their villages to attend religious ceremonies. In addition, the authorities of the 'TRNC' had not approved the appointment of further priests for the area, there being only one priest for the whole of the Karpas region; such restrictions prevented the organization of Greek Orthodox religious ceremonies in a normal and regular manner and amounted to a breach of Article 9 of the ECHR. Those restrictions essentially curtailed the ability of the enclaved Greek Cypriot population to observe their religious beliefs and, in particular, to access the places of worship outside their villages and to participate in other aspects of religious life.

§2. The Framework Convention for the Protection of National Minorities

I. The Provisions of the Framework Convention

272. The FCNM has been an important initiative of the Council of Europe, aiming to ensure that the signatory states respect the rights of national minorities and undertake to combat discrimination, promote equality, as well as preserve and develop the culture and identity of national minorities and encourage the participation of national minorities in public life.[322] Article 25 of the FCNM binds the signatory states to submit periodical reports to the Council of Europe containing full

319. *Modinos v. Cyprus*, Judgment of 22 Apr. 1993, Series A, No. 259; (1994) 16 EHRR 485.
320. *Selim v. Cyprus*, Judgment of the ECtHR of 16 Jul. 2002.
321. *Cyprus v. Turkey*, Judgment of 10 May 2001; (2002) 35 EHRR 731, paras 241–247.
322. *See* M. Weller (ed.), *The Rights of Minorities: A Commentary on the European Framework Convention for the Protection of National Minorities* (Oxford: Oxford University Press, 2006).

information on the legislative and other measures taken to give effect to the principles set out in the FCNM. The FCNM was adopted by the Committee of Ministers of the Council of Europe on 10 November 1994 and opened for signatures by the Member States of the Council of Europe on 1 February 1995. The Republic of Cyprus ratified the FCNM with Law 28(III)/1995, which entered into force on 1 February 1998.

273. It is important to note the statement of the Government of the Republic of Cyprus that it considers that the FCNM should apply to all three 'Religious Groups' of the Republic, namely, the Armenians, Maronites and Roman Catholics, as well as, and without prejudice to their constitutional position, to the Turkish Cypriots living in the non-occupied areas,[323] despite the fact that the Roman Catholics are a religious and not a national minority, and the fact that the Armenians and Maronites could probably be considered ethnic minorities, rather than national minorities.[324] In view of the above, the FCNM currently applies in Cyprus predominantly as an instrument for the protection of the major religious minorities of the island, and thus, it is of particular importance for the protection of religious human rights in Cyprus.

274. Article 3 of the FCNM provides that every person belonging to a national minority shall have the right freely to choose to be treated or not to be treated as such, and no disadvantage shall result from this choice or from the exercise of the rights which are connected to that choice. It is further provided that persons belonging to national minorities may exercise the rights and enjoy the freedoms flowing from the principles enshrined in the FCNM, individually as well as in community with others. Article 4 of the FCNM provides that the contracting Parties undertake to guarantee the right of equality before the law and of equal protection of the law to persons belonging to national minorities. In this respect, any discrimination based on belonging to a national minority shall be prohibited. The Parties further undertake to adopt, where necessary, adequate measures in order to promote, in all areas of economic, social, political and cultural life, full and effective equality between persons belonging to a national minority and those belonging to the majority. In this respect, they shall take due account of the specific conditions of the persons belonging to national minorities.

275. Article 5 of the FCNM further provides that the Parties undertake to promote the conditions necessary for persons belonging to national minorities to maintain and develop their culture and to preserve the essential elements of their identity, namely their religion, language, traditions and cultural heritage; the Parties shall refrain from policies or practices aimed at assimilation of persons belonging to national minorities against their will and shall protect these persons from any action aimed at such assimilation. In addition, Article 6 provides that the Parties shall

323. Report Submitted by Cyprus, 1 Mar. 1999, Part II, Art. 3.
324. *See* more generally G. Kentas & A. Emilianides, 'The Emergence and Regulation of Minority Religious Groups in Europe', in *How Groups Matter: Challenges of Toleration in Pluralist Societies* 260–285 (M. Bessone, G. Galder & F. Zuolo eds, London: Routledge, 2013).

encourage a spirit of tolerance and intercultural dialogue and take effective measures to promote mutual respect, understanding and cooperation among all persons living on their territory, irrespective of those persons' ethnic, cultural, linguistic or religious identity, in particular, in the fields of education, culture and the media; the Parties further undertake to take appropriate measures to protect persons who may be subject to threats or acts of discrimination, hostility or violence as a result of their ethnic, cultural, linguistic or religious identity.

276. Article 7 of the FCNM further stipulates that the Parties shall ensure respect for the right of every person belonging to a national minority to freedom of peaceful assembly, freedom of association, freedom of expression and freedom of thought, conscience and religion; Article 8 clarifies that the Parties undertake to recognize that every person belonging to a national minority has the right to manifest his/her religion or belief and to establish religious institutions, organizations and associations. In addition, by virtue of Article 9 of the FCNM, the Parties undertake to recognize that the right to freedom of expression of every person belonging to a national minority includes freedom to hold opinions and to receive and impart information and ideas in the minority language, without interference by public authorities and regardless of frontiers. The Parties shall ensure, within the framework of their legal systems, that persons belonging to a national minority are not discriminated against in their access to the media; in this respect, the Parties shall not hinder the creation and the use of print media by persons belonging to national minorities, while in the legal framework of sound radio and television broadcasting, they shall ensure, as far as possible, that persons belonging to national minorities are granted the possibility of creating and using their own media.

277. It is further provided in Article 12 of the FCNM that the Parties shall, where appropriate, take measures in the fields of education and research to foster knowledge of the culture, history, language and religion of their national minorities and of the majority and that they shall, *inter alia*, provide adequate opportunities for teacher training and access to textbooks, and facilitate contacts among students and teachers of different communities. The Parties further undertake to promote equal opportunities for access to education at all levels for persons belonging to national minorities, while Article 13 stipulates that within the framework of their education systems, the Parties shall recognize that persons belonging to a national minority have the right to set up and to manage their own private educational and training establishments.

II. Opinions and Resolutions on Cyprus

278. Cyprus was due to deliver its first cycle State Report on 1 February 1999; such Report was eventually delivered on 1 March 1999 with several omissions and without any prior consultation with the minorities concerned; that Report was supplemented by an additional Report received on 18 February 2000. The first cycle country visit of the Advisory Committee of the FCNM took place from 6 to 8 November 2000, while an Opinion of the Advisory Committee was adopted on 6

April 2001. Subsequently, the Government of Cyprus then submitted its comments on the Opinion of the Advisory Committee on 26 September 2001, and a Resolution was eventually adopted by the Council of Ministers of the Council of Europe on 21 February 2002. Cyprus was then due to deliver its second cycle State Report on 1 February 2004, although the Report was only delivered on 27 October 2006; this time, however, the Report was complete and was the result of prior consultation with the minorities concerned. The second cycle country visit of the Advisory Committee of the FCNM took place from 2 to 4 April 2007, and an Opinion was adopted on 7 June 2007. The comments of the Government of Cyprus on the Opinion were then submitted on 27 November 2007, and a Resolution was once again adopted by the Council of Ministers of the Council of Europe on 9 July 2008. The third cycle country visit of the Advisory Committee of the FCNM took place from 12 to 15 October 2009, and an Opinion was adopted on 19 March 2010. The comments of the Government of Cyprus on the Opinion were then submitted on 8 October 2010, and a Resolution was adopted by the Council of Ministers of the Council of Europe on 21 September 2011. The fourth cycle country visit took place from 15 to 17 December 2014, and an Opinion was adopted on 18 March 2015. The comments of the Government were then submitted on 25 September 2015, and a Resolution was adopted by the Council of Ministers on 11 May 2016. The fifth cycle country visit took place from 8 to 11 July 2019. An Opinion was adopted on 7 November 2019 and a Resolution by the Council of Ministers on 13 January 2021.

279. The first Opinion of the Advisory Committee, adopted on 6 April 2001, considered that, in general, the Republic of Cyprus respects the provisions of the FCNM and that it has, in many respects, made commendable efforts in the protection of national minorities. However, it observed that the information conveyed in the Report with regard to the practical implementation of the FCNM was rather limited and regretted that the authorities had not held any consultations with minority representatives, while the State Report was being prepared. The Advisory Committee further noted that awareness of the FCNM and its contents is limited, particularly among those persons who may directly benefit from its implementation. The Advisory Committee, therefore, encouraged the Government to take further measures to improve awareness of the FCNM, its explanatory report and the rules concerning its monitoring at the international level, including through the publication and dissemination of the State Report and other relevant documents. It was further suggested that the Government ought to identify ways and means of obtaining reliable statistical data to assess the size of the national minorities since, without such data, it would be very difficult for the authorities to implement and monitor measures aiming to ensure the effective equality of persons belonging to national minorities.

280. The Advisory Committee observed that the Constitution of Cyprus appears not to be compatible with the FCNM in a number of respects. In particular, the Advisory Committee suggested that the provisions of Article 2 of the Constitution, according to which members of the Religious Groups belong either to the Greek or to the Turkish Community, should be amended since they violate Article 3 of the FCNM, according to which each member of a minority group has the right to be considered, or not to be considered as such;[325] however, the Advisory Committee acknowledged that an amendment to the Constitution in that respect would currently be an extremely difficult task, in view of the abnormal situation prevailing in Cyprus. The Committee further noted that many persons belonging to the Latin Community are not satisfied with the term 'Latins', which the Government uses to designate them, as the expression does not properly reflect the essential element of their identity, namely the Roman Catholic rites they have in common. It was correctly suggested that it would be possible for the Government to address the issue in consultation with those concerned without undue difficulties, since no change to the Constitution would be required.[326]

281. The Advisory Committee further observed that the general legal obligation to vote in elections is indeed extended to the election of representatives of minorities so that persons belonging to Religious Groups are obliged to cast a vote in the parliamentary elections. While the Advisory Committee considered that it is to be welcomed that persons belonging to Religious Groups have the possibility to vote for a special representative in the House of Representatives, it also considered that this should be conceived as a right and not an obligation. It thus held that the obligation to elect special representatives for Religious Groups, failure of which may theoretically result in prosecution, is not compatible with Article 3 of the FCNM.[327] The Advisory Committee further noted, with approval, the creation of the post of Presidential Commissioner for Religious Groups, overseas Cypriots and repatriates. It was suggested that thought could be given to extending the scope of the mandate of the Presidential Commissioner, which is currently limited to relations with the Maronite, Armenian and Latin Communities.

282. In the second Opinion on Cyprus adopted on 7 June 2007, the Advisory Committee observed that since the adoption of the first Opinion, Cyprus had taken new steps to improve the implementation of the FCNM with respect to the Armenians, the Latins and the Maronites; efforts had been made to support the cultural activities of the three mentioned minority groups and to provide them with better opportunities to receive minority-specific education. Nevertheless, it noted that additional measures were necessary in order to meet the particular needs of these persons. The Advisory Committee welcomed the Cypriot authorities' willingness to pursue the dialogue on the implementation of the FCNM in Cyprus but noted that only limited consultations were held with the minorities concerned during the preparation of the Report; it thus considered that such consultations should be more extensive and effective in the future. In addition, the Advisory Committee regretted that the State Report had been submitted with a delay of more than two years, a situation which hampered the monitoring process.

283. The Advisory Committee reiterated that the constitutional obligation of members of the three Religious Groups to adhere either to the Greek or Turkish

325. Advisory Committee on the FCNM, *Opinion on Cyprus*, 6 Apr. 2001, para. 18.
326. *Ibid.*, para. 20.
327. *Ibid.*, para. 21.

Community is not consistent with the FCNM. In addition, the constitutional provision according to which a married woman shall belong to the Community to which her husband belongs was deemed to be contrary to the principle of self-determination and gender equality since both spouses ought to have the possibility to maintain their respective ethnic and religious affiliations.[328] The Committee further observed that members of the three minority groups are still obliged to vote for their representative, which is also not consistent with the FCNM; however, it also noted that nobody has been prosecuted since 2001 for non-compliance with the legal obligation to vote, and it was suggested that no such prosecutions should be initiated in the future. The Advisory Committee further regretted the fact that the measures intended to change the proper term of designating the Roman Catholic Religious Group had not been carried through.[329]

284. While the Advisory Committee welcomed the fact that the Government had obtained updated statistics on the numbers and the situations of the persons belonging to national minorities, derived from the population census organized in 2001, it noted that there were disparities between the official figures and the three minority groups' own estimates of their actual numbers. In addition, the Advisory Committee noted that if the obligation to carry out military service was to be extended, as indeed it was, to persons belonging to the three Religious Groups of the Republic, the authorities should seek ways of guaranteeing the effective exercise of the Religious Groups' right to manifest their own religion, including the right to opt out of any practices or activities which are specific to another religion.[330] It was also suggested that the authorities should identify measures, especially following the abolition of the position of the Presidential Commissioner for Religious Groups, in order to improve and institutionalize the management and coordination of the Government's minority policies and to ensure that consultation with the minorities is conducted on a regular basis.[331]

285. In the third Opinion on Cyprus adopted on 19 March 2010, the Advisory Committee observed that Cyprus had pursued its efforts to improve the protection of the Armenians, the Latins and the Maronites and had extended the provision provided by the FCNM to the Roma. It was noted that while the authorities had continued to provide support to the cultural activities of the three Religious Groups, they should further adjust this support to the existing needs of these groups and ensure more transparent procedures for accessing public subsidies. It was considered that the participation of the three Religious Groups in the decision-making process on issues concerning them should be made more effective.[332] The Resolution of the Council of Ministers adopted on 21 September 2011 recommended that the

328. Advisory Committee on the FCNM, *Opinion on Cyprus*, 7 Jun. 2007, para. 30.
329. *Ibid.*, para. 35.
330. *Ibid.*, para. 105.
331. *Ibid.*, para. 143.
332. Advisory Committee on the FCNM, *Third Opinion on Cyprus*, 19 Mar. 2010.

Republic of Cyprus should take adequate measures to ensure effective implementation of the principle of self-identification of the minorities and to combat and sanction all forms of discrimination and intolerance, including misconduct by members of the police force. It was also recommended that the Government should take additional measures to respond to the educational needs of the Religious Groups, especially as regards the availability of teaching materials and qualified teachers. The Republic was further called upon to pursue the dialogue with the Religious Groups concerning the potential recognition of the Armenians and the Maronites as national minorities and with respect to the designation of the Latins, as well as to enable the more effective participation of the Religious Groups in the House of Representatives through improved consultation mechanisms. It was further recommended that the obligation of the Religious Groups to affiliate themselves with either Community, as well as their statutory obligation to vote to elect their representative in the House of Representatives, ought to be reconsidered.[333]

286. It could be argued that, compared with their predecessors, the recommendations of the Advisory Committee and subsequently of the Resolution of the Council of Ministers during the Fourth reporting cycle were more vague and ideological. Instead of concrete proposals, the Advisory Committee called the Republic of Cyprus to ensure the enjoyment of the right to free self-identification in data collection exercises as a means to overcome ethnic divisions in daily life and to facilitate the formation of an open, multilingual and inclusive society. It further recommended that the Republic of Cyprus raise awareness of applicable human rights norms and anti-discrimination standards among the police force and the judiciary and enhance the support of minority languages and identities as an integral part of modern Cypriot society rather than merely as elements of cultural heritage. It further called for Roma protection and for strengthening the competencies of the representatives of the three Religious Groups.[334]

287. The Resolution adopted during the Fifth reporting cycle had more concrete proposals, including the implementation of the option of 'multiple affiliation' in the census so as to ensure that questions of ethnic and religious affiliation remain non-mandatory and open-ended, extending the possibility to intervene on all issues to the representatives of the three Religious Groups of the Republic, further supporting Greek language programmes for non-Greek speaking residents, further increasing financial training in Armenian and Cypriot Maronite Arabic, developing a detailed action plan for the social inclusion of Roma and increasing financial and human resources allocated to them, ensuring that complaints regarding discriminatory treatment are dealt with swiftly by the Ombudsman and that decisions are

333. Resolution CM/ResCMN (2011) 16 on the Implementation of the FCNM by Cyprus.

334. Advisory Committee on the FCNM, *Fourth Opinion on Cyprus*, 18 Mar. 2015, Resolution CM/ResCMN(2016) 8 on the Implementation of the FCNM by Cyprus, adopted on 11 May 2016.

enforced by public authorities, and considering the establishment of a state institution with a clear mandate and sufficient resources to address the needs of national minorities.[335]

335. Advisory Committee on the FCNM, *Fourth Opinion on Cyprus*, 7 Nov. 2015, Resolution CM/ResCMN(2016) 8 on the Implementation of the FCNM by Cyprus, adopted on 13 Jan. 2021.

Part V. Religion and Politics

Chapter 1. Religion Influence on Politics

§1. Religious Influence on Politics

I. The Makarios Era

288. There is no prohibition with regard to the election or appointment of religious functionaries in political or public offices. This is due to the fact that during the Turkish and British rule of Cyprus, the Orthodox Church constituted the nation-leading political organization of the Greeks under foreign sovereignty; thus, the Archbishop of Cyprus was also the leader of the Ethnarchy, acting as both the spiritual and political leader of Greek Cypriots. Makarios, the first president of the Republic of Cyprus, was also the Archbishop of the Greek Orthodox Church. Contrary to the importance of the Orthodox Church in Greek Cypriot political affairs, the role of religion in Turkish Cypriot politics was very limited; this was a direct result of the secularization of Turkey following the reforms of Kemalism.

289. From 1960 until his death in 1977, Makarios was not only the President of the Republic but also the most notable and influential political figure on the island. In the 'Times' editorial on the day following his death, Makarios was described as 'one of the most instantly recognizable figures of international politics'.[336] All parliamentary political parties supported, at least nominally, the policy of Makarios; while AKEL,[337] the communist party of Cyprus, had initially opposed Makarios, following 1960, Makarios enjoyed the continued and overwhelming support of AKEL as well. The only major political coalition besides AKEL, from 1960 to 1969, was the Patriotic Front, which was a coalition of all politicians who supported Makarios. When the first political parties were formed in 1969, Makarios' prior approval and blessing were provided;[338] prominent political figures of the island's history, including the centrist Presidents of the Republic Spyros Kyprianou and Tassos Papadopoulos and the socialist President of the House of Representatives Vasos Lyssarides, considered themselves the political successors of Makarios.

336. *The Times*, 4 Aug. 1977.
337. *See* T.W. Adams, *AKEL: The Communist Party of Cyprus* (Stanford: Hoover Institution Press, 1971).
338. *See* A. Emilianides, *Parliamentary History of the Republic of Cyprus 1964–1977* (Nicosia: Aigaion, 2007, in Greek).

290. As already noted, opponents of Makarios argued that his involvement in politics and his standing as a candidate for presidency violated the Holy Canons, which provide that no Bishop, priest or Deacon is allowed to undertake a secular position.[339] Makarios and his followers argued that, on the contrary, Makarios had continued to act as the leader of the Ethnarchy in view of the anomalous situation prevailing on the island; according to this view, the Holy Canons did not preclude Makarios from being the President of the Republic, since the Orthodox Greeks of Cyprus were struggling for their national survival, while under the circumstances, the holding of secular office did not confer on the Archbishop any personal reward, but was an onerous and bitter duty.[340] The Major Synod, which convened in 1973 with the participation of Patriarchs and Archbishops of other Orthodox Churches, endorsed Makarios' arguments.[341]

291. While from a Canon Law perspective, it is doubtful whether Makarios' position could be considered the correct one, the fact remains that during the early years of the Republic, a multi-party political environment had not yet developed, principally due to the anomalous situation prevailing in Cyprus and the Greco-Turkish conflict;[342] thus, the majority of the population considered Makarios as their natural leader, similarly to his predecessors and as if Cyprus was still under foreign rule.[343] Although it is true that the state respected the Constitutional provisions concerning religions during the period of Makarios' presidency, it could be argued that the fact that the President of the Republic was also the Archbishop of the Orthodox Church was undesirable for members of other religious communities, who might fear that the state would unavoidably favour the Orthodox Church.[344]

292. Makarios, however, seemed to maintain good relations with the Armenians, the Maronites and the Roman Catholics; his dual identity was mainly deemed to be problematic by members of the Orthodox Church who opposed Makarios politically and who considered that voters were religiously compelled to support their spiritual leader. Makarios represented both the Government and the Church in such a manner that criticism of the political activities of Makarios could be interpreted as opposition not only to the President but also to the Archbishop; this resulted in a peculiar situation which hindered the secularization process of the Republic.

---

339. Committee of Coordination of the Struggle for Union with Greece, *The Inconsistency of Being an Archbishop with Performing Secular Functions* (Nicosia: 1972, in Greek).
340. A. Gavrielides, *Nomocanonical and Political Study on the Defrocking of Bishops in Cyprus in Conjunction to the Exercise of Their Ethnarchical Rights* (Nicosia: 2nd ed. 1973, in Greek); C. Tornaritis, 'The Occupation of Secular Power by a Religious Minister According to the Law of the Orthodox Church of Cyprus', *Cyprus Law Tribune* 2–3, 3–10 (1973), (in Greek).
341. A. Mitsides, *The Major Synod of Nicosia* (Nicosia: 1973, in Greek).
342. *See* S. Zavou, *The Political Parties of Cyprus in the 20th Century* (Nicosia: Epifaniou 2nd ed. 2011, in Greek).
343. *See*, e.g., D. Assos, *Makarios. The Revolutionary Priest of Cyprus* (London: Tauris, 2018); P.N. Vanezis, *Makarios: Life and Leadership* (London: Abelard-Schuman, 1979).
344. *See*, e.g., G. Theodoulou, *The Origins and Evolution of Church – State Relations in Cyprus* (Nicosia: 2005).

II. After Makarios

293. Ever since the death of Archbishop Makarios in 1977, the political system of Cyprus has been completely secularized since religious functionaries, in principle, refrain from participating actively in elections and are not appointed to public offices. The Archbishop and other religious ministers restrict themselves, in general, to the exercise of their spiritual role without interfering in the exercise of the executive powers of the Republic. Consequently, religious influence in political life has diminished substantially; no political party claims that it is guided by spiritual truths or that it has the support of the Orthodox Church. In addition, the fact that the Archbishop or Metropolitans of the Church support a particular political party is of little significance to voters.

294. In the 1991 parliamentary elections, the former Archbishop Chrysostomos I secretly sponsored the short-lived Pancyprian Party of Displaced Persons (PAKOP); that party failed to surpass even 1% of the votes; furthermore, the fact that in the presidential elections of 1998, he supported the centrist candidate Paschalis Paschalides proved to be of little help, as Paschalides was supported by only 18.65% of the voters and failed to qualify for the second round of the elections. His successor Archbishop, Chrysostomos II, was a known supporter of the DIKO, without, however, his election to the office of the Archbishop or his known support of DIKO having enabled DIKO to increase its political power. The current Archbishop Georgios seems to be even more disengaged from political affairs than his predecessors.

295. During the first round of the 2008 Presidential elections, Archbishop Chrysostomos II supported former President Tassos Papadopoulos, and during the second round, after Papadopoulos had been eliminated, he supported the candidate of the DISY Ioannis Casoulides; both Papadopoulos and Casoulides lost the elections, despite enjoying the support of the Archbishop. During the second round of the Presidential elections, the great majority of the voters of DIKO voted for Christofias, who was supported by their party after the elimination of Papadopoulos, despite the fact that the Archbishop – also a supporter of DIKO – supported Casoulides. Other Metropolitans or members of the clergy also support or express their preference towards a particular presidential candidate, without this dictating the results of any Presidential, parliamentary or municipal elections; the political parties exercise much more influence over their supporters with respect to the outcome of any political elections, when compared to the Church.

296. Almost all political parties and many politicians have at times received funding from the Church during elections or with respect to their political activities; not only the Archdiocese but also the Monastery of Kykkos have funded many political activities of diverse political orientations. AKEL, the communist party of Cyprus, has also received funding from the Church on many occasions. In addition, many politicians regularly request the Church to assist their voters and arrange meetings with the Archbishop, the Bishop of Kykkos, or other Metropolitans in order to enable their voters to receive grants or other donations from the Church.

While in such cases the Church is exercising its role in helping the poor, or people in need, or in general, providing for their members, the politicians also satisfy their voters by arranging meetings with religious functionaries or by vouching for their voters who need assistance.

297. In view of the fact that the Orthodox Church engages in many economic activities in Cyprus and is a principal shareholder in various enterprises, the political role of the Church in funding political activities may also be exercised indirectly through its related commercial companies. However, it is not the case that the Church's funding of political activities is necessarily associated with the political beliefs of its Archbishop or of particular Bishops. The policy of the Church has been to support the political activities of different political parties; accordingly, many politicians who express political views different from those of the Archbishop with respect to the Cyprus Problem regularly receive funding or support from the Church.

§2. Religious Influence in Specific Political Affairs

I. The Role of the Church in the Cyprus Problem

298. Religious influence in politics may principally be traced in particular areas such as the Cyprus Problem and education. Archbishops of Cyprus who succeeded Makarios considered that the Church ought to freely express its opinion with respect to the Cyprus Problem since a potential solution to the Problem is of utmost concern to all Greek Orthodox Cypriots. Archbishop Chrysostomos I was considered to be a loyal supporter of Makarios and, in general, agreed with the policy expressed by the leader of the centrist DIKO and former President, Kyprianou, or the founder and leader of socialist EDEK, Lyssarides, who considered themselves to be the 'political children' of Makarios. Thus, Chrysostomos I supported the policy of the Government concerning the Cyprus Problem during the presidency of Kyprianou from Makarios' death until 1988; both Kyprianou and Chrysostomos I felt that the continuing occupation of northern Cyprus by Turkey amounted not only to a violation of international law but also to a failure of the international community and a disgrace for all civilized nations. Therefore, they considered that the removal of foreign military troops from Cyprus, the return of all displaced persons to their rightfully owned property, the expulsion of Turkish settlers from Cyprus, etc., were requirements for any viable and fair solution to the Cyprus Problem to be found.

299. Archbishop Chrysostomos I was, therefore, an opponent of the policy expressed by neo-liberal George Vassiliou during his term from 1988 to 1993, as well as part of the policy expressed by the right-wing President Glafkos Clerides, especially during his second term from 1998 to 2003. Both Vassiliou and Clerides were, in general, willing to settle for a solution to the Cyprus Problem which was based upon a bi-zonal, bi-communal federation of two states, one Greek and one Turkish, the viability of which would be explicitly interwoven with the process of Greco-Turkish relations and the EU accession process of Turkey. In essence, both

Vassiliou and Clerides considered that finding a solution was more important by itself than the content of such a solution; according to such a view, since Turkey already occupied northern Cyprus and the international community had failed to induce Turkey to adhere to the principles of international law, Cypriots would have to settle for a solution which would be deemed to be acceptable by the international community, even if such a solution seemed to Cypriots, unfair or undemocratic.

300. Archbishop, Chrysostomos II was also a staunch supporter of the policy of his immediate predecessor with respect to the Cyprus Problem. Thus, he strongly opposed the plan providing for a comprehensive solution to the Cyprus Problem submitted by the former Secretary-General of the United Nations, Kofi Annan. The Archbishop felt that such a plan was unacceptable, unfair and undemocratic since it essentially provided for the legalization of the ramifications of the military invasion of Turkey in Cyprus and transformed Cyprus into a protectorate of Turkey. Consequently, the Archbishop fully supported former President Papadopoulos, who called upon the people of Cyprus to reject the Plan during the referenda of 24 April 2004. This view of the Archbishop was shared almost unanimously by the Holy Synod of the Orthodox Church; however, while certain Metropolitans, such as the Metropolitan of the occupied town of Kyrenia, were vocal opponents of the Plan, other members of the Holy Synod, were reluctant to express their opposition to the Plan in public.

301. While the great majority of the people of Cyprus rejected the Annan Plan, this should not be considered to indicate that the political influence of the Church has increased; in the case of the Annan Plan, the position of the Church was consistent with the views of the majority of the population of Cyprus and was not ground on the basis of which such views were formed. While Greek Cypriots always respect the opinions of the Archbishop and other members of the Holy Synod or of clergymen, with respect to political issues, they are more influenced by the views of their respective political parties or by the views of political personalities or experts; in the case of the Annan Plan, the Church had a more limited role in opposing the Plan, when compared to the role played by former President Papadopoulos, various politicians, or even the non-governmental Pancyprian Citizens Movement.

302. Chrysostomos II criticized the former President of the Republic, Dimitris Christofias, very often whenever he considered that the latter's actions with respect to the Cyprus Problem of the economy were contrary to the best interests of the people of Cyprus. However, the Archbishop had been very supportive of and enjoyed a good relationship with President Nicos Anastasiades, despite the fact that he was a leading supporter of the Annan Plan and their opinions on the Cyprus Problem were theoretically incompatible. In 2008, a non-governmental organization called 'Movement for Liberty and Rule of Law for Cyprus' was founded; it was announced that this Movement was financially supported by the Archbishop and purported to inform Cypriots and the international community about the need to solve the Cyprus Problem in accordance with the fundamental principles of European democracy, international law, human rights and rule of law. It soon became evident that such a Movement opposed the policy of President Christofias with respect to the Cyprus Problem; the influence, however, of this Movement proved to be extremely limited, and eventually, its operations were essentially suspended.

303. With respect to the Cyprus Problem, the Church is most influential while funding non-governmental organizations, associations of citizens, or even political activities which purport to inform the international community about the tragedy that occurred in Cyprus in 1974. In addition, the Archbishop regularly meets with other Patriarchs or Archbishops of the Orthodox Church, with other primates of Christianity, including the Pope, or with foreign political leaders in order to inform them of developments concerning the Cyprus Problem and ask for their support. The Church further provides support to displaced persons, relatives of the missing persons and Cypriots who have lost their properties as a result of the Turkish invasion of 1974. It has also sponsored various publications and conferences which prove the desecration or pillage of Greek Orthodox churches and monasteries situated in the occupied areas.

II. The Role of the Church in Education

304. The Constitution of Cyprus provided that, *inter alia*, educational and religious matters of the Greek Community would come under the jurisdiction of the Greek Communal Chamber, while educational and religious matters of the Turkish Community would come under the jurisdiction of the Turkish Communal Chamber. Education – apart from religious education – has always been considered very important to the Greek Orthodox Church since, during the period of foreign rule over the island, education was the cornerstone of the preservation of Greek – and Orthodox – identity; consequently, the Church had funded the establishment of many public schools and had always encouraged the instruction of classical studies, such as Ancient Greek, Latin, literature, and history.[345] While the Church has always considered classical studies and the knowledge of Greek history, language, customs and ethics as essential for the preservation of Hellenism in Cyprus and, consequently, for the identity of Cypriots as Greek Orthodox, it has virtually had no role in the preparation of the analytical programmes concerning classical studies, or education in general; such programmes have always been prepared by the specialized public officers of the Ministry of Education, Sport and Youth, without any participation by the Church.

305. As a result, since the establishment of Independence, the Church's interest in the teaching of classical studies has not implied any further involvement of the Church in education; such competence is solely exercised by the Ministry of Education, Sport and Youth, without any religious involvement. On the other hand, the Church has never expressed even a theoretical interest with respect to other educational issues which were considered religiously controversial in other countries; thus, the Orthodox Church has not strongly opposed the teachings of Darwin in

345. P. Persianis, *Church and State in Cyprus Education* (Nicosia: 1978).

schools, nor has it ever seriously considered promoting the teaching of Creationism or Intelligent Design in schools. This is probably due to the fact that religious education has always been a cornerstone of education in general in Cypriot schools; hence, the Church has never felt that the introduction of alternative *scientific* lessons was necessary. Consequently, the teaching of physics, biology and similar subjects in Cypriot schools has always depended upon the findings of the scientific community and never upon religious considerations. Whereas the enactment of Law 205(I)/2022, which mandatorily introduced holistic sexual education in schools, has been aggressively opposed by various religiously-influenced groups, particularly due to the potential for incorporation of LGBT+ education, the Holy Synod and the official Church have refrained from engaging in any debate, with the Archbishop speaking in support of holistic sexual education.

306. Ever since the inter-communal conflict of 1963 and the self-dissolution of the Greek Communal Chamber, the Ministry of Education has been considered the functioning successor of the Greek Communal Chamber. Since the death of Makarios, the practice of Presidents of the Republic had been to consult the Greek Orthodox Church before appointing a new Minister of Education, Sport and Youth. While the President of the Republic has the power to appoint a new Minister of Education, Sport and Youth without consulting the Church, it had been considered that the Church ought to have the opportunity to express its opinion before the appointment of a new Minister of Education, Sport and Youth; this was due to the fact that education has been a matter of particular interest to the Church. However, after the Church expressed its opinion, the President could well appoint a Minister of Education, Sport and Youth who did not enjoy the support of the Church. Therefore, consulting the Church was a practice aimed at aiding the President in making an informed decision after consulting all interested parties rather than a procedure aiming to bind the President. Consequently, many Ministers of Education, Sport and Youth have not enjoyed the support of the Church and have been political appointees. Dimitris Christofias was the first President of the Republic who appointed a Minister of Education without previously consulting the Orthodox Church; this might have been due to the fact that Christofias did not enjoy a good personal relationship with Archbishop Chrysostomos II. The practice of consulting the Church for the appointment of the Minister of Education, Sport and Youth has, however, since waned.

307. The Church opposed the educational reform of the Christofias Government and the declared intention to reform Cypriot history books, so as to abolish 'chauvinistic and nationalistic elements' and in order to reconcile the two communities of the island. While the Church did not disagree with the abolition of such elements from the history books or with the reconciliation of the two communities, it disagreed with the formerly governing AKEL's views on the content of such history books. The official position of AKEL has always been to downgrade the EOKA liberation struggle, while the Church was the guiding force of that struggle, and it has always considered that struggle as the most glorious period of the recent history of Cyprus.

308. Furthermore, the Church, and indeed the majority of the population, considers that any amendments to the history books ought to occur on the basis of historical findings and research work by Cypriot and alien academics and not simply as an effort to reconcile the two communities. Thus, the Church's opposition to the declared reform of the history books is not based upon religious grounds but mainly upon disagreement as to what constitutes historical truth and how history should be evaluated; not simply the Church, but many prominent Cypriot historians and most political parties, have officially disagreed with the specific context of the declared intention to reform Cypriot history books, even though they all agree with reform in general.[346]

346. *See Sygxroni Apopsi* 7 (2008): 44–69 (in Greek).

Chapter 2. Political Influence in Religion

309. While there is no political influence in religious Canon Law, political parties have always shown a particular interest in the election of a new Archbishop of the Orthodox Church of Cyprus. After the death of Makarios, the nomination of Chrysostomos I was initially supported by AKEL, DIKO and EDEK; however, eventually, no elections were held, and Chrysostomos I was unanimously elected as Archbishop. The involvement of political parties in the election of a new Archbishop was more intense during the 2006 elections. AKEL, the communist party of Cyprus, officially supported the nomination of Bishop of Kykkos Nikiphoros; many of the laypersons elected as General Representatives in the Electoral Assembly on behalf of the Bishop of Kykkos were officials of AKEL; outside the polling stations, members of AKEL attempted to convince the voters to support the nomination of the Bishop of Kykkos. The Secretary-General of AKEL and now President of the Republic, Dimitris Christofias, had called upon all members of his party to support the candidacy of the Bishop of Kykkos as signifying a new prosperous era for the Church of Cyprus; such views were also expressed by other superior officials of AKEL.

310. Although AKEL was the only political party to officially support a candidate, the nomination of the Bishop of Kykkos was also supported by various politicians from all other political parties; a meeting organized by the Bishop of Kykkos prior to the elections was attended by the right-wing former President of the Republic Glafkos Clerides, members of the House of Representatives representing DISY, DIKO and EDEK, as well as other politicians and well-known businessmen; all expressed their support towards the nomination of the Bishop of Kykkos and called upon all members of the Orthodox Church to vote for him. While Athanasios, the Metropolitan of Limassol, never enjoyed the extent of political support enjoyed by the Bishop of Kykkos, he was also supported by a few members of the House of Representatives who hailed from Limassol; however, the main supporters of the Metropolitan of Limassol were Greek Orthodox Christians who attended Church more regularly and considered that the Church ought to focus on its spiritual role, rather than participate in political and financial activities.

311. Consequently, the Bishop of Kykkos was considered the representative of a Church participating in political and financial activities, while the Metropolitan of Limassol was considered the representative of a more spiritual-oriented Church. The third major candidate, the then Metropolitan of Paphos and current Archbishop Chrysostomos II, never enjoyed the public support that the other two candidates did; only ten of the 100 elected General Representatives supported the candidacy of the Metropolitan of Paphos, while the Bishop of Kykkos and the Metropolitan of Limassol had elected forty-five General Representatives each. Similarly, the Metropolitan of Paphos controlled only a minority of the ex officio members, while the Bishop of Kykkos and the Metropolitan of Limassol were supported by a nearly equal number of ex officio members as well.

312. However, due to the peculiarities of the electoral system, the Metropolitan of Paphos was elected as the new Archbishop of Cyprus; during the first two rounds of the elections, the Metropolitan of Paphos collaborated with the Metropolitan of Limassol so that the Metropolitan of Limassol was supported by a number of the General Representatives of the Metropolitan of Paphos, while the Metropolitan of Paphos was supported by a number of the ex officio members of the Metropolitan of Limassol. Consequently, the Metropolitan of Limassol was supported by the majority of the General Representatives, while the Metropolitan of Paphos was supported by the majority of the ex officio members, and they both proceeded to the third round of the elections, thereby eliminating the Bishop of Kykkos.

313. During the third round of elections, the Metropolitan of Paphos collaborated with the Bishop of Kykkos so that both the General Representatives and the ex officio members who had supported the Bishop of Kykkos in the first two rounds, now supported the Metropolitan of Paphos, who, consequently, supported by the majority of voters in the third round of the elections. In view of the above, the Metropolitan of Paphos was elected as the new Archbishop of the Orthodox Church of Cyprus, despite the fact that he did not enjoy support from political parties or politicians, as did the Bishop of Kykkos. Irrespective of political support during elections, it cannot really be argued that any political party exercises much influence over the decisions of the Holy Synod; political influence in religious affairs after the elections for a new Archbishop has always remained rather limited. During the 2022 elections for a new Archbishop, there was no widespread participation by political parties or politicians in the election campaign; this was partly due to the new electoral system, which limited the importance of popular elections compared to the 2006 elections.

Chapter 3. Interaction Between Religion and State on a Political and Legal Level

314. While the dialogue between the state and religions should be considered extremely important, until 1998, there had been no organ responsible for carrying out such a dialogue. This was probably due to the fact that in the early years of the Republic, Makarios was both the Archbishop and the President, so that any dialogue between the Orthodox Church and the Government would be mostly a theoretical notion. Following the death of Makarios, the fact that the Orthodox Church represented the great majority of the population and further enjoyed significant economic power enabled the Archbishop of the Orthodox Church to discuss his concerns with the President of the Republic as an equal. The representation of the three Religious Groups of the Republic in the House of Representatives, albeit in a limited manner, also enabled religious minorities to discuss their main concerns with the members of the House of Representatives and the Government. However, the lack of a central governmental service responsible for supervising the dialogue between the various religions and the State has proven, in many circumstances, to be problematic, especially for religious minorities.

315. From 1998 to 2003, the state had appointed a Presidential Commissioner for Religious Groups, Overseas Cypriots and Repatriates, who represented the state in this dialogue with the representatives of the three Religious Groups. The first Commissioner was Manolis Christophides, a former Minister of Health and former member of the House of Representatives on behalf of DISY.[347] Subsequent governments did not appoint a new Presidential Commissioner, arguing that since most of the issues of concern fall within the competence of the Ministry of Interior, a coordinator within the Ministry of Interior would be more capable of handling issues of concern to the Religious Groups, even if those issues fall within the competence of other ministries. The new consultation mechanism deals, among others, with issues of implementation of relevant international or regional treaties, the competencies of the Representatives of the three Religious Groups, the preservation of the social cohesion of the Religious Groups, the maintenance of monasteries and chapels, subsidization of students of Religious Groups, granting of Government land for cemeteries, payment of priests' salaries and other measures.

316. The wisdom of the aforementioned decision was doubtful since a Commissioner would be in a better position to handle issues concerning Religious Groups rather than the Ministry of Interior. The fact that reports on the application of the FCNM have been prepared by the Office of the Law Commissioner implies that the application of the FCNM, as well as legal provisions on the issue of religious freedom, are not, on the whole, handled by the Ministry of Interior. In any event, if the Ministry of Interior should be responsible for issues concerning religions, a department of religious affairs, not limited simply to the three Religious Groups of the

347. *See* Press and Information Office, *Ten Years of Government by Glafkos Clerides: 1993–2003* 255–261 (Nicosia: 2003), (in Greek); J. McMahon, 'Cyprus: Coping with a Quarter Century of Separation' 74–75 (Washington Report on Middle East Affairs, September 1999).

Republic, ought to be established; this was also suggested in 2001 by the Advisory Committee on the FCNM which noted that thought could be given to extending the scope of the mandate of the Presidential Commissioner.[348] Following the election of the new Anastassiades Government in March 2013, a new Presidential Commissioner for Religious Groups, Overseas Cypriots and Repatriates was appointed for the first time since 2003. The new Commissioner, Kate Clerides, was a former member of the House of Representatives and the daughter of the former President of the Republic and former President of DISY, Glafkos Clerides. On 30 September 2014, former Minister of Defence, Fotis Fotiou was appointed as a new Commissioner. The Resolution adopted during the Fifth reporting cycle of the FCNM suggested that the Republic should consider the establishment of a state institution with a clear mandate and sufficient resources to address the needs of national minorities.[349] However, the new President of the Republic, Nicos Christodoulides, has not, since undertaking his duties in March 2023, appointed a new Commissioner handling issues pertaining to either Religious Groups, as in the past or religious minorities.

348. Advisory Committee on the FCNM, *Opinion on Cyprus*, 6 Apr. 2001, para. 42.

349. Resolution CM/ResCMN(2016) 8 on the Implementation of the FCNM by Cyprus, adopted on 13 Jan. 2021.

Part VI. Labour Law Within Religious Communities

Chapter 1. Scope of Application of Labour Law

§1. Employment Law and Religious Communities

I. Introduction

317. The employment relationships in Cyprus are governed by ordinary contract law principles and are supplemented by statutory rights and obligations where appropriate.[350] A legal instrument of particular importance is the Termination of Employment Law 24/1967,[351] which was enacted pursuant to Recommendation 119/1963 of the International Labour Organization. It should be noted, at the outset, that in Cyprus, the terms of any collective employment relationship are of non-binding effect and should always form part of the specific individual employment relationship in order for such terms to apply in the latter case.[352] Otherwise, the terms of the individual employment relationship are considered to supersede the terms of the collective employment relationship in cases of conflict between them.

II. The Employment Relationships of Religious Communities

318. While the State pays the salary of several clergymen of the Orthodox Church, as well as of the three Religious Groups of the Republic and of the Orthodox Christians who follow the Old Calendar, this should not be taken to imply that such clergymen are public servants; the status of the clergymen of the Orthodox

350. *See* in general A. Emilianides & C. Ioannou, *Labour Law in Cyprus* (The Hague: Kluwer 2nd ed. 2019); P. Polyviou, *The Contract of Employment under Cypriot Law* (Nicosia: Chrysaffinis and Polyviou, 2016, Vols I–II, in Greek); P. Polyviou, *The Cypriot Labour Law: Theory and Practice* (Nicosia: Chryssafinis & Polyviou, 2018, in Greek); S. Yiannakourou, *Cypriot Labour Law* (Athens: Nomiki Vivliothiki, 2016, in Greek); N. Ktenas, 'Employment', in *Introduction to Cyprus Law* 991–1016 (Andreas Neocleous & Co ed., Limassol: 3rd ed. 2010); T. Papamiltiades, 'Labour Law', in *Corpus de Jure Cyprii*, Vol. II, 265–308 (Nicosia: Cyprus Bar Council, 1988, in Greek).
351. *See* M. Antoniou (ed.), *The Law of Termination of Employment in Cyprus* (Nicosia: Federation of Employers and Industrialists, 2000, in Greek).
352. For the collective employment agreements *see* C. Tornaritis, 'Collective Employment Contract', *Cyprus Law Tribune* 1–2, 14–17 (1972), (in Greek).

Church, of the three Religious Groups of the Republic and of the Orthodox Christians who follow the Old Calendar remains one of private law, and not one of public law, despite the fact that the salary of such clergymen may be paid by the State. This is due to the fact that the exact terms of the agreement between the State and the various constitutionally recognized religious communities are that the State has agreed to compensate the Orthodox Church, the three Religious Groups and the Orthodox Christians who follow the Old Calendar with respect to the payment of salaries of their clergymen; the agreement is therefore between the State and the religious communities and not between the State and the specific clergymen whose salaries are paid by the State.

319. The clergymen have employment contracts with, and receive instructions from, their respective Churches and not the State; consequently, the State does not itself function as the employer but simply funds the Churches, who function as the employers of the clergymen. The above view is consistent with the fact that the various religious organizations, including the Orthodox Church and the three Religious Groups, are not considered legal persons under public law but only legal persons under private law of a peculiar nature; therefore, the status of the employees of those Churches ought, in principle, to remain one of private law and not of public law. In view of the above, the employment relationship between a religious organization and an employee is governed by the general provisions of employment law.[353]

320. It could, however, be argued that in light of Article 110 of the Constitution, recognizing administrative religious autonomy to the Orthodox Church and the three Religious Groups, the general provisions of employment law should not apply with respect to religious ministers of the Orthodox Church, or the three Religious Groups of the Republic. According to this view, the employment relationship between the religious ministers and the Orthodox Church, or the members of the three Religious Groups, should be governed exclusively by the provisions of the Charter of the Orthodox Church or the internal law provisions of the three Religious Groups and not by the legislation of the State. In view, however, of the fact that the employment relationships do not constitute matters which would have fallen within the jurisdiction of the Greek Communal Chamber but instead matters which would have, in any case, fallen within the exclusive jurisdiction of the House of Representatives, the aforementioned view does not seem convincing.

321. The Orthodox Church and the three Religious Groups enjoy exclusive competence only with respect to matters of a religious nature which would have otherwise fallen within the competence of the Greek Communal Chamber and not to matters such as employment law. Consequently, so long as the relevant provisions of general employment law do not contain an exception clause concerning religious organizations, it is submitted that the employment law relationships of all religious organizations are governed by the general provisions of employment law. The above conclusion presents, however, certain problems. A religious minister is supposed to

353. *Sideras v. The Minister of Labour and Social Securities* [1989] 3 CLR (in Greek).

serve God continuously; thus, provisions concerning the maximum amount of working hours, as well as other employment law provisions, might be expected to be, in essence, inapplicable with respect to religious ministers, although they might well be applicable with respect to other employees of the religious organization.

322. Such conflicts might be more theoretical in nature than real; a religious minister has to perform certain functions which are crucial to his role and his spiritual mission. If a religious minister does not fulfil his role in an appropriate manner, then the religious organization might discipline such a religious minister. Furthermore, a religious minister normally undertakes certain responsibilities because he considers that they form part of his spiritual mission and because he has faith in the religion he belongs to and in its internal rules. Thus, problems concerning the application of the general provisions of employment law with regard to religious ministers might be more easily solved if the application of such provisions is considered within the wider context of the organizational religious freedom of each religious community and the spiritual role that each religious minister has to perform; therefore, each particular case ought to be examined within the framework of religious freedom protection. In any event, with respect to other employees of the religious organization, there seems to be no ground on the basis of which the application of the general provisions of employment law might be disqualified.

323. In so far as collective employment law is concerned, the ECtHR has held that whereas the right of members of the clergy to form a trade union falls under eleven of ECHR, the Romanian authorities acted within their margin of appreciation by refusing to register a trade union of the clergy and layperson of a Metropolis of the Orthodox Church of Romania. It was held that it was reasonable for the Romanian authorities to consider that the registration of a trade union would amount to a danger to the autonomy of the Romanian Orthodox Church, taking into account that the objective of the trade union was to safeguard the rights of its members and to accordingly demand for additional rights of participation in the Holy Synod, freedom of expression, audit of the financial situation, etc.[354]

III. Termination of Employment Law

324. The Termination of Employment Law 24/1967 defines the employer as any person under whom the employee has entered into employment or who is deemed by the Court to have the status of an employer, including the Government of Cyprus; hence, religious organizations are not excluded from the application of the Termination of Employment Law. According to the provisions of Law 24/67, in cases where a dismissal is declared unfair, the employer must compensate the employee. The cases where termination of employment of an employee is considered to be fair and which do not give rise to compensation are the following: (a) the employee fails to carry out his work efficiently; (b) the employee becomes redundant; (c) the termination is due to force majeure; (d) the contract is for a fixed term

354. App. 2330/2009, *Sindicatul Pastorum cel Bun v. Romania*, Judgment of 9 Jul. 2013.

and has expired; (e) the employee renders himself/herself liable to dismissal without notice; (f) the contract is such that it is clear that the employment relationship cannot reasonably be expected to continue, as in the case of gross misconduct, or where the employee commits a criminal offence in the course of his duties.

325. Redundancy can only be justified if it is based upon at least one of the grounds for dismissal which are expressly provided for in the Law. A dismissed employee will be entitled to receive payment from the Redundancy Fund if such employee: (a) has been dismissed on one of the legal grounds for dismissal on the basis of redundancy; and (b) has been employed by the same employer for a continuous period of at least 104 weeks before termination; and (c) has not reached the age of retirement before the date of termination. Such grounds for dismissal on the basis of redundancy are the following: (i) the employer has ceased, or intends to cease, to operate the business where the employee is employed; (ii) the employer has ceased, or intends to cease, to operate the business at the place (location) where the employee is employed; (iii) modernization, mechanization, or any other change in the method of production or organization, which necessitates a reduction in the number of employees, or a change in the products, the method of production, or the expertise required by the employees; (iv) abolition of a specific department (and not of a specific position), so long as such abolition does not arise from a transfer of such department to another legal entity, as a result of a merge, or a legal transfer; (v) reduction in the turnover of the business, or difficulties in placing products in the market, or credit difficulties, or lack of orders or lack of raw materials.[355]

326. In cases of redundancy, certain problems arise with respect to religious organizations. The Redundancy Fund is a public law legal entity, which is established by the Council of Ministers and which compensates employees who were dismissed on grounds of redundancy. Each employer is obliged to contribute to the Redundancy Fund. However, some religious organizations do not contribute to the Redundancy Fund, since they do not consider themselves as employers, a fact which may cause problems in practice should redundancy be alleged. In any event, if the Fund accepts the grounds stated by the employer and pays the employee, then the employee is redundant. If, however, the Fund rejects the application, the employee has to file an action in the Industrial Disputes Court claiming compensation for redundancy against the Fund, also claiming, alternatively, compensation for unfair dismissal against the employer. Therefore, the action is normally filed against both the employer and the Redundancy Fund. If the Industrial Disputes Court holds that the dismissal was not on the basis of a legal ground for dismissal due to redundancy, this will lead to the conclusion that the dismissal is unfair and that the employer must pay compensation to the employee for unfair dismissal.

327. The employee might not be entitled to receive compensation from the Redundancy Fund in the following circumstances: (a) if, before the termination of

355. *See* A. Emilianides, 'Redundancy Law in Cyprus', in *Redundancy Law in Europe* 29–35 (Van Kempen, Von Steinau & Ryley eds, The Hague: Kluwer Law International, 2008).

the employment contract, the employer offers to the employee a new adequate position or location of employment and the employee unreasonably rejects such offer; (b) if the employment contract has been terminated due to a change of employer, despite the fact that the new employer renewed the existing employment contract; (c) if the employer is a company and transfers the employee to another affiliated company, which is either a parent company, or a subsidiary, or they both belong to the same group of companies.

328. The amount of compensation awarded depends principally on the number of years that the employee has been employed. Therefore, the employee shall be entitled to two weeks' salary for each year of the first four years of continuous employment, two and a half weeks' salary for each year between the fifth and the tenth year of continuous employment, to three weeks' salary for each year between the eleventh and the fifteenth year of continuous employment, to three and a half weeks salary for each year between the sixteenth and the twentieth year of continuous employment and to four weeks salary for each year between the twenty-first and the twenty-fifth year of continuous employment of the employee. If any remaining period of continuous employment does not amount to fifty-two weeks, then a remaining period of twenty-two or more weeks shall amount to one full year of continuous employment for the purposes of awarding compensation. Any agreement between an employer and an employee to the effect that the latter will not claim any redundancy payment in return for any benefit provided by the employer is void and will have no effect. The amount of compensation awarded by the Fund is the minimum of compensation that would have been awarded by the employer in case of wrongful dismissal.

§2. Non-discrimination on the Grounds of Religion

329. The European Directive established a general framework for equal treatment in employment and occupation, Council Directive 2000/78/EC, which has been implemented into Cypriot Law with Law 58(I)/2004 concerning equal treatment in employment and occupation.[356] The purpose of Law 58(I)/2004 is, according to section 3 of the Law, to set out a framework in order to prevent discrimination on the grounds of, *inter alia*, religion or belief in the area of employment and occupation, so that the principle of equal treatment might be effected. Section 4 of Law 58(I)/2004 provides that the scope of this Law extends to all public and private sector bodies, including public authorities, local administrative authorities, as well as public or private organizations.

330. Thus, the scope of Law 58(I)/04 extends also to churches and other religious organizations. Indeed, section 2 of Law 58(I)/2004 clarifies that the term 'employer' covers, for the purposes of this Law, the Government of the Republic of Cyprus, local administrative authorities, as well as every natural or legal person in

356. *See* A. Emilianides, 'Age Discrimination in Cyprus', in *Age Discrimination in Europe* (Van Kempen, Von Steinau & Ryley eds, The Hague: Kluwer Law International, 2009).

the public or private sector or with respect to any other activity which entails occupying, or having occupied, employees. For the purposes of Law 58(I)/2004, an 'employee' is defined as any person who is employed or apprenticed, either full-time or part-time, for a defined or undefined period of time, continuously or not, irrespective of the place where such person is occupied and including persons who work from home; however, the notion of an 'employee' does not include self-employed persons.

331. Discrimination on the grounds of religion or belief is unlawful with respect to access to employment, self-employment or occupation, including selection criteria and recruitment conditions, whatever the branch of activity and at all levels of the professional hierarchy, including promotion. Discrimination on the grounds of religion is further prohibited with regard to access to all types and to all levels of vocational guidance, vocational training, advanced vocational training and retraining, including practical work experience, employment and working conditions, including dismissals and pay, membership of, and involvement in, an organization of workers or employers, or any organization whose members carry on a particular profession, including the benefits provided for by such organizations.

332. Discrimination on the grounds of religion exists if a person is treated less favourably on the grounds of religion than another person is, has been, or would be treated in a comparable situation. The assessment as to whether a less favourable treatment exists must be based on a comparator; hence, the notion of a 'comparable situation' is quite important; it should be proved that the claimant is treated less favourably than another person performing the same, or essentially similar, or comparable work as the claimant. In order to conclude whether the claimant is treated less favourably, an overall comparison of all types of work to be performed under the contract should be undertaken. The mere fact that the claimant is treated less favourably with respect to one aspect of the contract will thus not suffice if the claimant is treated more favourably with respect to other aspects; it is rather the overall assessment and comparison of the contract which is important. In the absence of a current comparator, comparators formerly employed have to be used for the comparison before an assessment can be made.

333. Section 6 of Law 58(I)/2004 further prohibits indirect discrimination on grounds of religion; section 2 of Law 58(I)/2004 provides that indirect discrimination shall be taken to occur where an apparently neutral provision, criterion or practice would put persons having a particular religion, at a particular disadvantage, compared with other persons, unless that provision, criterion or practice is objectively justified by a legitimate aim and the means of achieving that aim are appropriate and necessary. Indirect discrimination may occur where there is a failure to treat different individuals or groups differently, without any objective justification, in such a manner so that an apparently neutral provision which theoretically applies to everybody, in essence, constitutes a disguised discriminatory provision which discriminates between the claimant and other persons.

334. On the other hand, the aforementioned provisions are subject to certain exceptions with respect to religious organizations. Section 7 of Law 58(I)/2004 provides that in the case of occupational activities within churches and other public or private organizations whose ethos is based on religion or belief, a difference of treatment rooted in a person's religion or belief shall not constitute discrimination, provided that the nature of such an activity or treatment constitutes a genuine, legitimate and justified occupational requirement, with regard to the ethos of the organization.[357] Hence, section 7 of the Law allows a requirement that a person should be of a particular religion or belief in order to be employed in a church or any other religious organization; the application of the principle of non-discrimination with respect to employment loosens in favour of the application of the principle of organizational religious freedom.[358] It has been held that the willingness of an employer to take account of the wishes of a customer so as to force a worker to stop wearing an Islamic headscarf cannot be considered a genuine and determining occupational requirement.[359] On the contrary, it was held that an internal rule by the employer targeting all employees generally and without differentiation and thus neutrally, and which prohibited employees from wearing visible signs of their political, philosophical or religious beliefs in the workplace, including an Islamic headscarf, did not introduce any unjustified difference of treatment.[360]

335. Moreover, section 5 of Law 58(I)/2004, which corresponds to Article 4 of Council Directive 2000/78/EC, clarifies that a difference of treatment on any ground shall not constitute discrimination where, by reason of the nature of the particular occupational activities concerned or of the context in which they are carried out, such a characteristic constitutes a genuine and determining occupational requirement, provided that the objective is legitimate and the requirement is proportionate. It could be well argued that section 5 of Law 58(I)/04 covers the cases where a church refuses to employ women as members of the clergy; in the latter cases, it is indisputable that a difference of treatment on the grounds of sex is strictly related to the nature of the particular activities concerned and the context in which they are carried out, in view also of the principle of organizational religious freedom. However, whether the exemption could also apply with respect to other employees of the religious organization besides religious ministers is debatable; the church or the religious organization in question would have to prove that hiring a female layperson in order to perform certain duties might be problematic, for instance, due to the fact that this might be scandalizing for the male religious ministers who would have to work with the female employee. Whether, in such a case, the criteria of the existence of a genuine and legitimate occupational requirement or the principle of proportionality are fulfilled is quite doubtful.

357. Case C-414/16, *Egenberger v. Evangelisches Werk für Diakonie und Entwicklung e.V* EU:C:2018:257.
358. *See* in general R. Ahdar & I. Leigh, *Religious Freedom in the Liberal State* 305 ff. (Oxford: Oxford University Press, 2005).
359. Case C-188/15, *Bougnaoui and Another v. Micropole SA* EU:C:2017:204.
360. Case C-157/15, *Achbita and Another v. G4S Secure Solutions NV* EU:C:2017:203, Case C-344/20, *L.F. v. S.C.R.L* EU:C:2022:774, Cases C-804/18 and C-341/19, *IX v. WABE eV and MH Müller Handels GmbH* EU:C:2021:594.

336. It is further argued that should section 5 be considered a sufficient basis to justify differentiation of treatment on the grounds of sex, it could also justify differentiation on the grounds of sexual orientation, in so long as such differentiation was explicitly based upon Canon Law provisions and was related to the principle of organizational religious freedom. Again, it is doubtful whether such differentiation in treatment might equally apply with respect to laypersons who are employed by the church or the religious organization without performing religious duties, such as accountants, secretaries, or legal counsels. Therefore, while section 7 of Law 58(I)/04 explicitly exempts cases where religious organizations differentiate between their employees or refuse to hire employees on the grounds of religion or belief, section 5 also provides an exemption, in the proper cases, with respect to difference in treatment on the grounds of sex or sexual orientation.[361] The CJEU has held that a difference of treatment, as regards a requirement to act in good faith and with loyalty to that ethos, between employees in managerial positions according to the faith or lack of faith of those employees is consistent with that directive only if, bearing in mind the nature of the occupational activities concerned or the context in which they are carried out, the religion or belief constitutes an occupational requirement that is genuine, legitimate and justified in light of the ethos of the church or organization concerned and is consistent with the principle of proportionality.[362]

361. A. Emilianides, 'Discrimination Law in Cyprus', in *Religion and Discrimination Law in the European Union* 79–85 (M. Hill ed., Trier: European Consortium for State and Church Research, 2012).
362. Case C-68/17, *IR v. JQ* EU:C:2018:696.

Chapter 2. Religious Ministers and Labour Law

337. Religious ministers primarily perform a spiritual function; in the United Kingdom, it has been held that the duties owed by the pastor to the church are neither contractual nor enforceable.[363] According to the aforementioned view, religious ministers should not be considered employees of the religious organization but should rather be considered as performing a spiritual mission. The only Supreme Court case where the status of a religious minister was considered concerned a member of the clergy of the Greek Orthodox Church.[364] In the aforementioned case of *Sideras*, it was held that the relationship between the religious minister and the church is one of employee and employer, irrespective of the fact that the main purpose of the working relationship is a spiritual one. It was accordingly held that the purpose of the function carried out by a religious minister was not profit-making, and accordingly, a religious minister could not be considered a self-employed person. In accordance with the decision, religious ministers are properly considered employees, and thus, the general provisions of employment law are applicable with respect to their status as employees. This applies to ministers of all denominations, and accordingly, the status of religious ministers when working for their respective denominations will be the normal legal status of any other private law employee.

338. In view of the decision of the Supreme Court in the case of *Sideras*, religious ministers are properly considered employees, and thus, the general provisions of employment law are applicable with respect to their status as employees. However, as already observed, in view of the peculiar and unique characteristics that the status of a religious minister entails, certain exceptions from the general provisions of employment law might be recognized in the appropriate cases; the extent to which the principle of organizational religious freedom may circumvent the application of the general provisions of employment law has not yet been settled and has to be examined on a case by case basis and in light of all relevant considerations.[365]

---

363. *Davies v. Presbyterian Church of Wales* [1986] 1 WLR 323 (HL).
364. *Sideras v. The Minister of Labour and Social Securities* [1989] 3 CLR (in Greek).
365. *See also* A. Emilianides & C. Ioannou, 'Law and Religion at the Workplace in Cyprus', in *Law and Religion at the Workplace in the EU* 117–126 (M. Rodriguez Blanco ed., Granada: Comares, 2016).

Chapter 3. Other Church Employees and Labour Law

339. The former Charter of the Orthodox Church provided for the procedure by which laypersons were to be employed. According to Articles 52 and 75–79 of the 1980 Charter of the Orthodox Church of Cyprus, each of the metropolises could employ clergymen or laypersons to assist in the spiritual and administrative work of the Church. Employees were appointed for a probationary two-year period, after which the Bishop would decide whether they should become permanent. Any members of staff who were occupied full-time in the Church are entitled to insurance cover and medico-pharmaceutical care. However, in 2007, the Holy Synod decided that the new employees of the Metropolises would not enjoy pension or medical care, but they would become members of the Providence Fund of the Metropolises or the Archdiocese. The 2010 Charter does not contain any specific reference to the legal status of church employees; however, their status is that of a private employee. Other Churches or religious organizations also contain internal rules with respect to their employees. As already observed, there is no reason why the general provisions of employment law should not apply with respect to other church employees.

Part VII. Religious Communities and Protection of the Individual

Chapter 1. Protection of Privacy

§1. Human Rights Provisions

340. Article 15 of the Constitution of Cyprus provides that every person has the right to respect for his/her private and family life and that there shall be no interference with the exercise of this right except such as is in accordance with the Law and is necessary only in the interests of the security of the Republic or the constitutional order or the public safety or the public order or the public health or the public morals or for the protection of the rights and liberties guaranteed by this Constitution to any person.[366] Similarly, Article 8 of the ECHR provides that everyone has the right to respect for his/her private and family life and that there shall be no interference by a public authority with the exercise of this right, except such as is in accordance with the Law and is necessary in a democratic society in the interests of national security, public safety, or the economic well-being of the country for the prevention of disorder or crime, for the protection of health or morals or for the protection of the rights and freedoms of others.

341. Therefore, each individual has a right to privacy, which includes, *inter alia*, religious, philosophical, or moral beliefs, family and emotional life, friendship, or personal health, activities of a professional and business nature, as well as the right to establish and develop relationships with other human beings.[367] The right to privacy complements Article 9 of the Constitution, safeguarding the right to religious freedom, since it enhances the view that the Constitutional right to religious freedom further includes the negative aspects of such a right, namely the right not to disclose one's religion. The application of the right to privacy has, however, also led to the discomfort of religious authorities with respect to the controversial issue of whether private homosexual acts between consenting adult males should be criminalized.

366. *See* C. Tornaritis, *The State Law of the Republic of Cyprus* 128 ff. (Nicosia: Cyprus Research Centre, 1982, in Greek); A. Loizou, *Constitution of the Republic of Cyprus* 104 ff. (Nicosia: 2001, in Greek).
367. *Niemetz v. Germany*, Judgment of 16 Dec. 1992; (1993) 16 EHRR 97.

§2. Criminalization of Private Homosexual Acts

I. The *Dudgeon* Case

342. In *Dudgeon*, the applicant complained that under the law in force in Northern Ireland, he was liable to criminal prosecution on account of his homosexual conduct and that he had experienced fear, suffering and psychological distress due to the existence of such a law.[368] It should be observed that the applicant had never actually been prosecuted; however, he was questioned by the police with regard to certain homosexual activities, his house was searched, and personal papers belonging to him were seized during the search and returned to him more than a year later. The ECtHR held that the maintenance in force of the said legislation constituted a continuing interference with the applicant's right to respect for his private life under Article 8 of the ECHR; the applicant was forced to avoid engaging in homosexual acts in order to escape prosecution. It was further observed that the police investigation showed that the fear of prosecution was real.

343. The ECtHR went on to examine whether the impugned legislation was in pursuit of a legitimate aim under Article 8 of the ECHR. It was accepted that the objective pursued was the protection of morals in the sense of the prevailing conception of sexual morality in Northern Ireland. A second aim was the protection of the rights and freedoms of others, namely vulnerable members of society, such as young, immature or mentally disabled persons, from the consequences of homosexual ethos. It remained incumbent to establish whether the legislation could be justified as necessary in a democratic society. In this respect, the ECtHR considered several criteria. To begin with, the ECtHR acknowledged that space-based criteria of morals, namely, the prevailing opinion concerning morality in each particular state, should be considered a relevant factor; therefore, the impugned legislation might be considered necessary in the context of Northern Irish society, despite the fact that similar legislative measures were not considered necessary in other parts of the United Kingdom or in other Member States of the Council of Europe. The ECtHR accepted that Northern Irish society had different attitudes, with regard to sexual morality, than Great Britain; the Northern Irish society was more conservative and gave due weight to religious factors.

344. The ECtHR further considered time-based criteria of morals;[369] it was observed that compared with the time when the legislation was enacted, there was, at the time of judgment, a better understanding and an increased tolerance and acceptance with regard to homosexual behaviour. As a result, there was an increasing European tendency to decriminalize homosexual acts between consenting adults; even in Northern Ireland, it was an established fact that the authorities had refrained from enforcing the law prohibiting private homosexual acts of consenting

368. *Dudgeon v. United Kingdom*, Judgment of 22 Oct. 1981, Series A, No. 45; (1982) 4 EHRR 149.
369. *See also* R. Koering-Joulin, 'Public Morals', in *The European Convention for the Protection of Human Rights: International Protection versus National Restrictions* 84–86 (M. Delmas-Marty ed., Dordrecht: Martinus Nijhoff Publishers, 1992).

adult males without any proof of harm to moral standards, or even any public demand for stricter enforcement of the law. As a result, the ECtHR concluded that there was no pressing social need which could justify the criminalization of such acts.[370]

345. A third criterion that the ECtHR considered was the notion of proportionality. The prohibition of homosexual behaviour concerned a most intimate aspect of personal life; it is therefore accepted that any interference shall be considered to be necessary in a democratic society, only so long as there exist important reasons justifying the interference, which are proportionate to the aim pursued. In *Dudgeon*, the ECtHR held that the grave interference with the private life of a homosexual could not be justified simply because a part of the society may feel appalled or offended by such acts, despite the fact that they occur in private between consenting adults. The argument that such a decriminalization of certain homosexual acts would lead to the corruption of moral ethos of the society was also rejected since it could not justify interference to such extent with the applicant's personal life. The ECtHR held by fifteen votes to four that there had been a breach of Article 8 of the ECHR. The Cypriot Judge, the Turkish Cypriot Zekia, delivered a dissenting opinion.

346. Zekia noted that Christian and Muslim religions are all united in the condemnation of homosexual relations and sodomy; moral conceptions are thus, to a significant degree, rooted in religious beliefs. He further observed that while considering the respect due to the private life of a homosexual, respect is also due to the people holding the opposite view, especially in a country populated by a great majority of such people who vehemently oppose such 'unnatural immoral practices'. Zekia argued that in considering the necessity of respect for one's private life, the necessity of keeping a law in force for the protection of morals held in high esteem by the majority of the people should not be underestimated; Zekia further observed that:

> While on the one hand I may be thought biased for being a Cypriot Judge, on the other hand I may be considered to be in a better position in forecasting the public outcry and the turmoil which would ensue if such laws are repealed or amended in favour of homosexuals either in Cyprus or in Northern Ireland. Both countries are religious minded and adhere to moral standards which are centuries' old.

II. The *Costa* Case

347. The Supreme Court of Cyprus considered the constitutionality of the criminalization of private homosexual acts between consenting adults in the case of *Costa*.[371] The Court observed that in ascertaining the nature and scope of morals and

370. *Dudgeon v. United Kingdom*, Judgment of 22 Oct. 1981, Series A, No. 45; (1982) 4 EHRR 149.
371. *Costa v. The Republic* [1982] 2 CLR 120.

the degree of the necessity commensurate to their protection, the case law of the ECtHR and the European Commission of Human Rights had already held that the conception of morals changes from time to time and from place to place and that there was no uniform European conception of morals. It was therefore held that the Authorities of each country were in a better position than an international Judge to give an opinion as to the prevailing standards of morals in their Country.

348. Consequently, the Supreme Court opted to adopt the dissenting opinion of Judge Zekia and not to follow the majority view in the *Dudgeon* case because:

> It is convinced that it is entitled to apply the Convention and interpret the corresponding provisions of the Constitution in the light of its assessment of the present social and moral standards in this Country; that, therefore, in the light of the aforesaid principles and viewing the Cypriot realities this Court is not prepared to come to the conclusion that section 171(b) of our Criminal Code, as it stands, violates either the Convention or the Constitution, and that it is unnecessary for the protection of morals in our country; accordingly the appeal against conviction should fail.[372]

III. The *Modinos* Case

349. The principles of *Dudgeon* were confirmed in the subsequent judgments of *Norris*[373] and *Modinos*.[374] In *Modinos*, a recourse against Cyprus, the ECtHR held that an interference had occurred, regardless of the fact that the Attorney-General had followed a consistent policy of considering the law with regard to private homosexual conduct between consenting adults as dead letter; the ECtHR observed that such policy did not preclude the possibility that the law might be enforced in the future, especially in view of the opinion of the Supreme Court expressed in the case of *Costa*. In essence, the ECtHR established that the criminalization of private homosexual adults between consenting adults cannot be considered necessary in a democratic society within the meaning of Article 8 and thus, constitutes a violation of Article 8 of the ECHR.[375] Until 1998, various draft laws had been proposed before the House of Representatives with a view to lifting the criminalization, but each time, the legislation was blocked following opposition by the Orthodox Church; eventually, section 171 of the Criminal Code, Cap. 154, was amended in 1998 so that homosexual acts between consenting adults no longer constituted a criminal offence.[376] It should be noted, however, that whereas criminalization of homosexual acts with minors is necessary in order to safeguard minors who are

372. *Ibid.*

373. *Norris v. Ireland*, Judgment of 26 Oct. 1988, Series A, No. 142; (1991) 13 EHRR 186.

374. *Modinos v. Cyprus*, Judgment of 22 Apr. 1993, Series A, No. 259; (1994) 16 EHRR 485.

375. *See also* P. Van Dijk, 'The Treatment of Homosexuals under the European Convention on Human Rights', in *Homosexuality: A European Community Issue* 179 (K. Waaldijk & A. Clapham eds, Dordrecht: Martinus Nijhoff Publishers, 1993).

376. *See* further A. Emilianides, 'Homosexuality and Human Rights in the Cypriot Legal Order', in *Sexualities: Views, Studies and Experiences in the Cypriot and Greek Space* 130–151 (C. Phellas

more vulnerable due to their youth,[377] this does not imply that difference in treatment in the age of criminalization of sexual acts between heterosexuals and homosexuals is acceptable.[378] Cypriot law might thus remain incompatible with the ECHR in this respect.

§3. The Processing of Personal Data Law

350. The General Data Protection Regulation (GDPR) prohibits the processing of sensitive personal data revealing racial or ethnic origin, religious or political beliefs, trade union membership, as well as personal data concerning health, sex life, sexual orientation, genetic and biometric data.[379] Lawful processing may be permitted only in specific situations, namely when the data subject has given explicit consent or had previously made the data public or when the processing is necessary for a specific set of legitimate objectives explicitly provided in Article 9 of GDPR. The Cypriot Commissioner of Personal Data Protection issued an Opinion on 15 November 2022, pursuant to which the Ministry of Interior could share data from the electoral registry of state elections to the Orthodox Church of Cyprus, subject to appropriate safeguards, in order to enable the Church to carry out elections for a new Archbishop. The Commissioner observed that Article 110 of the Constitution authorized the Church to administer its internal affairs pursuant to its Charter in force, and that section 23 of the Charter of 2010 enabled the Church to cooperate with State officials for preparing the electoral registry. Hence, there was a sufficient legal basis for the processing of the personal data in question in accordance with the GDPR.[380] The CJEU has further held that a religious community, such as the Jehovah's Witnesses, should be considered a controller, jointly with its members who engage in preaching, for the processing of personal data carried out by the latter in the context of door-to-door preaching. Accordingly, the processing of personal data carried out in connection with door-to-door preaching must comply with the GDPR.[381] In compliance with the GDPR, large religious organizations, such as the Orthodox Church of Cyprus, have appointed Data Protection Officers in order to safeguard compliance with the new rules about data protection.

et al. eds, Athens: Polyxromos Planitis, 2014), (in Greek); A. Emilianides, 'The De-criminalisation of Homosexuality', in *History of the Republic of Cyprus* 108–111 (P. Papapolyviou ed., Nicosia: Phileleftheros, 2011, v. IV).

377. *Dudgeon v. United Kingdom*, Judgment of 22 Oct. 1981, para. 62.
378. *Sutherland v. United Kingdom*, Judgment of 27 Mar. 2001.
379. GDPR (EU) 2016/679 of the European Parliament and of the Council.
380. 'Announcement of the Commissioner of Personal Data Protection regarding the upcoming Elections for an Archbishop', 16 Nov. 2022, available in https://www.dataprotection.gov.cy/dataprotection/dataprotection.nsf/All/9FD211076958BE9AC22588FC0030407B?OpenDocument.
381. C-25/17, *Tietosuojavaltuutettu v. Jehovan todistajat* EU:C:2018:551.

Chapter 2. Freedom to Marry

351. Article 12 of the ECHR provides that men and women of marriageable age have the right to marry and to found a family according to the national laws governing the exercise of this right. Freedom to marry is further safeguarded by Article 22 §1 of the Constitution, which provides that any person reaching nubile age is free to marry and found a family according to the law relating to marriage applicable to this person under the provisions of the Constitution.[382] Marriage is, according to Cypriot Law, a contract formally and willingly entered into, conferring on the parties the status of husband and wife; it is, thus, a contractual agreement between a man and a woman to live together and to love one another as husband and wife to the exclusion of all others, by recognizing mutual and reciprocal obligations involving sharing a common home and a common domestic life.

352. However, marriage is a unique and peculiar contract. Special formalities need to be observed for a marriage to be concluded, and such contract cannot be discharged by agreement but only by a formal legal act pronounced by a court of competent jurisdiction. Hence, marriage is also an institution creating a specific status, namely the condition of belonging to a particular class of persons to whom the law assigns certain peculiar legal capacities or incapacities. The mutual rights and duties of the parties are largely fixed by law and not by agreement; such a law is obligatory and cannot be derogated from with the consent of the parties. This is due to the fact that the State has a special interest in the institution of marriage.[383]

353. The law relating to marriage applicable to such person under the provisions of the Constitution is further clarified in Article 22 §2 of the Constitution, which provides that:

> The provisions of paragraph 1 of this Article shall, in the following cases, be applied as follows: –
> (a) if the law relating to marriage applicable to the parties as provided under Article 111 is not the same, the parties may elect to have their marriage governed by the law applicable to either of them under such Article; (b) if the provisions of Article 111 are not applicable to any of the parties to the marriage and neither of such parties is a member of the Turkish Community, the marriage shall be governed by a law of the Republic which the House of Representatives shall make and which shall not contain any restrictions other than those relating to age, health, proximity of relationship and prohibition of polygamy; (c) if the provisions of Article 111 are applicable only to one of the parties to the marriage and the other party is not a member of the Turkish Community, the marriage shall be governed by the law of the Republic as in subparagraph (b) of this paragraph provided: Provided that the parties may elect

382. C. Tornaritis, 'The Right to Marry and Found a Family under the Law of Cyprus', *Cyprus Law Review* 4, 665–673 (1983).

383. *See* A. Emilianides, *The Cypriot Law of Marriage and Divorce* (Thessaloniki: Sakkoulas, 2006, in Greek); A. Emilianides, *Family and Succession Law in Cyprus* (The Hague: Kluwer 2nd ed. 2019).

to have their marriage governed by the law applicable, under Article 111, to one of such parties in so far as such law allows such marriage.

354. Article 22 §2 is supplementary and should be read in conjunction with Article 111 of the Constitution.[384] In view of the above, the right to marry may be exercised in the following manner:[385]

(i) If both parties belong to the Greek Orthodox Church of Cyprus, or if they both belong to the same Religious Group, then their marriage is governed by the provisions of Article 111 of the Constitution.
(ii) If one of the parties belongs to the Greek Orthodox Church and the other party does not belong to the Greek Orthodox Church and is not a member of the Turkish Community, then their marriage is governed by the Marriage Law 104(I)/2003. However, the parties may elect to have their marriage governed by the law applicable under Article 111 of the Constitution.
(iii) If one of the parties belongs to a Religious Group and the other party does not belong to the respective Religious Group and is not a member of the Turkish Community, then their marriage is governed by the Marriage Law 104(I)/2003. However, the parties may elect to have their marriage governed by the law applicable under Article 111 of the Constitution.
(iv) If none of the parties belongs to the Orthodox Church or a Religious Group and neither of such parties is a member of the Turkish Community, then their marriage is governed by the Marriage Law 104(I)/2003.

355. With respect to members of the Turkish Community, the Interim Committee on Turkish Affairs observed in its Report in 1949 that while the matrimonial relations of the Turkish Muslims ought to retain their religious character and derive their origin and basic principles from the Quran, they should also be modified on the basis of Kemalic reforms and the principles of Articles 82–145 of the Civil Code of Turkey of 1926.[386] On the basis of the observations of the Interim Committee, two laws were enacted: the Turkish Family (Marriage and Divorce) Law 4/1951, Cap. 339 in the 1959 Edition of the Laws of Cyprus and the Turkish Family Courts Law 3/1951, which was eventually replaced by the Turkish Family Courts Law 42/1954, Cap. 338 in the 1959 Edition. According to the aforementioned laws, the

384. A. Emilianides, *The Cypriot Law of Marriage and Divorce* 188 ff. (Thessaloniki: Sakkoulas, 2006, in Greek); G. Serghides, *Internal and External Conflict of Laws in Regard to Family Relations in Cyprus* 160 ff. (Nicosia: 1988).
385. *See* A. Emilianides, *The Cypriot Law of Marriage and Divorce* 188 ff. (Thessaloniki: Sakkoulas, 2006, in Greek). *See* further C. Tornaritis, 'On the Applicable Law in Case of Mixed Marriages', *Revue Hellenique de Droit International* 19, 289–293 (1966); C. Tornaritis, *The Marriage Law in General and Especially the Marriage of Mixed Marriages as Applies in Cyprus* (Nicosia: 1986, in Greek); A. Emilianides, 'Interracial and Interreligious Laws in Cyprus', *Revue Hellenique de Droit International* 11, 286–306 (1958).
386. Cyprus Government Printing Office, *Interim Report of the Committee on Turkish Affairs: An Investigation into Matters Concerning and Affecting the Turkish Community in Cyprus* (Nicosia: 1949).

Turkish Family Law applied to all marriages of parties, at least one of whom was a Turkish resident in Cyprus professing the Muslim faith.[387]

356. Article 22 does not safeguard the right to same-sex marriages or partnerships. The ECtHR has also held that Article 12 of the ECHR safeguarding the right to marry does not necessitate the Member States to recognize the right to marry or civil partnership to same-sex couples.[388] However, it has been held that once a State decides to recognize civil unions or registered partnerships as an alternative form to marriage, it would be a violation of the principle of non-discrimination if such was recognized for heterosexual partners only.[389] The right to celebrate a civil union instead of a marriage was eventually recognized by the enactment of the Civil Union Law 184(I)/2015. A civil union has the same legal validity and consequences as if a marriage, either religious or civil, had been celebrated,[390] with the exception of the right to adoption, which is precluded as it was deemed to be highly controversial. It should be noted, however, that the ECtHR has already recognized the right of adoption to single homosexual parents,[391] and hence its exception from the ambit of Law 184(I)/2015 might well be inconsistent with the principle of non-discrimination.

387. *See* J. Anderson, 'The Family Law of Turkish Cypriots', *Die Weit des Islams* 5, 161–187 (1958).
388. *Schalk and Kopf v. Austria*, Judgment of 22 Jan. 2008, *Gas and Dubois v. France*, Judgment of 15 Mar. 2012.
389. *Valianatos v. Greece*, Judgment of 7 Nov. 2013, *Oliari v. Italy*, Judgment of 9 Jul. 2016.
390. *See* S. Liasides, *Civil Union (Law 184(I)/2015). Legal Aspects* (Nicosia, 2016, in Greek); A. Tryfonidou, 'The Legal Position of LGBT Persons and Same-Sex Couples in Cyprus', *The Cyprus Review* 29, 183–213 (2017).
391. *E.B. v. France*, Judgment of 22 Jan. 2008.

Chapter 3. Freedom of Expression

§1. Human Rights Provisions

357. Article 19 of the Constitution provides that every person has the right to freedom of speech and expression in any form. This right includes the freedom to hold opinions and receive and impart information and ideas without interference by any public authority and regardless of frontiers. The exercise of such rights may be subject to such formalities, conditions, restrictions or penalties as are prescribed by law and are necessary only in the interests of the security of the Republic or the Constitutional order or the public safety or the public order or the public health or the public morals or for the protection of the reputation or rights of others or for preventing the disclosure of information received in confidence or for maintaining the authority and impartiality of the judiciary. It is further stipulated that seizure of newspapers or other printed matter is not allowed without the written permission of the Attorney-General of the Republic, which must be confirmed by the decision of a competent court within a period not exceeding seventy-two hours, failing which the seizure shall be reversed. In addition, the Republic may, in accordance with Article 19, require the licensing of auditory and visual broadcasting or cinema enterprises.[392]

358. Article 10 of the ECHR, which corresponds to Article 19 of the Constitution, provides that everyone has the right to freedom of expression; such right shall include freedom to hold opinions and to receive and impart information and ideas without interference by public authority and regardless of frontiers. It is provided, however, that Member States may require the licensing of broadcasting, television or cinema enterprises. The exercise of the freedoms safeguarded by Article 10 of the ECHR may be subject to such formalities, conditions, restrictions, or penalties as are prescribed by law and are necessary in a democratic society in the interests of national security, territorial integrity or public safety, for the prevention of disorder or crime, for the protection of health or morals, for the protection of the reputation or rights of others, for preventing the disclosure of information received in confidence, or for maintaining the authority and impartiality of the judiciary.[393]

359. The right to freedom of expression constitutes one of the essential foundations of a democratic, tolerant and pluralistic society and includes all forms of expression, such as paintings, books, films, statements in radio interviews and information pamphlets. It is not merely applicable to information or ideas regarded as inoffensive or indifferent, but also to 'those that offend, shock or disturb the State or any sector of the population'.[394] Thus, freedom of expression safeguards the manifestation of all kinds of religious beliefs, especially minority religious beliefs. In

392. C. Tornaritis, *The State Law of the Republic of Cyprus* 148 ff. (Nicosia: Cyprus Research Centre, 1982, in Greek); A. Loizou, *Constitution of the Republic of Cyprus* 114 ff. (Nicosia: 2001, in Greek).
393. *See* E. Barendt, *Freedom of Expression* (Oxford: Oxford University Press, 2005).
394. *Handyside v. United Kingdom*, Judgment of 7 Dec. 1976; (1979–1980) 1 EHRR 737.

order to declare whether a legislative measure was 'necessary' for the purposes of Article 19 of the Constitution, there should be a serious, though not inevitable, risk that one or more of the causes defined therein will be imperilled. It should be assessed whether the interference corresponded to a pressing social need, whether it was proportionate to the legitimate aim pursued and whether the reasons given by the authorities to justify it are relevant and sufficient. The nature and severity of the penalty or fine imposed are also factors to be taken into account when assessing the proportionality of the interference. The sanction should not be such as to have a chilling effect on the exercise of freedom of expression.

360. Hate speech is generally considered a legitimate restriction on the freedom of speech since the protection or reputation of others is a ground for restricting freedom of speech. There are several legislative provisions which restrict and/or punish hate speech. If any offence has been committed against a group of persons due to bias against their race, colour, national or ethnic descent, religious or other beliefs, sexual orientation or gender identity, a Court may consider such a bias as an aggravating factor during the sentencing and imposition of any penalty. The Supreme Court has generally defined hate speech within the context also of the Council Framework Decision 2008/913/JHA[395] as any speech publicly inciting to violence or hatred directed against a group of persons or a member of such a group defined by reference to race, colour, religion, descent or national or ethnic origin.[396] The Court has stressed that hate speech offences are extremely serious, and sentencing should be proportionate to the seriousness of the offences. It should be noted, however, that the European Commission against Racism and Intolerance has indicated in its latest Report of 7 March 2023 a number of areas where it suggests further action on behalf of Cypriot authorities to tackle hate speech.[397]

361. Section 3 of Law 134(I)/2011 on combating certain forms and expressions of racism and xenophobia by means of criminal law, which has incorporated the Framework Decision 2008/913/JHA in the Cypriot legal order, provides that any person publicly inciting, or publicly disseminating, in a way that incites violence or hatred directed against a group of persons or a member of such a group defined by reference to race, colour, religion, descent or national or ethnic origin, is subject to a penalty of five years imprisonment and/or a fine of up to EUR 10,000. The same penalty is also provided for any person publicly condoning, denying or grossly trivializing crimes of genocide, crimes against humanity and war crimes as defined in Articles 6, 7 and 8 of the Statute of the International Criminal Court or in Article 6 of the Charter of the International Military Tribunal appended to the London Agreement of 8 August 1945, to the extent that such crimes have been either recognized by an international court with a final judgment or by a unanimous decision of the House of Representatives. The speech penalized should be directed against a group

395. Of 28 Nov. 2008 on combating certain forms and expressions of racism and xenophobia by means of criminal law, as enacted in Cyprus by Law 134(I)/2011.
396. *Police v. AA and another*, Crim. App. 4/21, Judgment of 1 Jul. 2021 (in Greek).
397. Available in https://www.coe.int/en/web/european-commission-against-racism-and-intolerance/cyprus.

of persons or a member of such a group defined by reference to race, colour, religion, descent or national or ethnic origin when the conduct is carried out in a manner likely to incite violence or hatred against such a group or a member of such a group. Reference to religion is intended to cover, at least, conduct which is a pretext for directing acts against a group of persons or a member of such a group defined by reference to race, colour, descent, or national or ethnic origin.

§2. Blasphemy

362. A publication may sometimes be considered blasphemous or offensive to a particular religion; section 142 of Criminal Code, Cap. 154 criminalizes the circulation of defamatory publications, while section 141 criminalizes words or sounds which deliberately affront the religious sentiments of others. Section 142 of Cap. 154 provides that any person who publishes a book or pamphlet or any article or letter in a newspaper or periodical which any class of persons considers as a public insult to their religion, with intent to vilify such religion or to shock or to insult believers to such religion, is guilty of a misdemeanour. It is evident that the mere denial of the truth of the Christian religion does not constitute the offence of blasphemy;[398] any person can deny the Christian doctrines and inform the public of their views. It is also accepted that serious treatises which attempt to deny the truths and miracles of the New Testament do not constitute the offence of blasphemy, even if they contain opinions hostile to the Christian religion.[399] A different conclusion would invalidate the right to freedom of thought, conscience and religion, since it would mean that the only accepted religion in Cyprus is the Christian religion. It is thus accepted that it is not the *matter* which constitutes the offence of blasphemy but the 'manner'. Attacks on Christianity must be indecent and offensive in order to constitute an offence. A *decency test* should thus be applied; the court should examine whether the publications have crossed the line of decency due to a wilful intention to insult and mislead others. If the attack on Christianity has an element of vilification, ridicule or irreverence that would be likely to infuriate others,[400] then the publisher of the attack will be guilty of blasphemous libel. If, however, such publications neither offend nor vilify, then the 'attack' on the Christian religion does not constitute an offence.

363. In Cyprus, there have been no Supreme Court decisions holding that a publication is blasphemous or that a publication ought to be seized because of its blasphemous content; thus, the extent to which section 142 of Cap. 154 is consistent with Article 19 of the Constitution, or to which a publication might be seized because its content is considered to be blasphemous, has not been thoroughly considered by the Cypriot courts. It would seem that Cypriot prosecuting authorities have been unwilling to prosecute cases of blasphemy. The case law of the ECtHR

398. *R v. Ramsay and Foote* (1883) 15 Cox CC 231, at 236.
399. *R v. Lemon* (1978) 67 Cr App R 70, at 82.
400. *Bowman v. Secular Society Ltd* [1917] AC 406, HL, at 446.

would, however, suggest that the offence of blasphemy or the seizure of publications due to the fact that their content is deemed to be blasphemous does not necessarily violate Article 10 of the ECHR. The prevailing opinion, however, seems to be that the offence of blasphemy is only marginally acceptable in a modern European democratic society, and that therefore even if the prevailing moral opinion is supported by an overwhelming majority of the population and is marked by widespread indignation and disgust, this should not in principle mean that such majority can impose its views on a minority through the use of criminal law.[401]

364. In the British case *Gay News,* a homosexual magazine published a poem entitled *The Love that Dares to Speak Its Name* accompanied by an illustrative drawing.[402] The poem attempted to describe in detail acts of sodomy and fellatio with the body of Christ immediately after His death and to ascribe to Him homosexual practices with the Apostles and other men during His lifetime. The jury found the poem to be 'abusive' and to contain *vilification.* The majority of the House of Lords held that it was irrelevant whether the publisher intended to publish a blasphemy since that would make him a judge in his own cause. It was further held that it would be illogical to acquit the publisher due to the fact that he is *incapable, for some reason particular to himself,* of understanding the true nature of his publication in the same manner as the jury. The House of Lords thus held that it was sufficient for the prosecution to prove that the publisher had intentionally published the matter, which the jury held to be blasphemous.

365. The European Commission of Human Rights considered that the application against the United Kingdom was inadmissible;[403] it held that many laws seem inevitably vague and unclear, because of the use of terms which must be interpreted and applied in a variety of different and changing circumstances. The British courts had not gone beyond the limits of a reasonable interpretation of the existing law of blasphemy. In addition, the Commission noticed that the law was accessible to the applicants and that its interpretation was foreseeable for them so long as they had sought the appropriate legal advice. As a result, there had been no violation of Article 9, or any other Article of the ECHR.

366. The ECtHR was eventually called upon to examine the common law offence of blasphemy in *Wingrove.*[404] Wingrove, who is a British film director, was the director of a video entitled Visions of Ecstasy. The video, which contained no dialogue and ran for approximately eighteen minutes, portrayed a woman dressed

401. *See* A. Emilianides, 'Can God Be Offended? The Common Law Offence of Blasphemy and the European Convention on Human Rights' in *Contemporary Issues and Trends at the Beginning of the 21st Century* 232–239 (M. Moravcikova ed., Bratislava: Institute for State-Church Relations, 2008).

402. *Whitehouse v. Lemon* [1979] AC 617, HL.

403. App. 8710/79, *Gay News Ltd and Lemon v. United Kingdom*, Decision of 7 May 1982; (1983) 5 EHRR 123.

404. *Wingrove v. United Kingdom*, Judgment of 25 Nov. 1996 (1997) 24 EHRR 1. A similar judgment was delivered in *Otto Preminger Institut v. Austria*, Judgment of 20 Sep. 1994; (1995) 19 EHRR 34. *See also* App. 38450/12, *E.S. v. Austria*, Judgment of 25 Oct. 2018.

as a nun, who was described in the credits as Saint Teresa of Avila; this woman was having an erotic fantasy involving the crucified figure of Christ as well as a second female which was said to represent St Teresa's psyche. The British Board on Film Classification refused to grant the director a certificate for distribution on the grounds that the video was contrary to the law of blasphemy. The applicant alleged a violation of his rights to freedom of expression as guaranteed by Article 10 of the ECHR.

367. The ECtHR accepted that the British Board had interfered with the applicant's rights to freedom of expression. It observed, however, that such interference would not violate the ECHR so far as it was prescribed by law; it pursued a legitimate aim, and it was necessary in a democratic society. The ECtHR held that the offence was prescribed by law; although it noticed that the offence of blasphemy cannot, by its very nature, be defined in a precise manner, it accepted that the elements of the offence were adequately formulated by the House of Lords in the *Gay News* case. It also held that the interference pursued a legitimate aim, namely the aim to protect the religious feelings of Christians who might be outraged due to the treatment of Christ and St Teresa; the ECtHR held that such an aim corresponds to the protection of the rights of others within the meaning of Article 10(2) of the ECHR. It further held that the interference fell within the state's margin of appreciation and could, therefore, be considered necessary in a democratic society; it observed that there was not yet sufficient common ground in the legal and social orders of the Member States of the Council of Europe to conclude that the law of blasphemy is unnecessary in a democratic society. It also observed that the English Law of blasphemy does not prohibit the expression of all views hostile to the Christian religion, but only of those views which are expressed in an offensive manner, which is of significant extent. Having viewed the film for itself, the ECtHR was satisfied that the British authorities did not act arbitrarily. It thus held that there was no violation of Article 10 of the ECHR.

368. The Strasbourg organs have been unwilling to accept that the offence of blasphemy violates the ECHR. It has been suggested that these judgments arise out of the Court's unwillingness to impose a uniform conception of morality; the ECtHR gives priority to the uniform application of the standard of freedom of expression concerning political and public-concern speech, while at the same time, it allows a wide margin of appreciation with respect to cultural or artistic speech.[405] It could also be argued that the ECtHR is unlikely to decide on delicate issues concerning morality and religion without taking into account that many of the Member States of the Council of Europe still have blasphemy laws and accord privileged legal status to their established religions. It is suggested, however, that while law may be open-textured, novels and poems may not. Art should not be subject to only one interpretation. It is suggested that works of art are open to each specific reader's interpretation. A work of art is in search of its 'model reader' and, as such, is

405. *See* P. Mahoney, 'Universality Versus Subsidiarity in the Strasbourg Case Law on Free Speech: Explaining Some Recent Judgments', *European Human Rights Law Review,* 364 (1997).

distinct from its author. It is illogical that art should be considered to be blasphemous simply because a category of readers understands it as such. It is even more astonishing that while a person might express his/her own personal views without being prosecuted, an artist would be prosecuted for expressing the exact same views, which may not belong to him/her, simply because he/she expressed them in an artistic manner, which is considered to be contrary to the prevailing opinion about 'decency'.

369. Majorities have always used criminal law in order to suppress the opinions of minorities. However, while democracy may be based on majority rule, it should also be based on the protection of individual human rights, which should not be restricted simply because their exercise is unpleasant to the majority.[406] The right of the single individual to express oneself should be considered to be equally important to the right of a Religious Group to believe in whatever religion they want.[407] Religious freedom should not be taken to imply freedom without religion, but neither can it be interpreted as freedom only for the religious. While most would agree that any attempt to ridicule the religious feelings of many members of society should be avoided, fewer would also agree that any such attempt should be considered an offence or should be the object of legal enforcement. Even if the prevailing moral opinion is supported by an overwhelming majority of the population and is marked by widespread indignation and disgust, this should not mean that such majority can impose its views on a minority through the use of criminal law.

370. A recent incident in Cyprus re-ignited the debate about the limits of artistic freedom.[408] Gavriel, a director and teacher of art at a secondary education public school, who is also an artist in his leisure time, posted on social media in September 2020 pictures of some of his latest paintings. Some of them had a clear anti-Church theme, with one picture, in particular, showing a naked Jesus riding a motorcycle and wearing a scarf with the symbols of a well-known Cypriot soccer team and yet another picturing a dog urinating on the current Archbishop of the Orthodox Church of Cyprus. Other paintings were expressly political or were described as sexist and misogynistic due to the manner in which the female body was depicted. Following a public uproar and complaints by organized groups who called for Gavriel's dismissal, including a letter to this effect by the Archbishop himself to the Minister of Education, Sports and Youth, the Ministry (i.e., Gavriel's employer) launched a probe to examine whether the teacher-artist was liable for disciplinary offences. The alleged offence was the violation of section 48(1)(d) and (e) of the Public Education Law 10/1969, which provides that each educational officer must not act in a manner which might defame the educational service in general, or his office in particular, or which tends to hinder the trust of the public towards the educational service. The Ministry noted that the freedom of artistic creation could

406. *See* H.L.A. Hart, *Law, Liberty and Morality* (Oxford: Oxford University Press, 1963).

407. *See* A. Bradney, *Religions, Rights and Laws* 97 (Leicester: Leicester University Press, 1993); P. Kearns, 'Obscene and Blasphemous Libel: Misunderstanding Art', *Criminal Law Review,* 652 (2000).

408. *See* in detail A. Emilianides, 'Disciplinary Action and Freedom of Artistic Expression', *The Cambridge Journal of Law, Politics and Art* 1, 318–320 (2022).

not justify the insult to public feeling and the messages of the paintings that cultivate a sense of contempt or possibly a climate of intolerance within the student community when such expression derives from an official in the field of public education.

371. Many defended Gavriel's art, or at least his right to be provocative, and accused the Ministry of arbitrarily violating freedom of artistic expression. The debate included announcements by political parties and statements by individual politicians, as well as heated discussions and passionate statements by organized groups or the public at large, either supporting or criticizing the disciplinary action. The Cypriot Ombudsman, in a statement issued immediately after the probe was announced by the Ministry, held that Gavriel had crossed the acceptable boundaries for the exercise of his freedom of expression. The Ombudsman noted that the manner in which the artistic work in question was expressed had offended the rights and religious sentiments of third persons, which is a legitimate objective for restricting freedom of artistic expression in a democratic society. The Cypriot authorities neither prosecuted Gavriel for his paintings nor prohibited their dissemination; Gavriel has held exhibitions and shown his paintings to the public without any restrictions or problems. If disciplinary offences were found, this would be expected, considering prior practice of authorities in similar cases, to lead to minor sanctions at worse. There is little doubt that the paintings have been offensive to the religious feelings of Christians in a country where the majority of the population is religious. The paintings have also specifically targeted the Archbishop at a personal level.

372. An implied argument of the disciplinary probe, however, was that the right of artistic expression of Gavriel, the teacher, should not be equivalent to the said right of Gavriel, the artist. This distinction would be more convincing if Gavriel had expressed his anti-religion, political, or other sentiments during the exercise of his professional duties as a teacher. There was, however, no indication that Gavriel had, in this case, presented himself at any time as anything other than an artist, and there was no report of him acting in a given way during classes. Accordingly, the disciplinary offences, if any, referred to actions of Gavriel outside his working hours, or work as a teacher, and in particular to his artistic expression as an individual artist. It has therefore been suggested that the mere fact that artistic freedom expressed outside the school premises is offensive towards a – potentially large – group of the public should not lead to disciplinary proceedings because of the artist's parallel status as a member of the public educational service. Neither the public's trust towards the educational service is hindered, nor is the educational service defamed, simply because a teacher might be considered by part of the public as a bad or provocative artist. Eventually, the Council of Ministers decided to terminate the disciplinary action against Gavriel, taking into account the societal division this had caused.

Chapter 4. Due Process Norms and Religious Organizations

§1. Access to Courts

373. Article 30 of the Constitution provides that no person shall be denied access to the court assigned to him/her by or under this Constitution. The establishment of judicial committees or exceptional courts under any name whatsoever is prohibited. In the determination of his/her civil rights and obligations or of any criminal charge against him/her, every person is entitled to a fair and public hearing within a reasonable time by an independent, impartial and competent court established by law. Judgment shall be reasoned and pronounced in public sessions, but the press and the public may be excluded from all or any part of the trial upon a decision by the court where it is in the interest of the security of the Republic or the constitutional order or the public order or the public safety or the public morals or where the interests of juveniles or the protection of the private life of the parties so require or, in special circumstances where, in the opinion of the court, publicity would prejudice the interests of justice.

374. Every person has the right: (a) to be informed of the reasons why he/she is required to appear before the court; (b) to present his/her case before the court and to have sufficient time necessary for its preparation; (c) to adduce or cause to be adduced his/her evidence and to examine witnesses according to law; (d) to have a lawyer of his/her own choice and to have free legal assistance where the interests of justice so require and as provided by law; (e) to have free assistance of an interpreter if he/she cannot understand or speak the language used in court.[409]

375. Churches and other religious entities have the right to access to court, and indeed, most religious entities exercise such right when they consider that their rights have been violated; religious entities may have recourse to civil or administrative courts with respect not only to their constitutional rights, but also to rights arising from contract law, tort law, or immovable property law, or in order to seek the annulment of a decision of the administration. In addition, individual members of religious entities may have access to the courts in an appropriate case, not only as individuals but also as members of the religious entity. Consequently, a person may argue before a court that an act has offended his/her religious sentiments or beliefs or that his/her constitutional rights, such as religious freedom or non-discrimination on the grounds of religion, have been violated so that he/she may seek the issue of an injunction prohibiting the violation of his/her constitutional rights, or compensation and damages with respect to the violation.

376. Article 6 §1 of the ECHR further provides that in the determination of his/her civil rights and obligations or of any criminal charge against him/her, everyone is entitled to a fair and public hearing within a reasonable time by an independent and impartial tribunal established by law. Judgment shall be pronounced publicly,

409. A. Loizou, *Constitution of the Republic of Cyprus* 181 ff. (Nicosia: 2001, in Greek).

but the press and public may be excluded from all or part of the trial in the interests of morals, public order or national security in a democratic society, where the interests of juveniles or the protection of the private life of the parties so require, or to the extent strictly necessary in the opinion of the court in special circumstances where publicity would prejudice the interests of justice. It has been accepted that churches and other religious communities may apply before the ECtHR, alleging that there has been a violation of their rights under the ECHR; similarly, any individual member of a religious community may apply before the ECtHR and argue that his/her ECHR rights as a member of such religious community have been violated.

§2. Proof of Ecclesiastical Law

377. State courts have to apply ecclesiastical law in certain circumstances; when a family court is called upon to annul a marriage which was celebrated according to the rites of the Orthodox Church, it must apply the ecclesiastical law of the Orthodox Church. The question of whether ecclesiastical law should be considered a matter of law or fact during the procedure before the State courts was first considered before Independence in the case of *Stratoura*.[410] In *Stratoura,* the District Court had regarded the question as to what was considered necessary to make the marriage lawful according to the Canons of the Orthodox Church as a question of law on which the Court could take judicial cognizance.

378. The Supreme Court reversed the decision of the District Court and held that:

> The Greek Church of Cyprus although Autokephalous seems to rely largely on laws or canons in force in other branches of the Orthodox Greek Church of the origin of which we have small information, and which may perhaps be liable to changes of which the Court could have no official information. The Court will not take judicial cognizance of such laws. The law must be proved in the Court as a fact. Therefore questions of the legality of a marriage between Orthodox Greek Christians must in our opinion be treated as questions of fact to be decided upon the evidence in each particular case, and we are further of opinion that the Court did wrong in consulting outside the Court an expert in the law however eminent. The evidence of such an expert would be highly valuable in deciding the question of fact as to whether or not the marriage was legal, but it must be given in Court and the witness must be submitted to cross-examination like any other witness.

379. After Independence, the Courts have also adhered to the view that ecclesiastical law should be treated as a matter of fact. As a result, the Courts ought to call Canon lawyers as expert witnesses in order to provide evidence to the Court

410. *Stratoura v. Yakoumi* [1905] 6 CLR 91.

and enable it to decide how the internal Canon Law of the Church ought to be interpreted.[411] This was due to the fact that a judge was not expected to have adequate knowledge with respect to the law of the Orthodox Church or of the three Religious Groups. Thus, ecclesiastical law has to be proved as a matter of fact before the State courts[412] unless it has been incorporated in state laws; such was the case of the grounds of divorce, which were provided in the 1980 Charter of the Orthodox Church, which had been explicitly incorporated in Article 111 of the Constitution and therefore had to be treated by the Courts as a question of law.

411. *Michael v. Michael* [1971] 1 CLR 211; *Hjjovanni v. Hjijovanni* [1969] 1 CLR 207; *Metaxa v. Mita* [1977] 1 CLR 1.

412. *Papacharalambous v. Papacharalambous* [1998] 8 JSC 243 (in Greek).

Chapter 5. Professional Secrecy

380. People expect that what they confess to their pastor shall be kept in confidence. Christians habitually consult priests of their respective religion with respect to their spiritual anxieties and personal problems, asking God for forgiveness, specifically for criminal or other unlawful acts that they have committed.[413] Thus, Christian communities consider the role of the priest during confession as analogous to that of the lawyer, and they expect that confessional secrecy shall not be overridden by other considerations; members of the clergy expect that they will enjoy a privilege with respect to confessional secrets. However, according to the prevailing view, clergymen do not enjoy exemption in criminal or civil procedure as a result of any kind of confessional secret.[414] If a clergyman reveals a secret, then he may be liable only to Canonical offences of his respective church but not to criminal offences since it is not a criminal offence for a religious minister to reveal a secret he has obtained in the exercise of his duties.

413. *See* K. Greenawalt, *Religion and the Constitution: Free Exercise and Fairness* 246 ff. (Princeton: Princeton University Press, 2006).

414. N. Santis & T. Eliades, *The Law of Evidence: Substantial and Procedural Aspects* (Nicosia: Hippasus 2nd ed. 2016, in Greek).

Chapter 6. Medical Deontology

§1. Blood Transfusion

381. Parents who are Jehovah's Witnesses often object to their children receiving blood transfusions, no matter how life-threatening their children's condition might be. This situation was considered by the Supreme Court in the case of *Charalambous*.[415] The parents of a young girl, being Jehovah's Witnesses, refused to consent to their child receiving blood transfusion due to their religious beliefs; thus, the child's life was put at risk. The Director of the Welfare Department received the child into his care and undertook the parental rights of the child in order to allow for the necessary blood transfusion to take place without the parents' consent. The Director based his actions on sections 3 and 4 of the Children Law, Cap. 352. Section 3 of Cap. 352 provides that it shall be lawful for the Director to receive a child under the age of 16 into his/her care if it appears to him/her (a) that the child has neither parents nor guardian or has been and remains abandoned by his/her parents, or guardian, or is lost; (b) that his/her parents or guardians are, for the time being, or permanently, prevented by reason of mental or bodily disease, or infirmity or other incapacity or any other circumstances from providing for his/her proper accommodation, maintenance or upbringing and there is no available person or persons capable, fit or willing to undertake the care of the child; and (c) in either case, that the intervention of the Social Welfare Department under this section is necessary in the interests of the welfare of the child.

382. It is further provided that where the Director has received a child into his/her care, it shall be his/her duty to keep the child in his/her care so long as the welfare of the child appears to him/her to require it and the child has not attained the age of 18. However, nothing shall authorize the Director to keep a child in his/her care if any parent or guardian desires to take over the care of the child, and the Director should, in all cases where it appears to him/her to be consistent with the welfare of the child so to do, endeavour to secure that the care of the child is taken over either by a parent or guardian of his/hers or by a relative or friend of his/hers, being, where possible, a person of the same religious convictions as the child or who gives an undertaking that the child will be brought up under those religious convictions. Section 4 of Cap. 352 further provides that the Director may assume all parental rights over the child in his/her care, so long as the child's parents are dead and it has no guardian, or if the parent or guardian has abandoned or neglected the child or suffers from some permanent disability rendering the said person incapable of caring for the child, or is of such habits or mode of life as to be unfit to have the care of the child.

383. It was argued on behalf of the Director of the Social Welfare Department that the parents' refusal to allow for the necessary blood transfusion to take place meant that they were unfit to have the care of the child. The parents argued that the

415. *Charalambous v. Director of the Social Welfare Department* [1994] 1 CLR 396 (in Greek).

Director had no power to receive the child, contrary to the wishes of the parents, even on the basis of sections 3 and 4 of Cap. 352. The Court held that since there had been no express objection from the parents, the mere fact that they had not consented to the action of the Director did not signify that the exercise of his rights went beyond the scope of Cap. 352; it was held that since the parents could not consent due to their religious beliefs, it was proper for the Director to assume the parental rights over the child. It was further held that sections 3 and 4 of Cap. 352 do not violate the right to family life of the applicants, as safeguarded by Article 15 of the Constitution, since their aim is to guarantee the life and the welfare of the child, rights which are also enshrined in the Constitution.[416]

384. The aforementioned decision of the Supreme Court might be subject to criticism. To begin with, arguing that the Director may exercise his powers even without the consent of the parents does not necessarily explain why the parents should be considered to be unfit to have the care of the child; Article 18 §7 of the Constitution expressly stipulates that until a person attains the age of 16, the decision as to the religion to be professed by him/her shall be taken by the person having the lawful guardianship of that person. Thus, receiving blood transfusion is, in principle, assumed to be contrary not only to the religious beliefs of the parents but also to the religious beliefs of the child. Is the exercise of religious beliefs a ground on the basis of which the Director can unilaterally decide that the parents are unfit for the care of the child?[417]

385. The ECtHR has held that the extent of the right to private life should always be taken into account; in the *Glass* case, the mother of a severely mentally and physically disabled child had opposed the administration of morphine and diamorphine to her son, which the doctors considered necessary to relieve distress during what they considered the terminal phase of respiratory failure. The ECtHR held that the decision to impose treatment in the face of the mother's objections constituted an interference with respect to the child's private life, which could not be justified in a democratic society since the hospital could have made an early application to the courts of their determination of whether the administration of such medication had been in the best interests of the child.[418]

386. Section 18 of Law 216/90, providing for the relations between parents and children, stipulates that if the parents fail their duties to care for the child, or administer its property, or if they cannot perform their duties as parents, or if they perform such duties in an abusive manner, the Family Court may remove the parental rights from either, or both parents and provide that a guardian should exercise such parental rights. Removing parental rights is an extreme measure which may only be ordered if all other measures have proven to be inadequate in order to prevent bodily or mental harm to the child. While Law 216/90 provides that removing parental

416. *Ibid.*
417. *See* the discussion in A. Emilianides (ed.), *Welfare of the Child and Beliefs of the Parents* (Nicosia: University of Nicosia Press, 2010).
418. *Glass v. United Kingdom*, Judgment of 9 Mar. 2004; (2004) 39 EHRR 341.

rights is a measure to be exercised with caution, Cap. 352, as interpreted by the Supreme Court in *Charalambous*, provides that the powers of the Director of the Social Welfare Department are very wide.

387. It might be questioned whether, following the enactment of Law 216/90, the Director should still exercise such powers or whether removing parental rights should be for the Family Courts to decide. There is case law supporting the position that sections 3 and 4 of Cap. 352 providing for the powers of the Director have been implicitly repealed by Law 216/90 to the extent that they are inconsistent with the provisions of the said Law.[419] Cypriot Law thus provides that the Director may undertake the parental rights of the child in order to allow for the necessary blood transfusion to take place without the parents' consent. However, the case of *Charalambous* does not provide an authority that the Director may also undertake the parental rights of the child in those cases where the parents explicitly object; it is suggested that only the Family Court may issue a relevant order in the latter case.

§2. Medical Refusal of Treatment on Religious Grounds

388. Another issue that might arise concerning the medical professional is whether a doctor could, in principle, refuse treatment on religious grounds. Regulation 8 of the Regulations of Conduct of Doctors of 1991, issued under the Doctors (Council, Discipline and Pension Fund) Law 16/1967, provides that a doctor may refuse medical treatment to a patient, except in cases of emergency or humanitarian duty. Therefore, it could be argued *a contrario* that a doctor might refuse to provide medical treatment on the grounds of religion, such as refusing to provide contraception or proceeding to a blood transfusion.[420] However, such conduct might be viewed in certain circumstances as contrary to the principles of the medical profession and consequently forbidden by section 4 of Law 16/67, which prohibits any conduct which is disgraceful to, or inconsistent with, the medical profession.

§3. Premarital Regulation of the Health of Future Spouses

389. On 1 June 1983, the Church of Cyprus took an extremely important initiative for the premarital regulation of the health of future spouses, something that most Churches in other countries disapprove of. In Cyprus, several incidents of sickle-cell anaemia are reported each year. The Holy Synod decided that among the documents that the spouses-to-be are required to submit to the Church for the issuing of a licence for the solemnization of a religious wedding ceremony, there should

---

419. *Gerolemou*, Application no. 7/02, Judgment on habeas corpus application dated 6 Mar. 2002 (in Greek), *Petrou,* Application no. 158/95, Judgment on habeas corpus application dated 4 Oct. 1995 (in Greek). A different conclusion is supported by *Ioannou*, Application no. 19/95, Judgment on habeas corpus application dated 8 Mar. 1995 (in Greek).

420. *See* T. Christodoulidou, 'Religious Conscientious Objection in Cyprus', *Cyprus and European Law Review* 2, 330 (2006). *See*, in general, C. Ioannides, *Law in the Field of Health* (Nicosia: Hippasus, 2023).

be a certificate from a state-appointed doctor proving that they had been examined for sickle-cell anaemia. Even when the test shows signs of the disease, the marriage may still be celebrated; the aim of the test is exclusively to enable the prospective spouses to make informed decisions with regard to their family to be.[421]

§4. Abortion

390. Procuring abortion constitutes a criminal offence under Cypriot Law. Section 167 of the Criminal Code, Cap. 154 provides that any person who, with intent to procure the miscarriage of a woman, unlawfully administers to her, or causes her to take any poison or other noxious substance, or uses any force of any kind or any other means whatsoever, is guilty of a felony and is liable to imprisonment for fourteen years. Similarly, section 168 of Cap. 154 provides that any person who performs the above acts with intent to procure her own miscarriage is liable to imprisonment for seven years. Supplying drugs or instruments to procure abortion is also a criminal offence according to section 169 of Cap. 154.

391. However, section 169A of Cap. 154, as amended by Law 23(I)/2018, provides that no person shall be held guilty of any criminal offence, in cases where the abortion is carried out by a medical gynaecologist in an organized clinic and with the consent of the pregnant woman under the following circumstances: (a) twelve months of pregnancy have not yet been completed, (b) the pregnant woman (or in case of a minor, or mentally incapacitated person, her guardian or parent) declares in writing before the doctor that the pregnancy is the outcome of rape, sexual abuse or incest and so long as nineteen months of pregnancy have not yet been completed, (c) a competent medical doctor has opined after carrying out an examination with modern means of prenatal diagnosis, that there are signs of anomaly of the foetus which lead to the birth of a child with pathological problems, and (d) a competent doctor has opined that there is an irreversible danger to the life of the pregnant woman or danger of serious injury of her physical or mental health. While the Orthodox Church of Cyprus is, in principle, contrary to abortion, it has accepted that abortion may be justified in exceptional circumstances; thus, following the 1974 Turkish invasion, the Church essentially encouraged Greek Cypriot women who had been raped by Turkish soldiers to procure abortions. The Orthodox Church expressed its disagreement with the enactment of Law 23(I)/18, which, as explained above, effectively legalizes abortion during the first trimester of pregnancy. However, such disagreement was expressed rather mildly.

§5. Suppression Practices

392. A recent amendment to the Criminal Law, Cap. 154, with Law 39(I)/2023, has introduced a new section 233B, which criminalizes the offering of services or application of practices or techniques which aim to change, suppress or eliminate

---

421. *Apostolos Varnavas* 44 (1983): 63–64.

sexual orientation, gender identity or expression of another person. Any person violating section 233B is liable to two years imprisonment and/or a fine of up to EUR 5,000. The same penalty is also provided for persons advertising such services. If the services are offered, or the practices or techniques are applied, to minors or persons who are in a vulnerable position due to illness, incapacity, or mental condition, or by a person who has a position of power or influence over persons who are subject to such practices or techniques or who receive such services, the penalty imposed might be imprisonment imposed of up to three years and/or a fine of up to EUR 10,000. The same penalty is also provided for any lawful guardians who send their wards to receive such services or to be subject to such practices or techniques.

393. The legislator has clarified that the offering of consulting, psychological, or medical services, which refer to the free development of sexual orientation or gender identity of any person, or of scientifically established clinical acts by specialized health professionals, which are applied with regards to the sexual health of any person, do not amount to a criminal offence to the extent that they do not aim to the change, suppression or elimination of sexual orientation, gender identity or expression of another person. It has been further clarified that this section does not preclude the application of the constitutional principles safeguarding freedom of religion. This was an unnecessary addition since clearly any statutory legislation is subject to the Constitution, but was enacted pursuant to an intense request by the Orthodox Church of Cyprus. The Church issued an official announcement strongly disagreeing with the criminalization and expressing its concern that the ambit of the new section 233B might criminalize the expression or acts of Orthodox priests.[422] Although the Church of Cyprus has never applied any techniques or practices aiming to change, suppress, or eliminate gender identity or sexual identity, their concern was whether members of clergy might be held to act inconsistently with such criminal provision if they consult their faithful and express their, negative, views on homosexuality.

422. https://www.alphanews.live/cyprus/fylo-den-einai-epilogi-ti-apofasise-i-ekklisia-gia-therapeies-metastrofis, last accessed 15 Jul. 2023.

Chapter 7. Non-discrimination

§1. Human Rights Provisions

394. Article 28 §2 of the Constitution, implementing Article 14 of the ECHR, ordains that every person shall enjoy all the rights and liberties provided for in this Constitution without any direct or indirect discrimination against any person on the grounds of his/her community, race, religion, language, sex, political or other convictions, national or social descent, birth, colour, wealth, social class or on any ground whatsoever unless there is express provision to the contrary in this Constitution. It should be noted, however, that Article 28 is autonomous, and its application is not dependent upon a finding of violation of another article of the Constitution, contrary to Article 14 of the ECHR.[423] Article 1 of Protocol 12 of the ECHR, which has been ratified by the Republic of Cyprus, introduces a general and autonomous prohibition of discrimination, similar to Article 28 of the Constitution.

395. A difference in treatment is considered to be discriminatory if it has no objective and reasonable justification; thus, the courts will conclude that a law or an act is discriminatory if a difference in treatment does not pursue a legitimate aim or if there is no reasonable relationship of proportionality between the means employed and the aim sought to be realized; where the difference in treatment is based on the grounds of religion, very weighty reasons are required in order to justify such differential treatment. The Republic of Cyprus has further enacted legislation in harmonization with EU Law, which prohibits discrimination. The Equal Treatment (Racial or Ethnic Origin) Law 59(I)/2004 harmonized Council Directive 2000/43/EC on the implementation of the principle of equal treatment irrespective of racial or ethnic origin, in both public and private sectors, in matters of social protection, health treatment, social services, education and access to goods and services. Further, the Equal Treatment in Employment and Occupation Law 58(I)/2004 harmonized Council Directive 2000/78/EC and prohibits discrimination, specifically in the spheres of employment and occupation.

396. A violation of fundamental rights is actionable, and thus, an aggrieved person may file an action in civil courts against those perpetrating the violation, with the aim to recover just and reasonable compensation for any pecuniary or non-pecuniary damage that such person has suffered because of the discrimination; such discrimination may be either direct or indirect. The person may further demand that the Court holds that any discrimination inflicted upon him/her on the basis of a Law or an administrative act is illegal and, thus, should be declared invalid and with no

423. C. Tornaritis, 'The Right of Equality of Treatment and Absence of Discrimination', *Cyprus Law Tribune* 3–4, 5–6 (1973); G. Pikis, 'Equality of Citizens Before the Law as a Requirement of Safeguarding Rule of Law', in *Aspects of Cypriot Law*, Vol. II, 217–239 (Nicosia: Asselia, 1982, in Greek).

effect. By virtue of Article 35 of the Constitution, the executive, legislative and judicial authorities of the Republic are all bound to secure the efficient application of Part II of the Constitution, including Article 28 which safeguards the right of non-discrimination.

§2. The Ombudsman

397. In addition to the right to have access to courts, the Combating of Racism and Other Discrimination (Commissioner) Law 42(I)/2004 vests the Ombudsman, who is an independent officer of the Republic with special competencies, duties and powers for combating and eliminating discrimination in both public and private sectors. Any person or group of persons may lodge a complaint with the Ombudsman about having been subjected to discrimination prohibited by any law of the Republic, including legal instruments of EU origin, as well as the ECHR, the FCNM, the International Convention for the Elimination of all forms of Racial Discrimination, the Covenant for Civil and Political Rights, the Convention against Torture and Inhuman and Degrading Treatment or Punishment, the European Charter for Regional or Minority Languages, as well as any other international or religious human rights instrument ratified by the Republic.[424]

398. The Ombudsman is therefore authorized with the supervision of the implementation of the human rights instruments which the Republic has ratified. Discriminatory provisions or terms found in contracts of employment, collective agreements, articles of association of legal persons, bodies, or institutions, contracts for the supply of goods and services, as well as terms of membership of organizations, including professional ones, may be declared by the Ombudsman as discriminatory. In case of finding an incident of discrimination, the Ombudsman is empowered to order the person or authority responsible for such discrimination to take specific practical measures for ending and not repeating such discriminatory conduct or treatment, not only with respect to the complainant but also with respect to other persons who may find themselves in a similar situation in the future. The Ombudsman may also carry out investigations *ex proprio motu* into incidents of discrimination, prepare codes of practice concerning specific public authorities or persons in the private sector, oblige them to follow practical measures aimed at promoting non-discrimination and equality of treatment, irrespective, *inter alia*, of religion.

424. *See* Second Report submitted by Cyprus pursuant to Art. 25, para. 1 of the FCNM, 27 Oct. 2006, para. 22.

Chapter 8. Penal Law and Religion

399. The interaction between criminal law and religion in Cyprus has not so far been an issue of major debate. This is probably due to the system of coordination prevailing in Cyprus, which has, in general, promoted religious tolerance between the various religious communities. There is a lack of case law with respect to the penal protection of religions; indeed, the issue has almost never attracted social attention. Thus, the practical application or importance of the offences relating to religion, which are enumerated in the Criminal Code, has been limited.[425] Part IV of the Criminal Code Cap. 154, entitled 'Offences Injurious to the Public in General: Offences Relating to Religion', protects certain religious manifestations. The criminal offences that are characterized as religion-related in the Cypriot penal code are the following: (a) defamation of religions; (b) disturbing religious assemblies; (c) unlawful trespassing on burial places; (d) affront to religious sentiment by word or act; (e) circulation of defamatory publications; (f) impersonating clergy; and (g) offences linked with acts of worship.

400. The offence of defamation of religion is provided for in section 138 of Cap. 154, which provides that any person who destroys, damages or defiles any place of worship or any object which is held sacred by any class of persons, with the intention, thereby, of insulting their religion, or with the knowledge that such class of persons is likely to consider such destruction, damage or defilement as an insult to their religion, is guilty of a misdemeanour. Misdemeanour is any offence which is not a felony; section 35 of Cap. 154 provides that when no punishment is specially provided for any misdemeanour, it shall be punishable with imprisonment for a term not exceeding two years or with a fine not exceeding EUR 2,563 or with both punishments. The protected good is the public order, as well as the religious feelings of the believers, which may be offended by the act of destroying, damaging or defiling a particular place of worship or an object which is held to be sacred.

401. In order for the offence to take place, the court must be satisfied that there has been intention of insulting the religion of the class of persons who hold the destroyed, damaged, or defiled object as sacred or who attend the place of worship. Mental element is, therefore, a prerequisite for the existence of the offence. The offence of defamation of religions applies to all religions and not simply to Christianity. Although there has been no interpretation of the notion of religion in the Cypriot legal order, it is safe to assume that this only includes religions whose doctrines or rites are not secret and are included in the scope of protected religions since only such religions are considered not to be secret and therefore to be 'known' within the meaning of Article 18 §2 of the Constitution.

402. The offence of disturbing religious assemblies is provided for in section 139 of Cap. 154, which provides that any person who voluntarily causes disturbance to any assembly lawfully engaged in the performance of a religious worship

425. *See* A. Emilianides, 'Religion in the Criminal Law in Cyprus', in *Religion and Criminal Law* 35–40 (M. Kottiranta & N. Doe eds, Leuven: Peeters, 2013).

or religious ceremony is guilty of a misdemeanour. The protected good is the public order, which may be disturbed by the act of causing disturbance to the assembly which has lawfully been engaged in the performance of religious worship or religious ceremony. The court must be satisfied that there has been an intention of causing disturbance, and thus mental element is a prerequisite for the existence of the offence. The offence applies to all religions.

403. The offence of unlawful trespassing in burial places is provided for in section 140 of Cap. 154, which provides that any person who with the intention of wounding the feelings of any person or of insulting the religion of any person, or with the knowledge that the feelings of any person are likely to be wounded, or that the religion of any person is likely to be insulted thereby, commits any trespass in any place of worship or in any place of sepulchre or in any place set apart for the performance of funeral rites or as a depository for the remains of the dead, or offers any indignity to any human corpse, or causes disturbance to any persons assembled for the purpose of funeral ceremonies, is guilty of a misdemeanour. The protected good is the public order, as well as the religious feelings of believers, which are likely to be offended by the act of trespassing in the places of worship, sepulchre, or depositories or by the indignity offered to the human corpses or by the disturbance caused to the assembly of persons. Intention must be proved in order for the offence to take place. The offence applies to all religions.

404. The offence of affront to religious sentiment by word or act is provided for in section 141 of Cap. 154, which provides that any person who, with the deliberate intention of wounding the religious feelings of any person, utters any word or makes any sound in the hearing of that person, or makes any gesture in the sight of that person, or places any object in the sight of that person, is guilty of a misdemeanour and is liable to imprisonment not exceeding one year. The good protected is public order, as well as the religious feelings of believers, which may be offended by the words, sounds, gestures or objects placed. The intention of wounding the religious feelings is a prerequisite for the offence to take place. The offence applies to all religions.

405. The offence of circulation of defamatory publications is provided for in section 142 of Cap. 154. It is provided that any person who publishes a book or pamphlet or any article or letter in a newspaper or periodical which any class of persons considers as a public insult to their religion, with intent to vilify such religion or to shock or to insult believers to such religion, is guilty of a misdemeanour. The good protected is public order, as well as the religious feelings of believers, which may be offended by the publication. It could be argued that the *actus reus* of the offence is to be determined on the basis of the criteria prevailing in English Law with respect to the common law offence of blasphemy, and thus, the manner in which the views are expressed are more important than the views themselves.[426] The publication should have an element of vilification, ridicule or irreverence that would be

426. *R v. Ramsay and Foote* (1883) 15 Cox CC 231, which was approved by the House of Lords in *Bowman v. Secular Society Ltd* [1917] AC 406, HL.

likely to infuriate others. The court must be satisfied that the offender has intended to vilify such religion or shock or insult believers to such religion. The offence applies to all religions. A prosecution for the offence of circulation of defamatory publication may not be commenced except by, or with the consent of, the Attorney-General of the Republic of Cyprus.

406. The offence of impersonating clergy is provided for in section 109 of Cap. 154, which provides that any person who personifies persons employed in the public service on an occasion when the latter is required to do any act or attend in any place by virtue of his employment or who falsely represents himself to be a person employed in the public service, and assumes to commit any act or to attend in any place for the purpose of doing any act by virtue of such employment, is guilty of a misdemeanour and is liable to imprisonment not exceeding three years. For the purposes of Cap. 154, the notion of a 'person employed in the public service' includes a person acting as a minister of religion of whatsoever denomination in so far as he performs functions in respect of the notification of intending marriage or in respect of the solemnization of marriage, or in respect of the making or keeping of any register or certificate of marriage, birth, baptism, death or burial, but not in any other respect. Thus, impersonating a clergyman is not a criminal offence unless such impersonation is linked to the aforementioned specific function of a religious minister. The offence applies to ministers of all religions.

407. Offences linked to acts of worship are provided for in section 97 of Cap. 154, which provides that any person who holds or is responsible for a Muslim feast (a Muslim festival arranged for, or in connection with, a marriage or for circumcision) or is the occupier of premises on which such a Muslim feast is held and engages, whether with or without pay, or knowingly permits a dancing girl (a prostitute or a woman who dances or sings for pay at Muslim feasts) to dance or sing at such feast, is guilty of a misdemeanour and is liable to a fine not exceeding EUR 128, or to imprisonment for one month. It is questionable whether this law is consistent with the Constitution since it enacts a criminal offence linked to a specific religion, a fact which may be held to be contrary to the equality of religions safeguarded by Article 18 of the Constitution.

408. Section 233A of Cap. 154 further provides that female genital mutilation or female circumcision, unless performed by a medical doctor for health reasons, is an offence, irrespective of whether the female had consented to the act. The offender is liable to imprisonment not exceeding five years. Female genital mutilation, though often related to rituals, is not an offence linked exclusively with acts of worship under Cypriot Law; indeed, there is no mention of acts of worship or rites in the *actus reus* of the offence. There are no specific provisions in the Criminal Code or in other criminal laws, providing that religious motivation is either an aggravating or an attenuating circumstance of a specific offence. Moreover, ritual homicide is not considered to be an aggravation of homicide. However, a judge may have the discretion, on the basis of all relevant factors, to consider whether he should give weight to religious motivation when considering a specific offence.

Part VIII. Church Financing

Chapter 1. Direct Financing of Religious Communities

§1. Introduction

I. General Outline of the Current System of Financing

409. The current system of financing is a direct result of the constitutional provisions regarding the relations between the state and church in the Republic of Cyprus.[427] The right of the five major religions, namely the Greek Orthodox, the Islamic, the Armenian, the Maronite and the Roman Catholic, to exclusively regulate their own property is constitutionally recognized. The same status is essentially recognized by law with regard to the administration of their property to other religions. Consequently, each creed administers its own property without state intervention.

410. More specifically, the Orthodox Church administers its property according to the provisions of its 1980 Charter, the Armenian Church administers its property according to the 1950 Regulations of the Armenian Church, whereas the Roman Catholic and Maronite Churches administer their property according to their own Canonical Law. Prior to the Turkish occupation of northern Cyprus, it had also been accepted that the Islamic religion administered its property according to the Laws and Principles of Vakfs and the Laws and Regulations enacted or made by the Turkish Communal Chamber; due to the occupation, the aforementioned provisions concerning the Islamic religion cannot be implemented for the time being.

411. Article 23 §9 of the Constitution, as already mentioned, stipulates that no deprivation, restriction or limitation on the right to acquire, own, possess, enjoy or dispose of any movable or immovable property belonging to any See, monastery, church or any other ecclesiastical corporation, or any right over it or interest therein, shall be made, except with the written consent of the appropriate ecclesiastical

427. *See* A. Emilianides, 'Il Finanziamento delle cinque Religioni: Il Caso Cipriota', *Quaderni di Diritto e Politica Ecclesiastica* 1, 107–124 (2006); A. Emilianides, 'The Financing of Churches in Cyprus', in *The Financing of Churches in the European Union* (S. Berlingo ed., Leuven: Peeters, 2009).

authority being in control of such property. The same right is accorded to all Muslim religious institutions according to Article 23 §10 of the Constitution. It is, however, provided that restrictions or limitations for the purposes of town and country planning are exempted from the provisions of Articles 23 §9 and 23 §10 of the Constitution.

412. The ambit of Article 23 §9 of the Constitution was considered in the case of the *Holy Temple of Chryseleousis*.[428] The Republic had held that certain buildings belonging to the Holy Temple of Chryseleousis should be declared as ancient monuments without asking for the prior written consent of the appropriate ecclesiastical authority being in control of such property; it has been argued on behalf of the Republic that the act of declaring that the buildings were ancient monuments, did not amount to limitation or restriction on the right to property. The Court held that the said act amounted to a restriction of the Church's right to property, which could not be justified on grounds of town and country planning. Consequently, declaring that the buildings in question were ancient monuments without the prior written consent of the Holy Temple of Chryseleousis was unconstitutional.

413. Whereas the ambit of the near absolute prohibition of imposing restrictions or limitations to the property of religious organizations without their written consent is quite straightforward (exempting only restrictions and limitations for the purpose of town and country planning),[429] a recent judgment of the Supreme Court extended this exemption to virtually all limitations provided for in paragraphs 4, 7 and 8 of Article 23, citing the Greek text of the Constitution as proof of such an interpretation.[430] With all due respect to the Supreme Court, this is not only a misconceived interpretation of the Greek text of Article 23 §9, which clearly exempts the property of religious organizations from the application of the said paragraphs, but it is also contrary to the clear interpretation of the Turkish text of the Constitution, as well as the English text of the Constitution. It is hoped that the Supreme Court shall have the opportunity to overrule such mistaken interpretation in the future.[431]

414. The Republic of Cyprus does not provide funding to religions per se. Significant religious assistance is, however, provided to religious communities with regard to the construction or repair of their churches, monasteries and cemeteries, and for other religious purposes, in the form of state aid. It should be observed that such state aid is provided by the Central Government and is in practice, provided only to the five major religious communities and not to other religious organizations. The local government does not provide any funding to churches. By virtue of Article 18 §8 of the Constitution, no person shall be compelled to pay any tax or

---

428. *The Holy Temple of Chryseleousis v. The Republic* [1989] 3 CLR 3074. *See also The Holy Monastery of Kykkos v. The Republic* [1996] 3 CLR 3362 (in Greek).
429. *Ibid.*
430. *Holy Metropolis of Paphos v. Aristo Developers Ltd* [2011] 1 CLR 1377 (in Greek).
431. *See also* A. Emilianides, 'Reviewing the Review of Constitutionality: A Commentary on Three Recent Judgments of the Supreme Court', *Yearbook of Cyprus and European Law* 50 ff. (2013), (in Greek).

duty, the proceeds of which are specially allocated in whole or in part for the purposes of a religion other than his/her own.

415. Prior to the 1963 constitutional crisis, the Greek Communal Chamber had been responsible for providing State aid with regard to the educational and religious needs of its respective major religious communities, namely the Orthodox, the Armenian, the Maronite and the Roman Catholic, while the Turkish Communal Chamber had been equally responsible for providing State aid with regard to the educational and religious needs of the Islamic Community. Following the self-dissolution of the Greek Communal Chamber, the State aid towards religious organizations is currently provided only by the Central Government. The Republic of Cyprus does not impose any special religious tax. Furthermore, exemption from the income tax is provided with regard to the income of religious organizations and charitable associations. Other tax laws, however, do not provide for the exemption of religious organizations.

II. The Internal Organs of Administration of Property of the Orthodox Church

416. It is interesting to note that when the Orthodox church enacted its Charter on 1 January 1980, which was setting up central and peripheral organs for the administration of its property, it invited to the discussions the then Minister of Finance, the Attorney-General, the President of the Supreme Court, advocates and well-known Cypriot businessmen, in order to consider their views on the draft Charter.[432] The new 2010 Charter contains a detailed Annex III, which contains detailed rules on the administration of ecclesiastical property. The Orthodox Church has set up central and local institutions for the administration of its property. The central institutions are: (a) the Central Ecclesiastical Fund; (b) the Audit Department; and (c) the Fund for the Wages of the Clergy. All of these are situated in Nicosia. The local institutions are (i) the See Committee; (ii) the See Fund; (iii) the Parochial Fund; (iv) the Parochial Committee; (v) the Abbatial Council; and (vi) philanthropic and charitable ecclesiastical foundations in general.

417. The Central Ecclesiastical Fund is supervised by the Holy Synod. Its resources comprise percentages of the total resources of the Archdiocese, metropolises and monasteries, income from investments and donations (Charter, Annex III, Article 3). It pays the salaries of the clergy and subsidizes the various ecclesiastical educational establishments and activities, such as the publication of the official review 'Apostolos Varnavas' and Cypriot participation in inter-ecclesiastical and interreligious events (Annex III, Article 2). The Audit Department is supervised by the Holy Synod and inspects the management of the property of the Archdiocese, the metropolises and the 'royal' monasteries (Annex III, Article 5). It is staffed by laypersons, and it may also draft recommendations as to the best possible use of

432. *See* Chrysostomos, Archbishop of Cyprus, 'Introductory Report on the New Charter of the Church of Cyprus', *Apostolos Varnavas* 40, 375–377 (1979), (in Greek).

Church property. Nevertheless, the recommendations are not binding unless they are adopted by the Holy Synod. The Fund for the Wages of the Clergy is managed and administered by the Central Ecclesiastical Fund, and its aim is to safeguard the payment of salaries of the clergy (Annex III, Article 5).

418. There is a See Committee based in each Metropolis. Its chairman is the Metropolitan, and it consists of eight other members, four clergy and four lay (Article 35). The lay members of the Committee are elected, whereas the clergymen are appointed by the Metropolitan. The See Committee is charged with the study, supervision and management of the finances of its Diocese (Article 42). The See Fund operates under the directions of the See Committee, and it is responsible for the fiscal management of the finances of each metropolis (Annex III, Article 11).

419. The Parochial Committee manages the finances of the parish. This Committee is chaired by a member appointed by the Metropolitan, who may be either a member of the clergy or a layperson. Four additional members from among the laity are elected every four years by the parishioners (Article 53). The Parochial Fund is managed by the Committee, and it is responsible for the fiscal management of the finances of each parish (Annex III, Article 13). The Abbatial Council is chaired by the Abbot and manages the property of the monastery (Article 68). Each Metropolis may further establish philanthropic and other charitable foundations such as orphanages, old people's homes and boarding schools (Article 71). Foundations that have been instituted by virtue of a last will and testament and placed under the jurisdiction of the Church operate under the conditions of the testator.

§2. TYPES OF FINANCING

I. Salaries of Religious Ministers/Chaplaincy

420. Important assistance is provided by the State as far as the practice of religion is concerned. As a result of an agreement between the Republic of Cyprus and the Orthodox Church, the Church has transferred some of its immovable property to the Republic, which in return contributes to the payment of the salaries of the parish clergy in rural areas. The government decided that this agreement should also extend to the clergy of the three Religious Groups of the Republic, and as of 1 January 1999, the state has also begun to pay the salaries of a number of priests of the three Religious Groups, despite the fact that only the Orthodox Church had granted any immovable property to the Republic. This was due to the fact that the three Religious Groups and the Orthodox Church should be treated on an equal basis in view of the system of coordination, which is in force in the Republic of Cyprus.[433] The same treatment was also granted to the parochial priests of the Orthodox Christians who follow the Old Calendar.

433. *See* Report submitted by Cyprus pursuant to Art. 25, para. 1 of the FCNM, 1 Mar. 1999, Part II, Art. 5 D11.

421. The Republic of Cyprus does not contribute, however, to the payment of salaries of religious ministers of other religions or for lay people working either for the Orthodox Church or for the three Religious Groups. It should be further observed that the religious ministers of the three Religious Groups of the Republic enjoyed free medical treatment and medicines in Governmental hospitals, irrespective of their citizenship, despite the fact that such free medical treatment used to be provided for free only to Cypriot citizens. In addition to the above, the State provides an annual grant towards the churches of the three Religious Groups of the Republic in order to assist them in fulfilling their religious duties.

422. The salaries of religious ministers who work as chaplains in the National Guard are provided for by the Government since, in practice, such religious ministers are members of the Public Service of the Republic, who are temporarily seconded to the National Guard in order to perform such duties. It should be observed, however, that only religious ministers of the Greek Orthodox Church are seconded to the Army. The General Headquarters of the National Guard has established a Directorate for Religious Affairs, who is an Archimandrite of the Orthodox Church. The Director appoints a secretariat, whereas the Metropolitans of the Orthodox Church appoint priests as associates of the Director in order to cover the needs of the military camps of specific geographical areas which fall within the limits of their corresponding Metropolis. The priests of the Orthodox Church provide full chaplaincy services to members of the National Guard, either professional army officers or soldiers.[434] Furthermore, the Republic each year seconds several of the members of the Public Educational Service in order to perform duties related to the major church of the Republic.

423. In view of the positive obligation of the Republic to safeguard access to chaplaincy of adherents of other faiths or creeds, the Minister of Defence has instructed that members of other religions ought to be facilitated in the exercise of their religious beliefs and therefore army personnel is required to safeguard that chaplaincy is provided for all soldiers and army officers who are not Orthodox Christians. In order to achieve this aim, the National Guard coordinates with the various religions of the island on an ad hoc basis. Furthermore, the Ministry of Health has temporarily seconded religious ministers of the Orthodox Church in some hospitals in coordination with the Orthodox Church. The Orthodox Church coordinates with the Ministry of Health in order to ensure that there are chapels near major hospitals in a manner which enables the priests to provide chaplaincy services in a timely and comprehensive manner. The Ministry of Health aims to facilitate the exercise of religious beliefs by adherents of other faiths and thus aims to contact religious ministers of other religions, often with the assistance of the priests of the Orthodox Church, in order to secure chaplaincy services for the patients.

434. For a detailed description of the duties of the Directorship for Religious Affairs *see* the speech by the Director for Religious Affairs Ioannis Ioannou in the event 'The Work of the Church of Cyprus in the Armed Forces', 26 May 2012 (in Greek).

424. With respect to chaplaincy in prisons, Regulation 109 of the Prisons General Regulations 121/97, enacted in accordance with Prison Law 62(I)/96, provides that prisoners have a right, to the extent possible, to satisfy their religious needs.[435] In this respect, prisoners have an optional right to manifest and exercise their religious duties and to communicate with recognized representatives of their religion or creed. Proselytism of any kind is prohibited. In accordance with the Regulations, the prison authorities provide for the facilitation of chaplaincy services by religious authorities. As in other cases, the Orthodox Church enjoys a dominant role since an Orthodox priest is temporarily seconded in the Central Jail of Nicosia, which is the only correctional facility in Cyprus; the priest performs the Divine Liturgy on Sundays and carries out confessions. The prisoners have the opportunity to attend religious services, whereas additional priests occasionally visit the prisons for chaplaincy services if they are needed.[436] Furthermore, an Islamic Imam has been designated by the Embassy of Libya as an official representative of the Islamic religion and visits the prisons every Friday; other religious ministers of Islam, Christianity or other religions may visit the prisons pursuant to a request by the individual prisoners themselves.[437]

II. Education

425. All teachers of theology in public schools are appointed by the Government and are members of the educational service of the Republic. Thus, the Republic provides for all their salaries and pensions. Children belonging to the Turkish Cypriot, Maronite, Armenian and Roman Catholic groups are assisted by the State to attend private schools of their choice if they so wish. The state, therefore, covers all fees and expenses of Turkish Cypriot pupils whose families reside in the non-occupied areas, and who attend private schools of elementary and secondary education. It has been standard practice to fully subsidize Turkish Cypriot pupils who reside in the non-occupied areas to attend the English School, a private secondary school with very high fees.

426. For Turkish Cypriot pupils who reside in the territory that is not under the control of the Government and who wish to attend this school, a lump sum is allotted towards their fees. The subsidy is given regardless of the financial status of the pupils' parents. Free breakfast is provided to all Turkish-speaking pupils who attend public pre-primary and primary schools. Moreover, free breakfast is also provided to all pupils who attend schools which fall into the Educational Priority Zones; furthermore, free lunch is provided to all Turkish-speaking pupils who attend 'All Day' public primary schools, as well as to other children who have low economic status.

---

435. *See* A. Emilianides, 'Chaplaincy and the Law in Cyprus', in *Chaplaincy and the Law in the European Union* 75–82 (R. Balodis ed., Granada: Comares, 2018), (forthcoming).

436. *See* the speech of priest Christoforos Demetriou, 'The Pastoral Action of the Church of Cyprus in the Central Jail' (2010), (in Greek), available in http://archive.immorfou.org.cy/newsvarious-articles/305-the-pastoral-activity-of-the-church-of-cyprus-to-the-central-prison.html.

437. 'The Evangelical Clerics in Prisons', *Simerini*, 23 Jan. 2015 (in Greek). *See also* M. Demetriou, 'Discrimination for Evangelicals in Prisons', *Simerini*, 22 Jan. 2015 (in Greek).

427. The State also covers the expenses of the Armenian, Maronite, or Roman Catholic students who attend their own religious, ethnic, or national private schools. In particular, the State grants the annual fees of every Maronite or Roman Catholic student who attends pre-elementary education at the private schools of Terra Santa in Nicosia and of every Maronite or Roman Catholic student who attends elementary education in the aforementioned Catholic school. Moreover, the State grants an annual amount to every Maronite or Roman Catholic student who attends secondary education in the Terra Santa School.

428. Furthermore, the State provides an annual grant to every Armenian, Maronite, or Roman Catholic student who attends secondary education at the private school of St Mary's in Limassol. The State further grants a yearly amount to every Armenian, Maronite or Roman Catholic student who attends a private school of secondary education if such school does not provide education consistent with the religious beliefs of the pupils; such schools are the English School, Grammar School, GC School, Pascal, etc. Armenians have primary schools of their own in Nicosia, Limassol and Larnaca. Such schools are fully funded by the State; State aid includes the salaries of the teachers, as well as all expenses for the management of the schools. The same used to be true for Maronite schools; however, the Maronites lost their educational establishments as a result of the Turkish invasion. The State eventually decided to establish a new elementary school for Maronite pupils, while Maronite priests are compensated by the State for providing religious education to Maronite children.

III. Other Types of Financing

429. The Republic of Cyprus provides additional financial assistance to the three Religious Groups of the Republic with regard to their worship places and their cultural heritage. Land, as well as public grants, has been given to the three Religious Groups of the Republic for construction of their churches, monasteries and cemeteries. Grants are also given for repairs to existing churches and monasteries. In addition, the Ministry of Education finances cultural activities of the Greek Orthodox Church and the three Religious Groups of the Republic, including publications, performances, construction of libraries, seminaries, museums and keeping collections of archives or historic buildings. Financial assistance is also given to social and athletic clubs which relate to the Orthodox Church, or to the three Religious Groups. Any clubs which are approved by one of the three Religious Groups are therefore, entitled to receive annual grants from the Republic.

430. In addition to the above, it should be noted that the Republic pays all travel expenses of the Maronite priest, who visits Maronites who remained enclaved in their homes as a result of the Turkish occupation of Northern Cyprus. Furthermore, all the benefits provided by the Republic to the enclaved Maronites are given to the Maronite Religious Group. A grant is allocated for the repair and improvement of the houses of enclaved persons (Greek Orthodox and Maronites) in the occupied area. The Government further provides annually a grant to the Institution of Welfare of the Maronites of Cyprus. In order to facilitate links between Cypriot Maronites living in the non-occupied areas and those living in the occupied areas, the Government provides free transportation twice a week to all Maronites living in the non-occupied territories so as to enable them to visit their family members and to seek medical care. Free housing in the Government Refugee Housing Estates is provided to the Maronites who live permanently in the occupied areas in order to visit their children who attend school in the non-occupied areas. Free food supplies are also provided for once a week.

431. Since 1999 and the arson attempt on the Hala Sultan Tekke Mosque in Larnaca, all the mosques in the non-occupied areas have been guarded on a twenty-four-hour basis by periodic police patrols. A provision is made in the Annual Budget of the Republic for the repair, maintenance and cleaning of Turkish Cypriot ancient monuments, mosques and cemeteries (Budget of the Turkish Cypriot Properties Management Service and Budget of the Department of Antiquities of the Ministry of Communications and Works). During the period 2000–2005, the Government spent approximately EUR 1,500,000 for the repair and maintenance of the Turkish Cypriot mosques, ancient monuments and cemeteries. The budget allotted to the repair and maintenance of mosques has since substantially increased.

§3. Assessment

432. The current system of financing of the Republic of Cyprus is, as a whole, in accordance with the principles of the EU, including the ECHR and the FCNM. However, some aspects of the system need improvement. Insofar as the direct financing of churches is concerned, the Republic of Cyprus' substantial financial contributions assist the religious practices of the major religions of the Republic. Although members of the Religious Groups of the Republic might point out areas from time to time where more should be done, there is no doubt that the system is generally fair since it corresponds to the actual needs of the various religious communities of the Republic.

433. There is, however, one question which has not been examined so far by the Republic of Cyprus and which is bound to be examined in the future, namely, whether the Republic ought to also finance other religions. Should the State also finance religions or rites, such as the Jews, the Protestants, or the Buddhists? Although such cases have not yet occurred due to the small number of adherents to such religions or rites, it is quite possible that in the near future, one of these religious communities might also apply to the Government for financing. It is suggested that although there is a distinction in the Constitution between the five main religious communities of the Republic, the Government ought to be eager to assist other religious communities as well, on the basis of their actual needs, in order to assist them to best practice their religious beliefs within the boundaries of the

Republic.[438] It should be further noted that the dramatic deterioration of the Cypriot economy after 2011, which resulted in the imposition of a series of austerity measures and caused substantial property losses for the Church due to the loss of value of its stocks in Cypriot banks, has negatively affected the financial power of the Orthodox Church, as well as the power of the Government to fund religious minorities.

438. *See* A. Emilianides, 'Financing of Religions in Cyprus' in *The Financing of Religious Communities in the European Union* 111–117 (S. Berlingo ed., Peeters: Leuven, 2009); A. Emilianides, 'Equal Promotionist Neutralism and the Case of Cyprus', in *Financing of Churches and Religious Societies in the 21st Century* 135–144(M. Moravcicova ed., Bratislava: Institute for State-Church Relations, 2010); A. Emilianides, 'Il Finanziamento delle cinque Religioni: Il Caso Cipriota', *Quaderni di Diritto e Politica Ecclesiastica* 1, 123 ff. (2006).

Chapter 2. Indirect Financing of Religious Communities

§1. Income Tax

434. Income tax is levied on the income of any person, natural or legal, accruing in, derived from, or received in Cyprus in one fiscal year.[439] Religious institutions enjoy exemption from the income tax, according to section 8 §13 of the Income Tax Law 118(1)/2002, which provides that 'the income of a religious, charitable, or educational institution of public character' is exempted from the provisions of the Income Tax Law. There is no interpretation of the term 'religious institution' in Law 118(1)/02, and as a result, it is suggested that the institutions of any known religion which fulfils the criteria of Article 18 §2 of the Constitution should enjoy exemption from income tax. Article 18 §2 provides that any religions whose doctrines or rites are not secret are free; thus, religious institutions need not be officially recognized by state organs in order to enjoy exemption from the Income Tax Law; they only need to be 'known', in the sense that their doctrines and rites should not be secret. So far, applications by religious organizations to register as non-profit companies have promptly been accepted by the authorities of the Republic without any particular problems, and thus, there has been no legislative or judicial attempt to define 'religion'.

435. A question might arise whether section 8 §13 of Law 118(1)/02 should be interpreted as including only religious institutions 'of public character'. If such an interpretation is accepted, it could be further argued that only the income of the five constitutionally recognized religions could be exempted from the provisions of the Income Tax Law. Such an interpretation, however, does not seem convincing. To begin with, there are no official or established religions in the Republic of Cyprus. While the Constitution provides for certain explicit privileges granted to the five major religions of the Republic, it also provides that all religions are equal before the law. It should, therefore, be accepted that the House of Representatives cannot enact a law according to which some religions enjoy exemption from income tax, while other religions do not enjoy such an exemption since such law would be contrary to the constitutional mandate of equality of religions.

436. It is, therefore, suggested that section 8 §13 of Law 118(1)/02 should be interpreted in accordance with the constitutional provisions. Any interpretation according to which the five constitutionally recognized religions could be exempted from the provisions of Law 118(1)/02, while other religions could not be exempted, would be undesirable. In view of the fact that the Supreme Court of Cyprus has held that the Orthodox Church is not considered to be an '*organ*' or an '*authority*' in the Republic, under the sense of Article 139 of the Constitution,[440] and the fact that all

439. *See* in general A. Neocleous et al., 'Taxation', *Introduction to Cyprus Law* 541 ff. (Limassol: Andreas Neocleous & Co LLC 3rd ed. 2010).

440. *Autocephalous, Holy, Orthodox and Apostolic Church of Cyprus v. The House of Representatives* [1990] 3 CLR 338 (in Greek).

known religions are currently recognized as legal entities under private law, it is suggested that the *public character* argument could not really refer to the five major religions of the Republic.

437. Since the five major religions are recognized as legal entities under private law, and since they are not considered an *organ*, or an *authority* in the Republic, a status of 'public character' which would distinguish them from other religions would be illogical. Therefore, 'public character' with regard to religious institutions is not a requisite or even a relevant criterion. 'Public character' should refer to educational institutions but not to religious institutions. Such an interpretation is, in our view, in line with the constitutional provisions and the basic principles of teleological interpretation.

438. Such an exemption of religious organizations from the Income Tax Law is not without its critics. While other religious organizations do not really engage in important financial transactions due to the fact that their members in Cyprus are few, it is a well-known fact that the Orthodox Church takes part in all important economic activities of the island. Furthermore, the Orthodox Church contributes an important sum in order to purchase ecclesiastical material, furniture, vestments and articles for religious purposes. Due to the fact that the Orthodox Church is exempt from Income Tax Law, it is more difficult for the authorities to specify in an accurate manner the income made by those who engage in financial transactions with the Orthodox Church.

439. The Government had recently expressed the opinion that the financial transactions of the Orthodox Church should fall under the provisions of the Income Tax Law; however, the Orthodox Church disagreed with such view and argued that the Church is a non-profit organization and thus uses its income for charity purposes. It is further argued that while it is true that the Orthodox Church engages in financial transactions, each Metropolis is divided into a great number of parishes, and as a result, the annual income of each parish is not significant as such. It is also pointed out that only the Archdiocese and the Monastery of Kykkos actually engage in significant financial transactions.[441] In any case, for-profit companies where the Church is a shareholder are not exempted from the payment of income tax, nor is the Church arguing otherwise.

§2. Customs and Excise Duties

440. A further exemption from duty purposes with regard to religious authorities is provided for in section 3, Class P of Annex I of the Customs and Excise Duties Regulations (Exemptions from Import and Excise Duties) of 2004, 380/04. It is provided that all constructional material, fittings and furniture for churches or mosques and all vestments and other articles which are imported for religious purposes by Ecclesiastical and Religious Authorities are eligible for relief from duty.

441. *See Apopsi* 8 (2008), interview of Archbishop Chrysostomos II.

The aforementioned exemption concerns all religious authorities and not only the five constitutionally recognized religions of the Republic.

441. In addition to the above, and according to the provisions of Council Regulation 1186/2009,[442] there is an exemption from import duties for materials of little value, such as paints used in the building, fitting-out and decoration of temporary stands occupied by representatives of third countries at an event held mainly for religious reasons or reasons of worship and which are destroyed by being used, as well as unframed photographs, printed matter, prospectus, posters, calendar supplied free of charge in order to advertise goods manufactured outside the customs territory of the EU and displayed at an event held mainly for religious reasons or reasons of worship. Also, documentation intended to be distributed free of charge and with the principal purpose of encouraging the public to visit foreign countries in order to attend religious meetings or events is also excluded from import duties, provided that it contains no more than 25% of private commercial advertising matter. Furthermore, religious institutions who have been registered as non-profit organizations may admit free of import duties, a number of cultural or educational materials which are imported for non-commercial purposes.

§3. Value-Added Tax

442. Value-Added Tax is payable whenever there is: (a) a supply of goods or services in Cyprus by a Value-Added Tax registered person, natural or legal, within the activities or the promotion of activities of his/her business. The definition of supply of goods or services includes all types of supply but does not include anything that is not done with a consideration; (b) an import of goods in Cyprus from third countries; (c) a notional provision in Cyprus, of services received from abroad. Supplies of goods or services are further divided into taxable supplies and exempt supplies. Religious institutions may be registered for Value-Added Tax purposes, according to the Value-Added Tax Law 95(I)/2000, so long as the conditions of the aforementioned Law are fulfilled.

443. According to the Value-Added Tax Law 95(I)/00, all legal persons who engage in financial transactions may register and, thus, become taxable persons. A legal person who has engaged in taxable financial transactions exceeding the amount of EUR 15,600 within a period of a calendar year or who has reasons to believe that the value of its financial transactions shall exceed the amount of EUR 15,600 within the period of the subsequent thirty days, is obliged to register according to the provisions of the Value-Added Tax Law 95(I)/00. The following organs of the Greek Orthodox Church of Cyprus may be registered:

(a) Sees: the Value-Added Tax Form 101 is signed by the relevant Bishop, or an authorized representative.

442. Of 16 Nov. 2009 setting up a Community System of Reliefs from Customs Duty.

(b) Parishes: the Value-Added Tax Form 101 is signed by the parish priest, or a member of the Parochial Committee authorized by the relevant Bishop.
(c) Monasteries: the Value-Added Tax Form 101 is signed by the Abbot, or a member of the Abbatial Council who is authorized by the Abbot.
(d) Philanthropic and other charitable foundations in general, such as orphanages, old-age homes and boarding schools: the Value-Added Tax Form is signed by a person authorized in accordance with the internal regulations of the foundation.

§4. Capital Gains Tax and Immovable Property Tax

I. The Refusal of the Orthodox Church to Pay Capital Gains Tax

444. Capital gains tax is imposed on the gains accruing to any person, natural or legal, from a disposal of property which does not fall within the provisions of the Income Tax Law.[443] Furthermore, under the provisions of the Immovable Property Tax Law, all persons, natural or legal, are obliged to pay tax on all immovable property registered in their name. It should be further observed that due to the invasion and occupation of the northern part of Cyprus by Turkey, the Government has introduced a defence levy, deducted from salaries, pensions, dividends and interest, the proceeds of which are used for the defence of the country; such defence levy is called the Special Defence Contribution.

445. The Capital Gains Tax Law 52/1980, the Immovable Property Tax Law 24/1980, as well as the Special Defence Contribution Law 117(I)/2002 do not provide for the exemption of religious institutions in a manner similar to the Income Tax Law 118(I)/02. Thus, religious institutions have a legal obligation to pay taxes according to the aforementioned laws. However, Article 23(9) of the Constitution provides that the State may not interfere with the right to acquire, own, possess, enjoy, or dispose of any movable or immovable property of any ecclesiastical corporation, except with the written consent of the ecclesiastical authority who is in control of such property. It has been argued accordingly by the Orthodox Church that due to the aforementioned constitutional provision, any taxation of the property of the Church would be unconstitutional.

446. This argument of the Orthodox Church was considered by the Supreme Court of Cyprus in the case of *Attorney-General v. The Archdiocese of Cyprus*.[444] The facts of the case were the following: the Director of the Department of Lands had stressed that if the Archdiocese of Cyprus refused to pay the capital gains tax it owed with regard to the transfer of land, he would accordingly refuse to register and transfer the said land to the purchasers. The Archdiocese of Cyprus eventually agreed to pay the tax due, but it reserved its right to have recourse to the Supreme

443. *See* C. Demetriades, 'Republic of Cyprus: Capital Gains Tax of Immoveable Property', *European Taxation* 19, 250–256 (1979).
444. *Attorney-General v. The Archdiocese of Cyprus*, Judgment of 22 Mar. 1999 (in Greek).

Court of the Republic. When the Supreme Court held that the payment of the capital gains tax was not a requisite for the transfer of lands according to the provisions of the Transfer of Land Law 9/1965,[445] the Archdiocese of Cyprus argued that the Department of Lands should refund the paid tax, since a different outcome would violate Article 23 §9 of the Constitution.

447. The Supreme Court held that the question of whether the Orthodox Church is obliged to pay taxes is different from the question of whether the Republic may force the Church to fulfil its obligation. Even if it is accepted that any obligatory measures of collecting the taxes of the Orthodox Church are prohibited in view of Article 23 §9 of the Constitution, this should not mean that the ecclesiastical authorities are not obliged to pay such taxes; a different result would seriously undermine the importance of the obligation of all persons of the Republic to pay taxes and would inevitably lead to the unequal distribution of financial burdens.[446] Since the Archdiocese of Cyprus undoubtedly owed the tax, it would be contrary to the rules of equity to hold that the tax due should be refunded to the Archdiocese of Cyprus simply in order to revive the obligation of the Archdiocese to pay such tax.

448. The House of Representatives amended section 17 §2 of the Capital Gains Tax Law 52/1980 by Law 48/1999, in order to provide that:

> the tax ought to be paid before any transfer of property and irrespective of any recourse, or objection, unless the Director orders that the payment of such tax, or part of such tax, is suspended until a date specified in the aforementioned order. It is understood that no transfer of property may occur before the payment of the tax due, unless the Director orders that such payment is suspended.

The implications of the amended section 17 §2 of Law 48/99 were examined by the Supreme Court of Cyprus in the case of *The Archdiocese of Cyprus v. The Republic of Cyprus.*[447] The Court held that such a modification did not render the payment of the Capital Gains Tax as a prerequisite for the transfer of land since the Capital Gains Tax was not considered to be a tax which burdens the immovable property according to the provisions of the Transfer of Land Law 9/1965; thus, there was no obligation that the capital gains tax needed to be paid before the property was transferred.

449. The House of Representatives eventually amended the Transfer of Land Law 9/1965 by Law 181(I)/2002, which provided that in order to complete the process of transferring land, one should present: 'a certificate by the Director of Inland Revenue that any tax which is due to the transfer of the land in accordance with the provisions of the Capital Gains Tax Law, has been paid, or that its payment has been

445. *The Republic v. Kythreotis* [1992] 3 CLR 21.

446. *See also Rainbow v. Republic* [1984] 3 CLR 846; *Attorney-General v. Shizas* [1996] 2 CLR 175 (in Greek).

447. *The Archdiocese of Cyprus v. The Republic of Cyprus*, Judgment of 5 Jul. 2002 (in Greek).

suspended, or that no tax is due'. The Supreme Court held that despite such amendment of Law 9/1965, there is nothing in the said Law to explicitly prohibit the transfer of land in those cases where the capital gains tax has not been paid since the tax is imposed on the seller and not on the land.[448]

II. The Negotiations Between the State and the Orthodox Church

450. It is, therefore, clear that despite the successive amendments of Law 52/80 and Law 9/65, all attempts by the State to force the Orthodox Church, by indirect means, to pay the capital gains tax have been declared invalid by the Supreme Court. The State has made efforts to reach an informal agreement with the Orthodox Church with regard to the payment of the capital gains tax. Such an agreement was reached in 2002 between the Ministry of Finance, the House of Representatives and the Monastery of Kykkos, according to which the Monastery of Kykkos has agreed to pay in future, the capital gains tax, on the condition that all debts incurred before 2002 would be erased.

451. It was estimated that by 2007, the Orthodox Church had not yet paid to the Department of Inland Revenue the amount of EUR 85 million, namely EUR 20 million with regard to the Capital Gains Tax Law and EUR 65 million with regard to the Immovable Property Tax Law. Furthermore, the Orthodox Church did not pay the defence levy according to the Special Defence Contribution Law. However, it would seem that these estimates, which had always been rejected by the Church, were not entirely accurate. It should further be observed that private companies to which the Orthodox Church is a major stockholder, such as the Hellenic Bank, pay all relevant taxes without any problems. Following intense negotiations between the State and the Orthodox Church were kept a secret, it was announced that the former Government of Tassos Papadopoulos and the Orthodox Church had reached a thirteen-point interim agreement. According to this interim agreement, all past debts of the Orthodox Church would be deleted, and the Church would be exempted from the obligation to pay tax on its immovable property, which it does not intend to sell. The Church would, however, undertake the obligation to pay promptly all its future obligations arising out of the special defence levy and the capital gains tax.

452. In essence, the interim agreement between the State and the Church was based upon the same reasoning as the 2002 agreement between the Ministry of Finance and the Monastery of Kykkos. However, this interim agreement was deliberately finalized by the Council of Ministers of the subsequent Christofias Government. The new Government intended to renegotiate the terms of the agreement with the Orthodox Church; the Orthodox Church, however, refused to renegotiate the terms of the agreement. Eventually, following an unnecessary delay, the Orthodox Church and the Christofias Government finalized and signed the agreement in 2012.

---

448. *Ibid.*, Judgment of 1 Mar. 2005 (in Greek).

It is suggested that the agreement between the State and the Orthodox Church with regard to such taxes was a positive development as it ended a long period of disturbing dispute.[449]

453. From 2012 to 2017, it was estimated that the Orthodox Church paid the Department of Taxation of the Republic, in accordance with the terms of the agreement, the amount of approximately EUR 18 million, which referred to approximately EUR 16 million for capital gains tax and approximately 2 million for immovable property tax. However, an amount of approximately EUR 3 million was returned to the Church as a Value-Added Tax return since term 13 of the Agreement provided that the Orthodox Church would be relieved from the obligation to pay Value-Added Tax for the construction and maintenance of temples and immovable property situated around the temple, which are used for the Church's religious functions. The relief has taken the form of state aid provided in lieu of the paid Value-Added Tax. It should be noted, however, that whereas the Orthodox Church has transferred since 2012 a significant amount of immovable property exceeding EUR 150 million to the Bank of Cyprus and the Hellenic Bank as part of an agreement to restructure its loans, these transfers had been relieved from the obligation to pay capital tax gains tax due to a provision of general application regarding transfers made for the purpose of restructuring of loans.[450]

---

449. *See Syngxroni Apopsi* (2008) July: 46–48.

450. *See* K. Savva, 'What Has the Tax Agreement Between Church and State Brought?' *Politis*, 27 Nov. 2017 (in Greek), available in http://politis.com.cy/article/175-ekat-o-ovolos-ekklisias.

Part IX. Education

Chapter 1. Religious Education in Public and Private Schools

§1. Introduction

454. The Orthodox Church of Cyprus showed considerable interest in education during the Turkish and British rule of Cyprus; the Church considered that education was closely related to religion and the maintenance of the Greek Orthodox character of the island under foreign rule.[451] Education in Cyprus remained closely connected with religion in the early years following independence; education was one of the areas within the competencies of the Greek and Turkish Communal Chamber, respectively, and thus, while Turkish education was predominantly associated with the Islamic religion, Greek education was connected to the Orthodox Christian religion.

455. In addition, the three Religious Groups of the Republic were assisted in maintaining their own religious education. Consequently, Orthodox religion was an integral part of the curriculum, and no person of another religion could teach at a Greek elementary school. Most schools were established by the Church, which donated great amounts of money in order to support the proper functioning of primary and secondary schools. During British rule, Archbishop Makarios III established the Educational Council of the Ethnarchy, which coordinated the educational activities of the Greek schools.

456. Undoubtedly, the influence of the Orthodox Church on the curriculum has lessened after Independence; the non-Orthodox or atheists may well be appointed as teachers in Cypriot schools, while the Orthodox religion is no longer considered an integral part of the curriculum, as it used to be. In view of the fact that the Church no longer felt that Cyprus' identity was threatened because of foreign rule, the Republic followed international standards with respect to providing secular education. Consequently, education in state schools has been completely secularized, with the exception of religious education. However, the Church still retains a limited role with respect to educational activities since school festivities often relate to Christianity, such as the celebration of Easter or Christmas. In addition, students collectively go to church with their school, two or three times a

451. *See* P. Persianis, *Church and State in Cyprus Education* (Nicosia: 1978).

year, in order to participate in school worship. Furthermore, the first class of the day usually begins with a collective prayer.

457. Whereas the schools do not provide chaplaincy for Orthodox pupils, the wishes of students who opt to confess to a religious minister would be facilitated by the school authorities. In practice, there are chapels of the Orthodox Church near most schools so that students would have the opportunity to have access to chaplaincy if their parents so wished. The school authorities would normally facilitate pupils adhering to the Islamic, Roman Catholic, Maronite or Armenian religion whenever parents sought chaplaincy services of their corresponding religion to be offered to their children. However, the school authorities would not, in practice, be similarly eager to facilitate the provision of chaplaincy services for other religions, primarily because there is no central authority overseeing such a task, with each school unit having the responsibility to implement its own policy on the issue.

§2. The Right to Religious Education

458. Article 20 of the Constitution provides that every person has the right to receive, and every person or institution has the right to give instruction or education, subject to such formalities, conditions or restrictions as are in accordance with the relevant communal law and are necessary only in the interests of the security of the Republic or the constitutional order or the public safety or the public order or the public health or the public morals or the standard and quality of education or for the protection of the rights and liberties of others including the right of the parents to secure for their children, such education as is in conformity with their religious convictions. Similarly, Article 2 of the First Protocol of the ECHR provides that no person shall be denied the right to education and that in the exercise of any functions which it assumes in relation to education and teaching, the State shall respect the right of parents to ensure such education and teaching as is in conformity with their own religious and philosophical convictions. The stipulation that the parents have the right to secure for their children the education which conforms with their religious convictions, aims at safeguarding the possibility of pluralism in education.

459. The State is forbidden from pursuing an aim of indoctrination, which might be considered as not respecting the parents' religious convictions.[452] The ECtHR case of *Valsamis* is relevant.[453] The ECtHR held that the duty to respect religious convictions arose not only in relation to the contents of education and the manner of its provisions but also in relation to the performances of all the functions assumed by the State. Respect involves more than mere acknowledgement; hence, the State should genuinely consider all possible options during the organization of education so that the religious convictions of the parents will not be violated. While it is true that individual interests have to be subordinated, in some circumstances, to the

452. *Kjeldsen, Busk Madsen and Pedersen v. Denmark*, Judgment of 7 Dec. 1976 (1979–1980) 1 EHRR 711.

453. *Valsamis v. Greece*, Judgment of 18 Dec. 1996; (1997) 24 EHRR 294.

views of the majority, the State ought to attempt to achieve a balance which shall ensure the fair and proper treatment of minorities and avoid any abuse of the position of the majority group.

460. In *Valsamis*, the applicants were a family of Jehovah's Witnesses who considered that their daughter's attendance at a school parade to mark National Day in Greece was contrary to their religious beliefs, which opposed events with military overtones. When their daughter was punished by the school authorities for not attending the school parade, the parents complained that their religious convictions had not been respected. The ECtHR held that there was no violation of the right to education since the school had exempted the daughter from religious classes, and there was nothing in the requirement to attend the school parade which could offend the applicants' pacifist convictions since such celebrations serve both pacifist objectives and the public interest.

461. Similar were the facts in the Cypriot case of *Petrides*.[454] The applicants, who were Jehovah's Witnesses, objected to their daughter's attendance at a school parade, claiming that such a parade was contrary to their religious beliefs. However, the substance of their claim was never examined by the Supreme Court since it was held that the decision of the school authorities to punish the applicant's daughter was an internal act of the administration, which could therefore not be reviewed by the Court; the exercise of school discipline was not considered to be a proper subject for judicial review.

§3. Religious Education in Public Schools

I. The Doctrinal Character of Religious Education

462. Religious lessons given in primary and secondary schools follow the doctrine of the Eastern Orthodox Church. In secondary education, the courses are given by graduates of university schools of divinity, while in primary education, they are given by the class teacher. Attendance is compulsory for Orthodox pupils; atheists or members of other religions, however, may be excused. In the 1996 Curriculum of the Ministry of Education, Sport and Youth, the subject of religious education was under the title 'Christian Orthodox Education', and it was provided that the aim of the lesson was to enable the students to realize that they are members of the Christian Orthodox Church, to learn the fundamental truths of Christianity and to experience a loving relationship with God. According to the Curriculum, pupils needed to be assisted in understanding the presence of God throughout history and the apocalypse of God as an answer to the fundamental questions of human existence; they needed to experience the figure and teachings of Jesus Christ and experience the Christian way of love towards all people, regardless of colour, religion and race.

454. *Petrides v. The Republic* [1995] 3 CLR 1793.

463. It is further provided that pupils ought to be introduced to the basic aspects of other religions and develop a critical attitude towards them so as to become able to understand and respect the religious beliefs of others. Orthodox education should provide pupils, according to the Curriculum, with the skills to appreciate the meaning of Orthodox ethics, traditions and prayer and the beneficial influence of the Church on the development and progress of civilization. In addition to the above, Orthodox education should develop the understanding of the collective worship of the Church, encourage the students to participate in such worship, and teach them to respect the value and importance of the various ecclesiastical monuments. It should also promote each individual's responsibilities towards the continuation of the Orthodox faith and way of life.[455]

464. Some of the textbooks used in Cypriot schools are edited by the Ministry of Education, Sport and Youth, while some other textbooks are edited by the Ministry of Education of Greece. The objectives of religious education in the Greek curriculum are nearly identical to the aims of religious education in the Cypriot curriculum, namely, to teach the pupils the Christian Orthodox way of life, tradition and values, to develop their religious identity and to enrich their relationship with God. In addition, Orthodox education in Greece aims to teach children the meanings of the symbols and tradition of the Orthodox faith, the meanings of the Gospels and the moral and spiritual values of Orthodox Christianity. Religious education textbooks are written by committees appointed by the Government of Cyprus, or Greece respectively. Cypriot textbooks are edited by the Ministry of Education, Sport and Youth and distributed to every pupil in public schools for free. Teachers of theology in public schools are required to teach the content of such textbooks in order to promote the aims of the Curriculum; certain teachers of theology are even members of the clergy. Textbooks include topics from the Bible, both the Old and the New Testament, the history of the Orthodox Church, the lives of the Saints, hymnography and hagiography, as well as moral teachings.[456] In view of the increase of students adhering to religious beliefs other than Orthodox Christina, there has been, in recent years, an increase in the educational material concerning other religions.

II. Exceptions

465. There is no possibility of religious education for members of other religions in public schools, with the exception of Maronites and Turkish Cypriots; the religious instruction of Maronite children who attend public schools is taught by

455. Ministry of Education, *The National Curriculum of Cyprus* 128 (Nicosia: 1996, in Greek). *See also* A. Emilianides & C. Hadjisoteriou, 'Cyprus', in *Balancing Freedom, Autonomy and Accountability in* Education 1–25 (J. deGroof & C. Glenn eds, John Hopkins School of Education and European Association for Education Law and Policy, Baltimore, 2020).

456. *See also* A. Tapakis, *Religious Education in Primary and Pre-primary Schools. A Guidebook for Primary and Pre-primary School Teachers* (Nicosia: Holy Monastery of Kykkos, 2003, in Greek), S. Fotiou, 'Religious Education at Schools in the Republic of Cyprus', in *Religious Education at Schools in Europe* 41–55 (M. Rothangel et al. eds, Vienna: Vienna University Press, 2020).

Maronite priests who receive a monthly salary from the state. Similarly, where there is an adequate number, Turkish Cypriot pupils may be religiously educated in their mother language and in their own religion, even in Greek-speaking schools. The fact that the State cannot offer religious education consistent with every single individual religion or creed is not, of course, surprising; the greater majority of the pupils in each non-Turkish public school adhere to the Orthodox Christian religion, and thus, it would be practically unfeasible for the State to provide religious education which would meet the demands of all parents. This is why the State has opted to assist children belonging to Religious Groups to attend private schools of their choice if they so desire, and further, why non-Orthodox Christian pupils may request to be exempted from religious education, including collective worship.

466. In any event, parents (or lawful guardians, as the case may be) have the right to request in writing that their children be exempted from religious education if they are not Orthodox Christians. In the case of *Arvanitakis*, the school had refused to exempt from religious education, pupils who were Jehovah's Witnesses.[457] The applicants had stressed that in the textbooks used in the classes, Jehovah's Witnesses are referred to as an anti-Christian and anti-social sect and are generally presented in a negative manner; however, their arguments were rejected by the school, which declared that attendance to all classes is obligatory for all students, irrespective of their religion. The Supreme Court had no difficulty in holding that the school had exercised its competencies in an unlawful manner.

467. Exempting, however, only pupils who do not belong to the Orthodox Church might present certain problems; parents who belong to the Orthodox Christian religion might not wish for their children to receive doctrinal religious education. Furthermore, atheists or the non-Orthodox might not wish to declare their religious beliefs to the school authorities in order to be exempted from religious education. Similar to the principle that religion should not be referred to in public documents because it might lead to indirect discrimination on the grounds of religion, revealing one's religious beliefs for the purpose of exempting one from religious education might, in a predominantly Orthodox society, also lead to discrimination; the exercise of the right to opt out of religious activities, might entail significant discomfort or embarrassment for the students, or entrench religious differences at an early stage of the students' lives. On 15 September 2016, the Ministry of Education sent directions to the schools whereby the possibility of parents adhering to the Orthodox Christian religion to request for exemption was left open, depending on the grounds to be substantiated.

III. Objections and Considerations on Reform

468. Objections might be raised with respect to the doctrinal character of religious education in Cyprus; undoubtedly, religious education in Cypriot schools does not refer to an objective study of the various religions and creeds but rather consists

457. *Arvanitakis v. The Republic* [1994] 3 CLR 859 (in Greek).

of a purely doctrinal presentation from the point of view of the Orthodox Church. This becomes evident not only from a mere reading of the purposes of the curriculum of the Ministry of Education, Sport and Youth of the Republic of Cyprus but also from the everyday manner in which religious education is carried out in Greek-speaking primary or secondary schools. In addition, collective worship only takes place in Orthodox Christian churches. Collective prayer is based on the Orthodox tradition, while religious festivities in schools follow the Orthodox tradition. It could be argued that substituting this doctrinal character of religious education with lessons of neutral religiosity, or neutral religiosity in addition to doctrinal education, could be more education-friendly towards non-Orthodox pupils and could promote pluralism.[458]

469. It could further be argued that religion is a private matter, and as such, it is not appropriate within a state-funded public school; there is no doubt that such an educational reform would definitely be strictly opposed by the Church. Actual criticism of the content of religious education in Cyprus has been relatively rare until now, a situation which could be explained by the fact that the State assists pupils belonging to Religious Groups to attend private schools of their choice by covering all fees and expenses of such students, and by the fact that non-Orthodox Christian pupils had, until recently, been few, in Greek-speaking primary and secondary schools.

470. In order to avoid the possibility of discrimination, there are two possible ways of reforming the system: either religious education could consist of neutral religiosity instead of doctrinal education, or, if the doctrinal character of religious education is to be retained, students could be asked to opt for religious education as a non-compulsory course; the latter option would have the advantage of allowing parents to ensure that their children receive religious education according to their own religion, while at the same time avoiding, or at least restricting circumstances of indirect discrimination on grounds of religion. A solution should intend, in principle, to achieve a balance between the will of the majority to have a religious education of its choice, on the one hand, and the right of the minority not to be embarrassed, on the other.[459]

IV. The Debate about Confessionals in Public Schools

471. In 2003, the Metropolitan of Limassol, Athanasios, proposed to the Ministry of Education and Culture (as it was then named) that it establish confessionals in public schools situated in the district of Limassol. According to the Metropolitans' proposal, such confessionals would function on a purely optional basis and

458. *See also* M. Zembylas, L. Loucaidis & M. Antoniou, 'The Politicisation and Securitisation of Religious Education in Greek-Cypriot Schools', *European Educational Research Journal* 18(1), 69 (2018).

459. A. Emilianides, 'Religion in Public Education in Cyprus', in *Religion in Public Education* 87–98 (G. Robbers ed., Trier: European Consortium for State and Church Research, 2011).

would only serve the needs of those pupils who wanted to confess to a religious minister of the Orthodox Church. The proposal of the Metropolitan of Limassol enjoyed the support of a unanimous Holy Synod but was rejected by the Ministry of Education and Culture, which considered that a reform of the current system was not necessary. Currently, the decision as to whether there is a need for a confessional in a school is a matter which should be decided by each particular school, following a consultation with parents, teachers and governmental authorities.

472. The proposal of the Metropolitan of Limassol was harshly criticized by certain politicians and educators who argued that it would promote the establishment of the Orthodox Christian religion in public schools and would be contrary to the principle of religious freedom. The Metropolitan of Limassol clarified that he would not insist on the implementation of his proposal, although he considered that the reactions were unjustified since confessions have always taken place in schools in a non-uniform manner; he further clarified that his proposal only aimed at a uniform approach with respect to confessions, in order to facilitate those students who wanted to confess to a religious minister.

§4. Religious Education in Private Schools

473. There are two categories of private schools in Cyprus. The first category consists of schools regularly attended by members of the three religious communities of the island. The Terra Santa primary and secondary school and the Saint Mary's private secondary school are schools regularly attended by members of the Maronite and Roman Catholic Religious Groups. The Armenians operate their own primary and secondary schools; however, the national secondary education school of the Armenians, the Melconian Educational Institute, has closed down from the academic year 2005–2006 following a decision taken by the Central Board of the Armenian General Benevolent Union at its headquarters in the United States, and despite a governmental attempt to prevent such a decision from being taken.

474. The Government has decided that the NAREG primary Armenian school shall also operate as the new secondary education school of the Armenians. The State grants annual fees in order to assist members of the Religious Groups who wish to attend such schools, while the operation of schools by religious communities, such as in the case of the Armenians, is fully funded by the State. It should be noted, however, that a significant number of pupils hailing from the three Religious Groups do not attend private schools but rather prefer to attend public schools.

475. The second category of private schools consists of mostly English-speaking private schools, such as the English School or Grammar School. It has been standard practice to fully subsidize Turkish Cypriot pupils who reside in the Government-controlled area to attend the English School. Moreover, members of the three Religious Groups who wish to attend a private school other than one associated with their own religion are subsidized, albeit not fully, since it is considered that this does not contribute to the maintenance of their culture or religious beliefs, so as to warrant full subsidization.

476. Section 25 §2 of the Private Schools Law 5/1971, which applies to both categories of private schools, stipulates that the use of physical or moral compulsion for the purpose of making a person change or preventing him/her from changing his/her religion is strictly prohibited in all private schools. As a result, the compulsory religious education of a religion or rite different from that to which the pupil belongs is not permitted. Moral compulsion within the meaning of section 25 §2 of Law 5/71 includes all attempts to change the religious convictions of a pupil through deceitful means or by abusing his/her trust or inexperience or his/her intellectual or physical incapacity.

477. An interesting case arose when the parents of students of the English School applied before the Supreme Court requesting that an order of mandamus be issued, whereby the Court would order the English School authorities to declare as a national holiday the Turkish days of Bayram. They relied on a report issued by the Ombudsman dated 14 February 2014, where she suggested that the Islamic national holidays be introduced as national holidays for all students so as to promote the principles of a multi-faith and pluralistic society. The English School has declared the days of Bayram as a national holiday for Turkish Cypriot students only, and according to the petitioners, this discriminated between Turkish Cypriot and Greek Cypriot students of the English School. The Supreme Court rejected the application on procedural grounds; it was noted that a mandamus order can only be granted against a public authority, and since the English School is a private school, no such order could be granted.[460]

§5. Teachers of Religious Education

478. At the University of Cyprus, as well as at private Universities in Cyprus, there was no School of Divinity or Theology. Those who wished to study theology resort primarily to Greece, as well as to other countries, where Orthodox theological academies enjoy the status of a University college.[461] However, in 2015, the Orthodox Church of Cyprus received a licence from the Ministry of Education and Culture (as it was then named) to register a School of Theology; the School operates as a not-for-profit charitable private educational organization. Since the academic year 2015–2016, the School offers an undergraduate degree in Theology (4 years/240 European Credit Transfer and Accumulation System (ECTS)); the programme was positively accredited in April 2017 by the Cyprus Agency of Quality

460. *Constantinou and Another* [2015] 1 CLR 1591 (in Greek).
461. *See also* A. Emilianides, 'Public Authorities and the Training of Religious Personnel in Cyprus', in *Public Authorities and the Training of Religious Personnel in Europe* 173–182 (F. Messner ed., Granada: Comares, 2015).

Assurance and Accreditation in Higher Education. It should further be noted that two private universities, the University of Nicosia and the Neapolis University of Paphos, have introduced accredited Master's programmes in Theology, which are taught in Greek. The Neapolis University was the first to introduce a Master's programme since the academic year 2011–2012, whereas the University of Nicosia introduced its own Master's programme, as well as a PhD programme, in the academic year 2015–2016. The majority of the academic faculty are, for the time being, retired Professors from the University of Athens and the Aristotle University of Thessaloniki. The graduate programmes offered by the private universities have been supported by the Orthodox Church and especially the Monastery of Kykkos, which provided a significant number of scholarships for students of the programmes.

479. A person may become a teacher of religious education, called a teacher of theology, in secondary education, only so long as he/she has graduated from a theological academy of a Greek University or from an equivalent Greek Orthodox theological school. In the case of *Stavrou*, the applicant was a teacher of religious education in the private school of the American Academy of Larnaca;[462] the applicant was a Greek Orthodox Christian, holding a Bachelor's in Religious Studies from the University of Lancaster. The Consulting Committee for Education had concluded that the applicant did not possess the necessary legal requirements for being a teacher of theology. While the recourse of the applicant was pending before the Supreme Court, the Ministry of Education decided that graduates of non-Orthodox universities may also teach in private schools, so long as they are Orthodox Christians and the teaching is in Greek.

480. What counts as service for a teacher of theology was examined in the case of *Ioannou.*[463] According to Regulation 3 §1(f)(i) of the Regulations of 1997 regarding Educational Officers (Determining Recognised Service for the Purpose of Appointment, Promotion and Remuneration), educational service also includes service in the respective Offices of Religious Elucidation of the Archdiocese or the Metropolises, *so long as it contains the element of guidance and teaching*. The applicant had been a teacher of theology in secondary education since 2002; however, from 1989 to 2000, he had been working in the Office of Religious Elucidation under the Metropolis of Paphos. The applicant requested that the Educational Service Committee recognize his prior service to the aforementioned Office.

481. The Education Service Committee decided that such a service was, in general, of an administrative character; however, it considered that his service as a teacher at Sunday schools, which had been confirmed by the local ecclesiastical committees, could be recognized as prior educational service. The Supreme Court held that the decision of the Educational Service Committee was flawed; not only teaching at Sunday schools but also guiding young couples with respect to their

462. *Stavrou v. The Republic* [1996] 3 CLR 2796 (in Greek).
463. *Ioannou v. The Republic*, App. 1131/2002, Judgment of the Supreme Court of Cyprus of 12 May 2004 (in Greek).

potential marriage, delivering religious speeches and providing guidance to the youth in order to join the church's activities and solve their various problems, were all activities containing the necessary element of guidance and teaching provided for in the Regulations of 1997. Therefore, prior service for the purpose of the Regulations of 1997 is not restricted to teaching theology.

Chapter 2. Religious Schools

482. The right of Religious Groups to set up and operate their own schools is safeguarded, and such schools are financially assisted by the State.[464] It could well be argued that there is a continuous effort to maintain the special characteristics of the various religious communities with regard to education. In principle, financial assistance is provided to the three Religious Groups of the island; religions and creeds other than the five major religions of the island may set up and operate their own schools if they so wish but will not be financially assisted by the State. The Orthodox Church and the other Christian creeds operate Sunday schools without State intervention; the right to operate Sunday schools or provide private religious education in houses or other establishments is allowed for all religions and creeds.

483. The hieratic school *Apostolos Vanavas*, bearing the name of the founder of the Orthodox Church of Cyprus, operates in Nicosia, under the supervision of the Holy Synod, as a dependence of the Monastery of Kykkos. The school was founded in 1949 and currently offers two distinct levels of courses for persons who seek to become priests. The lower level of courses is designated for graduates of elementary schools, gymnasiums, or technical schools, while the higher level is designated for graduates of lyceums. Graduates of the lower level of courses may, however, proceed to the higher level. Pupils are enabled to become acquainted with the main aspects of the Orthodox Christian teaching and the various ecclesiastical ceremonies while also acquiring general knowledge which is deemed to be necessary for carrying out their duties. The school also functions as a boarding house for those pupils who wish to stay there during their courses. In practice, the great majority of pupils of the hieratic school reside in the school during the entire duration of their courses so as to become better acquainted with their spiritual mission. There are no fees for studying in the school and the pupils further receive a monthly stipend of EUR 250 to cover their immediate everyday needs. All expenses of the school are covered by the Monastery of Kykkos.[465] Following the licensing of the Theology School of the Church,[466] the number of students attending the hieratic school significantly decreased, and its operations were terminated. Other than the hieratic school, the Orthodox Church does not operate any training programmes (other than occasional seminars) for its religious personnel, either clergymen or laypersons.

464. *See* Second Report submitted by Cyprus pursuant to Art. 25, para. 1 of the FCNM, 27 Oct. 2006, paras 28 ff. For the period before 1974 *see* C. Tornaritis, *Promotion and Protection of Human Rights of National, Ethnic and Other Religious Minorities in the Republic of Cyprus* 7 (Nicosia: 1974).

465. *See* C. Kokkinoftas, 'The Hieratical School of Apostolos Varnavas and the Education of the Cyprus Clergy' (in Greek), available in http://ieratiki.cy.net/about/201509171127.pdf. *See also* the interview of the Director of the hieratic school Antonis Kalogirou, *Simerini*, 11 Mar. 2012.

466. Paragraph 478 above.

Part X. Matrimonial and Family Law

Chapter 1. Legal Position of Religious Marriage

§1. Introduction

484. According to Article 111 of the Constitution, any family matters of the members of the Greek Orthodox Church were governed by the law of the Greek Orthodox Church and were cognizable by a tribunal of such a Church. All the aforementioned rights of the Orthodox Church were also granted to the ecclesiastical groups of the three *Religious Groups* of the Republic. Thus, Article 111 provided that the competence of the ecclesiastical courts of the Greek Orthodox Church or the ecclesiastical courts of the three Religious Groups related to any matter relating to betrothal, marriage, divorce, nullity of marriage, judicial separation, restitution of conjugal rights or to family relations other than legitimation by order of the court, or abortion.

485. In the case of *Tylliros*, however, it was held that Article 111 was intended to preserve and not to extend the competencies of the ecclesiastical tribunals of the Greek Orthodox Church (as well as of the three Religious Groups), as exercised at the time of the coming into operation of the Constitution. It was thus held that the term 'matter relating to marriage or to family relations' did not include applications for maintenance since the ecclesiastical courts did not exercise competence with respect to maintenance applications prior to Independence.[467]

486. Accordingly, marital disputes between members of the Orthodox Church, who had celebrated a religious marriage according to the rites of such a Church, used to fall under the jurisdiction of the ecclesiastical courts of the Orthodox Church. When both of the spouses-to-be were Orthodox and citizens of Cyprus, it was not possible for them to celebrate a civil marriage in Cyprus.[468] In 1977, the Supreme Court of Cyprus held that a civil marriage between members of the Orthodox Church is null to begin with, wherever it has been celebrated;[469] consequently,

467. *Tylliros v. Tylliros* [1962] 3 RSCC 21.
468. *HjiHanna v. HjiHanna* [1973] 1 CLR 186; *De Stefano v. De Stefano* [1982] 1 CLR 367.
469. *Metaxa v. Mita* [1977] 1 CLR 1, adopted in *Neophytou v. Neophytou* [1979] 1 CLR 685; *Platritis v. Platritis* [1980] 1 CLR 324; *Panayiotou v. Constantinou* [1980] 1 CLR 533; *Koutsokoumnis v. Christodoulou* [1981] 1 CLR 58; *Farmakallidou v. Theocharides* [1981] 1 CLR 724; *Venglis v. Venglis* [1982] 1 CLR 223; *Papasavvas v. Johnstone* [1984] 1 CLR 38; *Televantos v. Kyza* [1985] 1 CLR 412.

the only appropriate form of marriage for the Orthodox, the Armenians, the Maronites and the Roman Catholics was the religious form according to the rites of their respective churches. The 1980 Charter of the Orthodox Church included detailed provisions with regard to the institutions of family law that came under the jurisdiction of ecclesiastical courts, namely betrothal, marriage, divorce and adoption (Articles 217–235), as well as the organization and operation of the ecclesiastical courts (Articles 236–335).

487. The compulsory character of religious marriage and the jurisdiction of ecclesiastical law were criticized as being inconsistent with contemporary legal principles and social perceptions.[470] The need to adjust all matters relating to personal institutions to the commitments of the Republic of Cyprus towards international conventions led to the First Amendment of the Constitution (Law 95/1989), which amended Article 111.[471] The First Amendment was held to be constitutional on the basis of the doctrine of necessity.[472] According to the provisions of Law 95/1989:

(a) All matters relating to divorce, judicial separation or restitution of conjugal rights or to family relations of the members of the Orthodox Church came under the jurisdiction of a Family Court. In divorce cases, the court is composed of three members. It is presided over by a clergyman, while two laypersons act as its other two judges. If the Church does not appoint a presiding judge, which has been the practice until today, a judge is appointed by the Supreme Court of the Republic. The Family Courts came into force with Law 23/1990.
(b) All matters relating to divorce, judicial separation or restitution of conjugal rights or to family relations of the members of the three Religious Groups came under the jurisdiction of the Family Courts of the Religious Groups, which eventually came into force with Law 87/1994.
(c) The Constitution specifically provides for grounds for divorce. The grounds of irretrievable breakdown rendering the marital relationship intolerable for the plaintiff is added, while the grounds of divorce mentioned in the Charter remain in force. The House of Representatives may establish with law any other grounds for divorce; such new grounds for divorce were eventually established with the promulgation of Law 46(I)/1999 and then Law 104(I)/2003.
(d) All members of the Greek Community, including members of the Greek Orthodox Church or of the three Religious Groups, may choose to celebrate a civil marriage. This became possible after the promulgation of Law 21/1990, which established a dual regime relative to religious marriage.

---

470. *See* L. Savvides, 'Sex Discrimination in Family Law in Cyprus', *Cyprus Law Review* 4, 708–714 (1983); C. Tornaritis, *Is Reform Needed in Family Law and on Which Areas?* (Nicosia: 1979, in Greek).
471. *See* A. Emilianides, *The Cypriot Law of Marriage and Divorce* 145 ff. (Thessaloniki: Sakkoulas, 2006, in Greek).
472. *Nicolaou v. Nicolaou* [1992] 1 CLR 1338 (in Greek).

(e) Matters relating to betrothal, marriage and nullity of marriage continue to be governed by the law of the Greek Orthodox Church or the Church of the corresponding Religious Group, as the case may be.

488. The Orthodox Church considered the First Amendment of the Constitution as an affront to the religious sentiments of its members.[473] In a decision of the Holy Synod, it was declared that: 'no one had ever imagined that one day, representatives of our people in the House of Representatives, would try to take such rights away from the Church'.[474] The Holy Synod decided that the celebration of a civil marriage by a member of the Greek Orthodox Church, or the petition to the Family Courts for the dissolution of a religious marriage, would be punished by the deprival of the participation of such persons in every aspect of religious life. However, the Holy Synod eventually mellowed, since in 1991, it acknowledged that petitioning before the Family Courts is obligatory so as to have the religious dissolution of marriage recognized by the State; the Church, therefore, accepts that its members may petition the Family Courts for divorce, so long as they first petition the ecclesiastical courts and a dissolution of their marriage is granted by both courts. The Roman Catholic and Maronite Church also refused to recognize the competencies of the Family Courts of the Religious Groups.

489. The 1989 amendment to the Constitution was a step in the right direction; Cypriot family law has been modernized, and its religious character might be said to have diminished. However, the church membership of the parties remained the most important criterion for the division of people for the purposes of family law; church membership was important not only with respect to the application of the provisions of Article 111 of the Constitution but also with respect to the interpretation of the Cypriot Law of marriage and divorce.[475] Thus, family matters of members of the Greek Orthodox Church or of the three Religious Groups continued to be treated specifically in Article 111 of the Constitution, despite the fact that the competence with respect to such family matters belonged to the (State) Family Courts and not to the (religious) ecclesiastical court.

490. In addition, in view of the fact that the Orthodox Church, as well as the Maronite and Roman Catholic Church, refused to recognize the competencies of the Family Courts, in essence, if a person wanted to obtain a divorce and then celebrate a new religious marriage according to the rites of his/her respective Church, he/she had to obtain both a divorce from the Family courts which would be recognized by the State only, as well as a divorce from the ecclesiastical courts which would be

473. *See* A. Emilianides, 'The Dispute Between Church and State for the Revision of the Family Institutions', in *History of the Republic of Cyprus* 110–115 (P. Papapolyviou ed., Nicosia: Phileleftheros, 2011, Vol. III, in Greek); G. Antoniou, 'Family Law: An Ecclesiastical Approach', *Cyprus Law Review* 8, 1353–1361 (1984), (in Greek); G. Antoniou, 'Church's Opinion on Divorce', *Cyprus Law Review* 41, 6149–6157 (1993), (in Greek); P. Mpoumis, 'Dissolution of Marriage from State Courts', *Apostolos Varnavas* 51, 43–49 (1990), (in Greek).

474. *Apostolos Varnavas* 50 (1989): 324 (in Greek).

475. *See* A. Emilianides, *The Cypriot Law of Marriage and Divorce* (Thessaloniki: Sakkoulas, 2006, in Greek).

recognized by the Church authorities only; if, however, a person did not wish to celebrate a new religious marriage, but he/she wished to celebrate a civil marriage, then he/she only had to obtain a divorce from the Family courts. This peculiar situation undoubtedly caused many problems with respect to the application of family law with regard to members of the Orthodox Church and the Religious Groups of the Republic.[476] Eventually, however, with the enactment of its new Charter in 2010, the Orthodox Church impliedly recognized the jurisdiction of the Family Courts, retaining only its competencies for spiritual dissolution of the marriage. Since then the Family Courts are the only courts exercising jurisdiction with regards to marriage and divorce of members of the Orthodox Church.

491. Article 111 of the Constitution was further amended with the Eighteenth Amendment of the Constitution, Law 3(I)/2023. It is no longer provided that the Family Court adjudicating the family relations of the members of the Orthodox Church is constituted of three members, and presided by a clergyman. The composition of the Family Courts shall be determined by Law. Moreover, the Family Courts of the Religious Groups are abolished, and the Family Courts shall have jurisdiction over all family relations of the members of the three Religious Groups. The Appellate Family Court has also been abolished, and appeals shall be determined by Law. In addition, the Constitution no longer provides for grounds for divorce. The new amendment effectively further weakens the significance of religious elements in the adjudication of family law disputes. The Family Court has jurisdiction over all family law matters and applies the same law, irrespective of the religion of the parties, with the sole exception of the validity of religious marriage celebrated in accordance with the rites of the Orthodox Church or of the Religious Groups.

§2. The Extent of the Application of Article 111 of the Constitution

I. Members of the Greek Orthodox Church and Article 111 of the Constitution

492. Article 111 of the Constitution refers to members of the Greek Orthodox Church and to members of the three Religious Groups of the Republic. The definition of 'members of the three Religious Groups of the Republic' has already been considered in Part I of this monograph; this part shall define 'members of the Greek Orthodox Church' for the purposes of Article 111 of the Constitution. The courts of the Republic of Cyprus have generally accepted that since there is no definition of membership of the Greek Orthodox Community in the Constitution itself, the expression 'members of the Greek Orthodox Church' should be interpreted as referring to membership of the church, under the rules of the church itself.[477]

476. *See* G. Serghides, 'Observations on the Cypriot Marriage Law of 2003', *Armenopoulos* 58, 677 (2004), (in Greek); E. Nicolaou, 'Family Law: Legislative and Procedural Problems', *Cyprus Law Review* 49–50, 7259 ff. (1995), (in Greek).

477. *Tsivitanides v. Tsivitanides* (1956) 21 CLR 111.

493. It is doubtful, however, whether membership of the Greek Orthodox Church has to be restricted to membership of the Greek Orthodox Church of Cyprus. There are no cases of the Supreme Court of Cyprus, which provide a settled answer to such a question. There are some cases which imply that membership of the Greek Orthodox Church in terms of Article 111 of the Constitution may only cover membership of the Greek Orthodox Church of Cyprus,[478] as well as some cases which favour the view that membership of the Greek Orthodox Church in terms of Article 111 of the Constitution may cover membership of any Greek Orthodox Church.[479]

494. It is suggested that Article 111 of the Constitution relates only to members of the Greek Orthodox Church of Cyprus and not to members of other Orthodox Churches.[480] Article 111 should not be construed as a solitary provision but within the context of Part V of the Constitution, dealing with Communal Chambers, and Article 110 of the Constitution, which refers to the Autocephalous Greek Orthodox Church of Cyprus; indeed, it would be quite peculiar if the Constitution referred to members of other Orthodox Churches, or if it conferred jurisdiction – before the First Constitutional Amendment – to ecclesiastical courts of other Orthodox Churches. In any event, irrespective of whether it is accepted that membership of the Greek Orthodox Church should be confined only to the Greek Orthodox Church of Cyprus or not, membership to the Greek Orthodox Church does not require residence in Cyprus, according to the rules of the Church itself. This is due to the fact that according to Article 1 § 2 of the 2010 Charter of the Greek Orthodox Church of Cyprus, members of the Greek Orthodox Church of Cyprus are all Christian Orthodox who reside in Cyprus. Since the amendment of Article 111 of the Constitution by Law 3(I)/2023, the distinction does not anyway seem to be as significant as it used to be, as it might be of importance only in marginal cases relating to the validity of religious marriages celebrated in accordance with the rites of the Orthodox Church.

II. Is Cypriot Citizenship a Requirement for the Application of Article 111?

495. It is not clear from the wording of Article 111 of the Constitution whether the Family Courts have jurisdiction only if the parties are both citizens of Cyprus. The view that Article 111, relating to jurisdiction, applies only to citizens of Cyprus was first adopted in the case of *HjiJovanni*,[481] where the Supreme Court held that:

478. *Cosgrove v. Cosgrove* [1961] CLR 221; [1964] CLR 77; *Papasavvas v. Johnstone* [1984] 1 CLR 38. *See also* C. Tornaritis, *The Law of Marriage, as Applied in Cyprus* (Nicosia: 1986), 13.
479. *Christodoulou v. Christodoulou* [1962] CLR 68; *Antoniou v. Antoniou* [1969] 1 CLR 307. *See also* G. Serghides, *Internal and External Conflict of Laws in Regard to Family Relations in Cyprus* 142 (Nicosia: 1988).
480. *See* A. Emilianides, *The Cypriot Law of Marriage and Divorce* 159 ff. (Thessaloniki: Sakkoulas, 2006, in Greek).
481. *HjiJovanni v. HjiJovanni* [1969] 1 CLR 207.

> Considering that Article 111(1) should be read in conjunction with Article 2 (3), in which express reference is made to citizens of the Republic and having regard to the exclusion of the competence of the Communal Chambers, which have competence only on citizens of the Republic, I am of the view that Article 111 should be construed as being applicable to citizens of the Republic only, that is to say, where both parties to the cause are citizens of the Republic.

496. The view expressed in *HjiJovanni* was adopted by the Supreme Court in a series of matrimonial cases.[482] According to the above view, it is immaterial whether the parties have their residence, or their domicile in Cyprus. The only important criterion is whether they are Cypriot citizens and members of the Greek Orthodox Church. A different approach, however, was adopted by the Supreme Court in a subsequent series of cases, where it was held that the nationality of the parties was immaterial and that the only requisite for the application of Article 111 of the Constitution was the domicile of the parties in Cyprus.[483]

497. In *Papasavvas*, the Supreme Court held that the application of Article 111 of the Constitution:

> Is not confined to members of the Greek Community stricto senso, as defined in Article 2, but extends to all members of the Greek Orthodox Church, provided that they are domiciled in Cyprus. Membership of the Greek Orthodox Church under Article 111, need not of necessity coincide with membership of the Greek Community under Article 2 of the Constitution. The division of the citizens of the Republic into communities, under Article 2 of the Constitution, is directly relevant to the composition, function and jurisdiction of Communal Chambers. The application of Article 111 extends to every member of the Greek Orthodox Church of Cyprus, provided they are domiciled in Cyprus. Any other interpretation would defy the rule of private international law that the laws of the country of domicile define personal status and offend in this regard the comity of nations. It can be argued that only domiciliaries of the Greek Orthodox Church may properly be regarded as members of the Greek Orthodox Church of Cyprus.[484]

498. Also, in *Tooley*, it was held that:

> The application of the provisions of Article 111 is confined to cases where both parties are not only members of the Greek Orthodox Church, but domiciled in Cyprus as well. Any other construction would offend the rule of Private International Law that lays down that the laws of the country of domicile define personal status. Also it could lead to some strange results that could not have been intended by the makers of the Constitution, such as nullification of marriages

482. *Achcar v. Saad* [1979] 1 CLR 627; *Dokidhou v. Dokidhes* [1970] 1 CLR 124; *Papa Alexandrou v. Andreou* [1970] 1 CLR 297.

483. *Medjel v. Medjel* [1983] 1 CLR 944; *Papasavvas v. Johnstone* [1984] 1 CLR 38; *Tooley v. Tooley* [1984] 1 CLR 279.

484. *Papasavvas v. Johnstone* [1984] 1 CLR 38.

contracted in distant parts of the world between a Greek Cypriot member of the Greek Orthodox Church of Cyprus and a Greek Orthodox domiciled on that part of the world.[485]

499. The view adopted in *HjiJovanni* according to which nationality, and not domicile, is the important factor for the application of Article 111 of the Constitution was, however, once again adopted by the Supreme Court in the subsequent cases of *Chahine*[486] and *Televantos*[487] where it was held that the application of Article 111 of the Constitution was confined to Cypriot nationals. Domicile or residence of the parties was not considered to be a factor in order for the Cypriot courts to accept jurisdiction. The same view also seems to have been adopted by the House of Parliament since the introductory report of Law 95/1989, which amended Article 111 of the Constitution, held that: 'Article 111 of the Constitution refers to matters of personal status of citizens of the Republic, who belong to the Greek Community.'

500. The view according to which Article 111(2)(a) applies only with regard to matters of personal status of citizens of the Republic who belong to the Greek Community was also adopted in a series of cases subsequent to the amendment of Article 111 of the Constitution with Law 95/1989.[488] However, two other cases of the Supreme Court have adopted the approach of *Tooley*, according to which domicile, and not nationality of the parties is the important factor in order to determine whether Article 111 of the Constitution should apply.[489] Law 3(I)/2023 has further confused the issue by distinctly providing that members of the Greek Community or the Greek Orthodox Church or a Religious Group may freely opt to celebrate a civil marriage; the separate mention of members of the Greek Orthodox Church seems to indicate that the House of Representatives impliedly recognized that there could be members of the Greek Orthodox Church referred to in Article 111 §1 of the Constitution who are not Cypriot citizens.

501. The question of whether Article 111 applies only to citizens of the Republic has been the subject of much debate; however, it is suggested that the initial position of the Supreme Court in *HjiJovanni* was undoubtedly correct and that subsequent case law simply confused a rather straightforward issue.[490] Article 111 intended to remove from the competence of the Communal Chambers, those matters of family status which concerned members of the Orthodox Church or of the three Religious Groups. Article 111 is, therefore, part of Part V of the Constitution, which concerns Communal Chambers and relates to competencies otherwise

485. *Tooley v. Tooley* [1984] 1 CLR 279.
486. *Chahine v. Chahine* [1984] 1 CLR 167.
487. *Televantos v. Televantou* [1985] 1 CLR 412.
488. *Demetriou v. Demetriou* [1991] 1 CLR 1153 (in Greek); *Elia* No. 3 [1995] 1 CLR 412 (in Greek). *See* further *Mantzafou v. Demetriades* [1995] 1 CLR 762 (in Greek).
489. *Koupparis v. Koupparis* [1996] 1 CLR 670 (in Greek); *Markitanis v. Moutzouri* [1997] 1 CLR 314 (in Greek).
490. *See* A. Emilianides, *The Cypriot Law of Marriage and Divorce* 174 ff. (Thessaloniki: Sakkoulas, 2006, in Greek).

belonging to the Greek Communal Chamber; it therefore concerns members of the Greek Communal Chamber, namely Cypriot citizens. If Article 111 was intended to apply with respect to parties who were not Cypriot citizens, then Article 111 ought to also exclude competencies otherwise exercised by the House of Representatives and not simply competencies otherwise exercised by the Communal Chambers.[491] Since the amendment of Article 111 of the Constitution by Law 3(I)/2023, the distinction does not anyway seem to be as significant as it used to be, as it might be of importance only in marginal cases relating to the validity of religious marriages celebrated in accordance with the rites of the Orthodox Church.

§3. The Regime for Solemnization of Marriages in Cyprus

I. Marriages of Members of the Greek Orthodox Church and of the Three Religious Groups

502. The First Amendment of the Constitution introduced a dual system for the solemnization of marriage with respect to members of the Greek Community; hence, members of the Greek Orthodox Church or of the three Religious Groups may choose to celebrate either a civil marriage or a religious marriage according to the rites of their respective Church. A person may further celebrate both a civil and a religious marriage with the same person. Article 111 of the Constitution, however, provides that matters relating to betrothal, marriage, and nullity of religious marriage of members of the Greek Orthodox Church continue to be governed by the law of the Greek Orthodox Church or of the respective Religious Group.

503. Consequently, in case the members of the Greek Orthodox Church opt to celebrate a religious marriage, such marriage shall be solemnized according to the relevant provisions of the Charter of the Orthodox Church and so long as all requirements provided by the Charter are fulfilled.[492] Similarly, religious marriages of members of the three religious churches must be solemnized according to the Canon Law provisions of the respective Religious Group. The requirements for celebrating a religious marriage in accordance with the rites and doctrine of the Orthodox Church are set out in Articles 83 and 84 of the 2010 Charter of the Orthodox Church.[493]

504. In order to solemnize a religious marriage according to the rites of the Greek Orthodox Church, both parties have to state their consent in writing before a

491. *See* G. Serghides, *Internal and External Conflict of Laws in Regard to Family Relations in Cyprus* 201 ff. and 488 ff. (Nicosia: 1988).

492. *See* in detail A. Emilianides, *The Cypriot Law of Marriage and Divorce* 306 ff. (Thessaloniki: Sakkoulas, 2006, in Greek).

493. For a detailed analysis *see* A. Emilianides, 'The Family Law Provisions of the Charter of the Church of Cyprus' *Family Law Review* 2, 21 ff. (2011), (in Greek), S. Liasides, 'Comments – Observations on the New Charter of the Church of Cyprus' *Family Law Review* 1, 23 ff. (2011), (in Greek). *See* further A. Emilianides, *The Cypriot Law of Marriage and Divorce* 309 ff. (Thessaloniki: Sakkoulas, 2006, in Greek).

member of the clergy of the Greek Orthodox Church; their consent must be genuine and complete in accordance with section 83 §1 of the 2010 Charter of the Orthodox Church. A religious marriage may only occur so long as the parties belong to different sexes; marriage therefore denotes a marriage between a husband and wife. Both parties must further be of marriageable age, which is set at 18 years in accordance with section 83 of the 2010 Charter; however, the parties may legally celebrate a marriage even if they are below 18 years of age, so long as they have completed their 16th year of age, there is an important ground (such as pregnancy) and there is the consent of the persons having parental responsibility, as well as of the Archbishop or Bishop of the place of solemnization of the marriage.

505. The Archbishop or Bishop of the place of solemnization of the marriage may waive the consent of the persons having parental responsibility if such persons may not be found. In addition to the above, it is provided that the age difference between the husband and the wife should not exceed twenty-five years; a competent Bishop may, however, waive this requirement. For a marriage to be performed, the parties have to provide a certificate of birth, a certificate that they have not been married before and a marriage licence by the Archdiocese or the Metropolis in the area in which the marriage shall be solemnized. If the future wife, or her mother, is a displaced person who resides in an Episcopal region different than the one where she stayed prior to 1974, two marriage licences need to be issued; the future wife has to first receive a marriage licence from the Archdiocese or the Metropolis where she resided prior to 1974 and present it to the offices of the Episcopal Region where the marriage is to be solemnized in order to receive the second marriage licence.

506. Moreover, both parties must belong to the Orthodox Church; nevertheless, a competent Bishop may permit a marriage to be performed between a member of the Orthodox Church and a member of another Christian Church so long as the non-Orthodox party declares that he/she shall not interfere with the exercise of the religious duties of the Orthodox spouse and he/she shall not be opposed to the children being baptized and raised according to the rites of the Orthodox Church. An Orthodox religious marriage between a member of the Orthodox Church and a member of a non-Christian Church is prohibited. Furthermore, members of the clergy who have been consecrated, or monks, may not celebrate a marriage according to the rites of the Orthodox Church. While it is not explicitly provided for, persons who wish to solemnize a marriage should be mentally capable of understanding the consequences of their decision.

507. A person may not celebrate a valid religious marriage according to the rites of the Greek Orthodox Church unless all previous marriages, if any, have already been dissolved or annulled by a competent court. Furthermore, a person may not celebrate a marriage if he/she has already celebrated three valid marriages. In addition to the above, the parties may not celebrate a valid marriage if they are within the prohibited degrees of marriage, either in consanguinity or from affinity; a marriage between ancestors and descendants is always prohibited irrespective of the degree of relationship between the parties, as is the marriage between parties related up to the fifth degree in consanguinity, or third degree in affinity. Marriages between godparents and godchildren are also prohibited, as are marriages between the siblings of two spouses. It is further provided that neither party may celebrate a marriage within ten months from the date that the decree of dissolution or annulment of a previous marriage becomes final; such requirement may be waived in an appropriate case.

508. Since the requirements to celebrate a valid religious marriage according to the rites of the Greek Orthodox Church are provided in the Charter of the Orthodox Church, the grounds for the nullity of such marriages are also provided in the Charter. Any marriage performed in violation of the provisions of the Charter concerning the religion of the parties, the existence of previous marriages, or the prohibited degrees of marriages is null and void *ab initio*. Such a marriage shall be invalid, even if performed in another Orthodox Church abroad, so long as the solemnization of the marriage is prohibited by the Orthodox Church of Cyprus. On the contrary, a marriage performed in violation of the provisions concerning marriageable age, due to duress, or due to a mistake as to the identity of the person is voidable; consequently, such a marriage will be considered valid if the minor spouse becomes an adult without seeking the annulment of the marriage, or if the party who performed the marriage under duress or lack of consent, does not immediately seek the annulment of the marriage.

II. The Marriage Law of 2003

509. Law 21/1990 provided for the celebration of civil marriages of members of the Greek Community in accordance with the provisions of the Constitution. It should be noted that a marriage could be celebrated on the basis of the provisions of Law 21/1990 only so long as both spouses-to-be belonged to the Greek Community; civil marriages between members of the Greek Community and members of the Turkish Community or non-Cypriots could not be celebrated in accordance with the provisions of Law 21/1990. Civil marriages between members of the Greek Community and non-Cypriots or between non-Cypriots could be celebrated in Cyprus only in accordance with the provisions of the pre-existing Marriage Law Cap. 279; Cap. 279 was held to be in force in accordance with the provisions of Article 188 of the Constitution.

510. Article 22 §2(b) of the Constitution provides that if the provisions of Article 111 are not applicable to any of the parties to the marriage and neither of such parties is a member of the Turkish Community, the marriage shall be governed by a law of the Republic, enacted by the House of Representatives; similarly Article 22 §2(c) provides that if the provisions of Article 111 are applicable only to one of the parties to the marriage and the other party is not a member of the Turkish Community, the marriage shall be governed by the same law of the Republic enacted in the House of Representatives. In view of the fact that the House of Representatives had enacted no relevant law until 2003, the Supreme Court held that the Marriage Law, Cap. 279, would continue to be in force by virtue of Article 188 of the Constitution, which provides that laws enacted during British rule may continue to be in force even after the date of the coming into operation of the Constitution, to the extent that they have not been repealed and are not contrary to the provisions of the Constitution.[494]

511. Cap. 279 not only provided for the celebration of civil marriages, but also for the solemnization of religious marriages between members of the Greek Community and non-Cypriots, as well as between non-Cypriots. In addition, Cap. 279 provided for the solemnization of religious marriages between members of the Greek Community who did not belong to the Greek Orthodox Church or to a Religious Group. Such religious marriages could be solemnized so long as the respective Church had registered its marriage officers in accordance with the provisions of Cap. 279. In a case concerning Jehovah's Witnesses, the Supreme Court held that Law 21/1990 and Cap. 279 have an entirely different meaning, and thus, the registered ministers of a Church should continue to solemnize religious marriages of members of their respective Church, irrespective of whether such members belong to the Greek Community.[495]

512. In 2003, the House of Representatives enacted the new Marriage Law 104(I)/2003, which replaced both Law 21/1990 and Cap. 279. It has been debated whether the new Marriage Law provides only for the celebration of civil marriages or whether it also provides for the celebration of religious marriages, similar to the pre-existing Cap. 279. Section 3 of Law 104(I)/2003 defines marriage as a contractual agreement between a man and a woman, celebrated by a marriage officer in accordance with the provisions of Law 104(I)/2003 or by a registered religious minister in accordance with the rites of the Greek Orthodox Church or the three Religious Groups. It has been noted that the explicit reference to marriages solemnized by registered religious ministers in accordance with the rites of the Greek Orthodox Church or the three Religious Groups might imply that the solemnization of religious marriages by registered religious ministers of other religions is no longer permitted.[496] It is suggested that this is not the case.[497] Section 40 §2 of Law 104(I)/2003 provides that religious ministers who had been registered in accordance with the provisions of Cap. 279 shall continue to have the right to solemnize marriages, also in accordance with the provisions of Law 104(I)/2003; moreover, section 40 §3 of Law 104(I)/2003 provides that the Minister of Interior is authorized to register any new ministers of any religion or creed.

513. Sections 13–24 of Law 104(I)/2003 provide the requirements for performing a valid marriage, for both civil and religious marriages, celebrated in Cyprus. A

494. *Michael v. Malkiel* [1976] 1 CLR 272; *Karanikki v. The Republic* [1984] 2 CLR 144; *Mohamed* [1998] 1 CLR 1304 (in Greek).

495. *The Minister of Interior v. The Jehovah's Witnesses Congregation (Cyprus) Ltd* [1995] 3 CLR 78 (in Greek). *See* comments in A. Emilianides, *The Cypriot Law of Marriage and Divorce* 212–213 (Thessaloniki: Sakkoulas, 2006, in Greek).

496. *See* G. Serghides, 'Observations on the New Cypriot Marriage Law of 2003', *Armenopoulos* 58, 661 ff. (2003), (in Greek).

497. *See* in detail A. Emilianides, *The Cypriot Law of Marriage and Divorce* 214 ff. (Thessaloniki: Sakkoulas, 2006, in Greek).

marriage may be declared void if either party has already been validly married at the time of performing the marriage, or if the parties are related within the fifth degree of consanguinity or the third degree of affinity, or if either party had not reached the legal minimum age which is set at 18 years of age. A marriage is further considered to be *void ab initio* if it has not been registered by a registered marriage officer or religious minister, if there was no consent of the parties, or if the marriage was performed despite the fact that a competent court had issued a prohibitive decree, or if the marriage was a sham. Voidable marriages may be invalidated if there was a lack of consent due to duress, mistake or unsoundness of mind.

514. Law 104(I)/2003 provides that its provisions regarding the nullity of marriage also apply to religious marriages, which were celebrated according to the rites of the Orthodox Church or the three Religious Groups of the Republic. However, such provisions of Law 104(I)/2003 are inconsistent with Article 111 of the Constitution since Article 111 explicitly provides that matters relating to betrothal, marriage and nullity of marriage continue to be governed by the law of the Greek Orthodox Church or the Church of the corresponding Religious Group as the case may be. Therefore, a state law, such as Law 104(I)/2003, may not provide for the requirements of celebrating a religious marriage according to the rites of the Orthodox Church or the three Religious Groups of the Republic or for the grounds for declaring such a religious marriage null and void; such requirements and grounds of nullity have to be considered on the basis of the internal Canon Law of the Orthodox Church and of the three Religious Groups.[498]

III. Marriage of Members of the Turkish Cypriot Community

515. According to section 2 of the Turkish Family Courts Law, Cap. 338, the term *religious matters* for which the Turkish Family Courts have exclusive competence was defined as covering any matters concerning marriage, divorce, alimony and registration of Vakfs, but not matters concerning hereditary succession or wills. Following the enactment of the Constitution, the Turkish Family Courts essentially functioned as Turkish Communal Courts under the relevant constitutional provisions and continued to have exclusive competence with regard to marriage and divorce of Turkish Muslims, according to the provisions of the Turkish Family (Marriage and Divorce) Law, Cap. 339. The Turkish Family Law applied to all marriages of parties, at least one of whom was a Turkish resident in Cyprus professing the Muslim faith. In the case of a Muslim male, he could marry any woman, irrespective of the latter's religion. Muslim women, however, were prohibited from marrying a non-Muslim man.[499]

---

498. *See* A. Emilianides, 'What Is the Legal Status with Regard to the Adjudication of Cases of Nullity of Marriage?', *Cyprus and European Law Review* 1, 113–127 (2006).

499. *See* A. Emilianides, 'Islamic Faith as One of the Main Religions: The Case of Cyprus', in *Islam in Europe* 220–228 (M. Moravcikova ed., Bratislava: Institute for State-Church Relations, 2005).

516. As a result of the 1974 Turkish invasion and the subsequent occupation of the northern part of the Republic of Cyprus, it became impossible for any Turkish Muslims to celebrate marriages in the areas controlled by the Republic of Cyprus; this was due to the fact that section 34 of the Marriage Law, Cap. 279, provided that the provisions of that Law could not apply in marriages of parties, one of which was a Turk professing the Muslim faith. In addition, there was no court which had competence with regard to the matrimonial affairs of Turkish Muslims.

517. The right of Turkish Muslims to celebrate legal marriages in the Republic was eventually recognized by Law 46(I)/2002, which extended the application of Cap. 279 to members of the Turkish Community. The Law was enacted on the basis of the doctrine of necessity and was the result of an application to the ECtHR by the Turkish Cypriot Kemal Selim, who had complained of a violation of his right to celebrate a marriage and found a family according to Articles 8 and 12 of the ECHR.[500] When the Marriage Law, Cap. 279, was replaced by the Marriage Law 104(I)/2003, Law 120(I)/2003 provided that the provisions of Law 104(I)/03 would also apply with respect to the marriages of members of the Turkish Community, on the basis of the doctrine of necessity.

518. It was therefore provided that the application of Caps. 338 and 339 in the Republic of Cyprus would be suspended for as long as the Republic is prevented from exercising effective control over the occupied territories. The Presidents of the District Courts have the exclusive competence to adjudicate the matrimonial affairs of members of the Turkish Community who have performed their marriage under the provisions of either Cap. 279, or Law 104(I)/03. It should be observed, however, that the dissolution of the marriage may be declared only on the grounds of the English Matrimonial Causes Act, 1950, namely adultery, desertion, cruelty and mental illness. This provision is definitely a drawback and needs to be amended as soon as possible.[501] It should also be observed that the Supreme Court of Cyprus has decided that the competence with regard to marriages of members of the Turkish Community, which were performed outside of Cyprus, belongs to the Family Courts, established under the Family Courts Law 23/1990.[502]

---

500. App. 47293/99, *Selim v. Cyprus*, Judgment of 16 Jul. 2002.
501. *See also* G. Serghides, 'Observations on the Marriage Law of 2003', *Armenopoulos* 58, 6664 (2004), (in Greek).
502. *Holubova v. Mehmet Ali* [2003] 1 CLR 643 (in Greek).

Chapter 2. Legal Position of Religious Family Law

§1. The 'Right' of the Orthodox Church to Appoint the President of the Family Court

519. Article 111(2)(A) of the Constitution, as amended by Law 95/89, provided that any matter of members of the Greek Orthodox Church relating to divorce, judicial separation or restitution of conjugal rights, or to family relations, shall be cognizable by a Family Court. In the case where a member of the Greek Orthodox Church performs a religious marriage and seeks dissolution, such a Court is composed, in divorce cases, of three members: it is presided over by a clergyman, while two laypersons act as its other two judges. If the Church does not appoint a presiding judge, which had been the practice, a judge is appointed by the Supreme Court of the Republic. The Family Courts came into force with Law 23/1990. However, in addition to their constitutionally derived competencies with respect to the dissolution of religious marriages of members of the Greek Orthodox Church, the Family Courts also have jurisdiction in accordance with the provisions of Law 23/1990 with respect to the dissolution of all other religious or civil marriages, so long as such marriages do not fall within the jurisdiction of the Family Courts of Religious Groups (or do not concern marriages of members of the Turkish Cypriot Community celebrated in Cyprus).

520. The Family Courts are therefore competent to dissolve a religious or civil marriage, irrespective of the religion or creed of the parties. However, Law 23/1990 provided that in all divorce cases, the Family Courts would be composed of three members, as provided for in Article 111(2)(A) of the Constitution; namely, it is provided for that a clergyman of the Orthodox Church might be the President of the Family Court, even with respect to the dissolution of civil marriages or religious marriages which have not been celebrated according to the rites of the Orthodox Church. In view of the refusal of the Orthodox Church to appoint the President of the Family Courts or to recognize the Family Courts, the issue of the participation of a clergyman in the composition of the Family Court remained of theoretical interest only. However, in 2008, following discussions between the Church and the State, the Archbishop of Cyprus suggested to the Supreme Court that he was willing to appoint the new President of the Family Court of Larnaca-Famagusta when the previous President retired, as provided for in Article 111 of the Constitution. Despite the fact that this right of the Orthodox Church was constitutionally provided for, the Supreme Court disregarded the submission of the Archbishop and appointed a judge as the new President of the Family Court of Larnaca-Famagusta.

521. The amendment of Article 111 of the Constitution by Law 3(I)/2023 abolished the provision that the Family Courts would include a presiding member of the clergy or that they should be composed of three judges in divorce cases. The amended Article 111 §1B of the Constitution merely provides that the composition of the Family Courts shall be determined by Law. Section 3 of Law 23/1990, as amended by Law 2(I)/2023, provides that the Family Courts are composed of professional judges only and that they adjudicate in a panel of a single judge; hence, the three-judge panel for divorce cases has been abolished. Therefore, there is no longer a provision, however theoretical in nature, questioning the secular character of the Family Courts.

§2. The Family Courts of Religious Groups

522. Only the Armenian Religious Group had established its own ecclesiastical courts in Cyprus when the Constitution came into force. The ecclesiastical courts of the Roman Catholic Religious Group were situated in Jerusalem, while the ecclesiastical courts of the Maronite Religious Group were situated in Lebanon. Thus, there were no ecclesiastical courts of the Maronite and Roman Catholic Religious Groups in Cyprus, but only preparatory fact-finding committees, which then sent their report to the ecclesiastical courts situated in Lebanon and Jerusalem, respectively. This awkward situation was considered to be very problematic by the Supreme Court.[503] Since the First Amendment to the Constitution with Law 95/89, all matters relating to divorce, judicial separation or restitution of conjugal rights or to family relations of the members of the three Religious Groups came under the jurisdiction of the Family Courts of the respective Religious Groups.

523. Article 111 §3 of the Constitution, which provided for the establishment of the Family Courts of the Religious Groups, specified that such courts would be separate from the Family Courts referred to in Article 111 §2 of the Constitution. It is further provided that a relevant law will regulate matters relating to the establishment, composition and jurisdiction of the Family Courts of Religious Groups, in line with the provisions for Family Courts of members belonging to the Greek Orthodox Church. The relevant law is the Family Courts (Religious Groups) Law 87 (I)/1994, which came into effect on 1 January 1995 and established Family Courts for the Religious Groups of the Armenian, Maronite and Latins with headquarters in Nicosia.[504] The amendment of Article 111 of the Constitution by Law 3(I)/2023 abolished the Family Courts of the Religious Groups; the Family Courts have since jurisdiction regarding all family matters of members of the Religious Groups.

§3. Religious Influence on Divorce

I. Attempt of Reconciliation and Spiritual Dissolution of Religious Marriages

524. Article 111 of the Constitution stipulates that a law shall provide for the spiritual dissolution of the marriage and for the attempt at reconciliation before a

503. *Christodoulou v. Christodoulou* [1962] CLR 68; *HjiJovanni v. HjiJovanni* [1969] 1 CLR 207. *See* further G. Serghides, *Internal and External Conflict of Laws in Regard to Family Relations in Cyprus* 300 ff. (Nicosia: 1988).

504. *See* the previous edition of this monograph for details on the composition and jurisdiction of the Family Courts of Religious Groups.

Bishop; such Laws are the Attempt at Reconciliation and Spiritual Dissolution of the Marriage Law 22/1990, as amended by Law 226(I)/2022, with respect to marriages celebrated according to the rites of the Orthodox Church or according to the rites of the three Religious Groups of the Republic. There is no need for an attempt at reconciliation or for a spiritual dissolution of civil marriages or religious marriages which were not celebrated according to the rites of the Orthodox Church or the three Religious Groups. According to Law 22/1990, the person who intends to file a petition for the dissolution of a religious marriage celebrated according to the rites of the Orthodox Church must first notify the Bishop of the habitual residence of either party of such an intention. No attempt of reconciliation needs to take place if the ground for divorce is the death in absentia or insanity of the other party or if the ground of divorce is irreparable breakdown of the marriage due to violence against the other spouse or a child and there has been an official complaint to the police or to the Welfare Services of the Deputy Ministry of Social Welfare.

525. No petition for a divorce may be filed unless the competent Bishop provides the petitioner with a certificate that there has been an attempt at reconciliation which has failed or if six weeks have lapsed from the date when the notification was sent to the Bishop. In any event, a party may file the petition for a divorce after the lapse of the six-week period. In cases where a party has not complied with the requirements of Law 22/1990, the petition shall be dismissed as premature;[505] in the case of *Papapetrou,* the petition was dismissed because the notification had been sent to the Bishop of Salamis, despite the fact that the Bishop of the habitual residence of the parties was the Metropolitan of Limassol.[506] The geographical limits of the Archdiocese, as well as the Metropolises of Paphos, Kition, Kyrenia, Limassol, Morphou, Constantia and Famagusta, Kykkou and Tillyrias, Tamasou and Oreinis, Trimythountos and Lefkaron, as well as the Dioceses of Karpasia, Arsinoes and Amathous, are determined in Annex I of the 2010 Charter of the Orthodox Church. Upon receiving the notification, the Bishop should invite by written notification both spouses to appear in person before him and then attempt to reconcile them with all the appropriate, at his discretion, spiritual means, in accordance with section 4 of Law 22/90; the means employed by the Bishop may not be judicially reviewed.

526. In practice, the Orthodox Church of Cyprus was not attempting any reconciliation of the marriage up to 2010 since it did not recognize the jurisdiction of the Family Courts; instead, it was sending a formal letter whose text was determined by the Holy Synod on 2 May 1991 and which informed the parties that the Family Courts have no jurisdiction to dissolve a marriage which was celebrated in accordance with the rites of the Orthodox Church. Ever since the enactment of its new Charter in 2010, however, the Orthodox Church has attempted the reconciliation of all religious marriages celebrated according to its rites.

---

505. *Zeniou v. Zeniou* [2002] 1 CLR 1175 (in Greek).
506. *Papapetrou v. Papapetrou* [2001] 1 CLR 1578 (in Greek).

527. Article 87 of the 2010 Charter provides that prior to the spiritual dissolution of the marriage and, consequently, the petition for divorce, there should be an attempt at reconciliation of the spouses before the Bishop of the habitual residence of either spouse in Cyprus; no attempt of reconciliation should take place if the ground for divorce is the death in absentia or insanity of the other party. If, due to exceptional circumstances, it is impossible for one of the spouses to participate in the attempt for reconciliation, the Bishop may waive it. Attempt for reconciliation is not considered by the Church as a judicial or legal act but rather a demonstration of the pastoral care and responsibility of the Church. A person has to appear in person before the Bishop or an experienced priest who has been authorized by the Bishop to conduct the attempt for reconciliation. The attempt for reconciliation has to be completed within a period of three months.

528. Until the enactment of its new Charter of 2010, the Orthodox Church did not spiritually dissolve the marriage in accordance with the procedure provided for in section 7 of Law 22/90; this was due to the fact that the ecclesiastical courts of the Orthodox Church continued to function and issue divorces even after the amendment of Article 111 of the Constitution by Law 95/89, contrary to the provisions of the Constitution. However, the new Charter of 2010 no longer provides for the functioning of ecclesiastical courts but only for the spiritual dissolution of the marriage. Article 88 of the 2010 Charter provides that the Bishop who undertook the attempt to reconcile the parties, or if that could not take place, the Bishop of the place where the petitioner habitually resides, may spiritually dissolve the marriage. The petition for spiritual dissolution is not subject to a specific form and can be filed either personally, through a proxy, or even through the priest of the petitioner's parish.

529. The petitioner ought to personally, or if there are exceptional circumstances by a proxy, appear before a Council of Spiritual Dissolution of the Marriage composed of the three clergymen appointed by the Bishop. It is provided that the Council should make every effort, if, of course there is such a possibility, to maintain the marriage; if this is not possible, then the Council should propose to the Bishop the spiritual dissolution of the marriage. If the marriage has objectively or subjectively dissolved and its spiritual dissolution shall not further burden the established legal and factual situation, the spiritual dissolution shall be granted. There is no time limit for submitting a petition for a spiritual dissolution of the marriage.

530. It has been suggested that the procedure set out by Article 88 of the 2010 Charter is incompatible with section 7 of Law 22/90, which provides that the Bishop should spiritually dissolve the marriage within fifteen days.[507] This is correct; however, it should be noted that the spiritual dissolution is part of the ecclesiastical legal order and not of the state legal order. The Orthodox Church has set out a procedure in accordance with which the spiritual dissolution of the marriage is a condition for

507. S. Liasides, 'Comments – Observations on the New Charter of the Church of Cyprus' *Family Law Review* 1, 33–34 (2011), (in Greek), G. Serghides, 'Cyprus Family Jurisdiction: Ratione Personae and Ratione Materiae', *Family Law Review* 2, 14–16 (2011).

celebrating a second religious marriage and not as a pre-condition for the dissolution of the marriage by the Family Courts. The new Charter has abolished the ecclesiastical courts and the dual, unconstitutional divorce proceedings; the role of the Church is now only to spiritually dissolve the marriage in accordance with the Constitution. The aim of the procedure for spiritual dissolution is not to replicate the divorce proceedings held before the Family Courts but rather to force the parties to attend before the Bishop for an attempt at reconciliation.

531. By providing that the appearance for the attempt of reconciliation is a prerequisite for the marriage to be spiritually dissolved, the Orthodox Church has ensured that the parties would have to attend for the attempt of reconciliation; otherwise, the spouses would simply wait for the lapse of six-week period in order to file a petition before the Family Court. It is, of course, regrettable that the new Charter does not expressly refer to the Family Courts and the procedure held before them; however, the Holy Synod did not wish to explicitly recognize the jurisdiction of the Family Courts. Taking that into account, the provisions of the new Charter safeguard that if the Family Court has granted a decree of divorce, then the marriage shall be considered as having been objectively dissolved, and the spiritual dissolution shall be granted. Any practical problems may be solved by the relevant Directions of the Holy Synod.[508]

532. With respect to the three Religious Groups of the Republic, sections 9–16 of Law 22/90, as amended by Law 226(I)/22, provide that the notification must be sent to the competent religious leader of the respective Religious Group of the parties. However, no notification needs to be sent in cases where a decree of divorce is not recognized by the Canon Law of the respective Religious Group; thus, no notification needs to be sent in cases of dissolution of marriages of members of either the Roman Catholic Religious Group or the Maronite Religious Group. Furthermore, no attempt at reconciliation should take place if the ground for divorce is the death in absentia or insanity of the other party or if the ground of divorce is irreparable breakdown of the marriage due to violence against the other spouse or a child and there has been an official complaint to the police or to the Welfare Services of the Deputy Ministry of Social Welfare. In view of the above, a notification need only be sent in the case of marriages celebrated according to the rites of the Armenian Religious Group; such notification should be sent to the Prelate of the Armenian Church. The Prelate may attempt to reconcile the parties within the period of six weeks; once the six-week period has lapsed, each party may file the petition for divorce before the Family Court.

---

508. A. Emilianides, *Family and Succession Law in Cyprus* (The Hague: Kluwer 2nd ed. 2019): A. Emilianides, 'The Family Law Provisions of the Charter of the Church of Cyprus' *Family Law Review* 2, 21 ff. (2011), (in Greek), C. Katsaros, 'The Attempt for Reconciliation and the Spiritual Dissolution of the Marriage', in *The New Charter of the Church of Cyprus* 137–165(A. Emilianides & C. Katsaros eds, Nicosia: Hippasus, 2013, in Greek).

II. Grounds for Divorce

533. Article 111 of the Constitution, as amended by Law 95/89, provided that the ten grounds for divorce stipulated in the 1980 Charter of the Orthodox Church would remain in force with respect to marriages of members of the Greek Orthodox Church; such grounds for divorce were the following: (a) adultery of the other party; (b) immoral or otherwise unacceptable conduct of the other party, so that the petitioner may no longer be expected to live with him/her; (c) intention of the other party to murder the petitioner; (d) insanity of the other party for at least three years; (e) conviction of the other party for imprisonment for a term of at least seven years (f) disappearance of the other party for at least three years; (g) incapacity of the other party to consummate the marriage for at least six months after the celebration of the marriage; (h) desertion of the petitioner by the other party for at least two years; (i) change of religion by the other party; or (j) for deliberately preventing child-bearing, despite the will of the petitioner. Thus, all grounds for divorce stipulated in the 1980 Charter of the Orthodox Church required that the defendant was at fault and that the petitioner was an innocent party.[509] The 2010 Charter of the Orthodox Church did not, however, include any grounds for divorce. The amendment of Article 111 of the Constitution by Law 3(I)/2023 eventually abolished the ten grounds of divorce of the 1980 Charter.

534. Article 111 of the Constitution introduced the ground of irretrievable breakdown rendering the marital relationship intolerable for the petitioner, with respect to marriages of members of the Greek Orthodox Church. Irretrievable breakdown may occur, either due to the conduct of the defendant or due to the conduct of both parties. Thus, contrary to what was provided in the 1980 Charter of the Orthodox Church, the ground of irretrievable breakdown may be proved even if both parties are at fault; however, divorce will not be granted if the only party who is at fault is the petitioner.[510] The Constitution further provided that the House of Representatives may establish any other grounds for divorce; the House of Representatives eventually established new grounds for divorce with the promulgation of Law 46(I)/1999, which introduced as a ground for divorce, the fact that the parties have lived apart for a period of at least five years immediately preceding the petition. The ground of the five-year separation of the parties does not depend upon proof of fault of either party and was deemed to be constitutional in the case of *Zenios*.[511] Law 104(I)/2003 further introduced four other grounds for divorce, namely: (a) change

---

509. *See* in detail G. Serghides, *Grounds of Divorce* (Nicosia, 2007, Vols I–II, in Greek); A. Emilianides, *The Cypriot Law of Marriage and Divorce* 250 ff. (Thessaloniki: Sakkoulas, 2006, in Greek). *See* further E. Nicolaou, 'Grounds for Divorce in Cypriot Family Law and Cypriot Case-Law', *Cyprus Law Review* 41, 6171–6179 (1993), (in Greek); L. Loucaides, 'Grounds for Divorce', *Cyprus Law Review* 4, 681–696 (1983), (in Greek); C. Melas, 'Grounds for Divorce in Cypriot Family Law and Relevant Problems of Interpretation', *Cyprus Law Review* 41, 6159–6170 (1993), (in Greek); C. Tornaritis, *Divorce* (Nicosia: 1979).

510. *See* G. Serghides, 'Grounds for Divorce under the Law of Cyprus: The Road to Europe', *Paneuropean Law Review* 1, 31–43 (1997).

511. *Zenios v. Zenios* [2002] 1 CLR 445 (in Greek).

of sex of the other party; (b) desertion of the petitioner; (c) intention of the other party to murder the petitioner; and (d) four-year separation.[512]

535. The amendment of Article 111 of the Constitution by Law 3(I)/2023 abolished any reference to grounds of divorce in the Constitution. Section 27 of Law 104(I)/03, as amended by Law 1(I)/2023, provides for the following grounds of divorce: (a) irretrievable breakdown rendering the marital relationship intolerable for the petitioner, due to the conduct of the defendant or of both parties; there is a rebuttable presumption that there is irretrievable breakdown if there is bigamy, adultery, desertion of the petitioner, attempt to murder the petitioner, or violence against the other spouse or a child, (b) separation of the spouses for at least two years; this amounts to an irrebutable presumption that the marriage has broken down and is not affected by attempts for reconciliation not exceeding three months in total, (c) divorce by consent; this also amounts to an irrebutable presumption that the marriage has broken down. The spouses should declare freely and without external influence before the Family Court that they wish to divorce. The petition may be filed by both spouses, or either spouse, six months after the marriage was celebrated, (d) change of sex of the other party, and (e) absentia of the other party. The grounds of divorce provided in section 27 of Law 104(I)/03 apply with regards to all mariages, including marriages of members of the three Religious Groups. The amendments introduced by Law 3(I)/2023 are welcome and in accordance with the previous edition of this monograph, where it was observed that the attempt to regulate divorce on the basis of the religion of the parties was extremely complicated and unnecessary and that there should be a radical reform of the Law of marriage and divorce.

512. For criticism *see* G. Serghides, 'Observations on the Marriage Law of 2003', *Armenopoulos* 58, 674 (2004), (in Greek); A. Emilianides, *The Cypriot Law of Marriage and Divorce* 267–269 (Thessaloniki: Sakkoulas, 2006, in Greek).

Part XI. Religion and Culture

Chapter 1. Religion and Art

536. Byzantine art is the term commonly used to describe the artistic products of the Byzantine Empire; Byzantine art was influenced, in particular, by the Orthodox Christian tradition so that the two are often considered intrinsically linked. Orthodox Christians have continued to produce art influenced by the artistic traditions of the Byzantine era, particularly with regard to icon painting and church architecture; as a result, the art of the Orthodox Churches in Cyprus, similar to other parts of Eastern Christianity, is influenced by religion and by artistic traditions which originate from the Byzantine era. Orthodox Churches in Cyprus were built with altars, thrones, iconostases, icons, ecclesiastical vessels, gospels and hymn books and are considered to represent a purely religious artistic tradition associated with Eastern Christianity.

537. The 1974 Turkish invasion resulted, among other effects, in the continuing occupation of more than 500 churches, chapels, temples and monasteries. Since then, Turkey has refused to cooperate in any way with the Church of Cyprus or with the Government of the Republic in order to safeguard the maintenance and conservation of the occupied churches. Consequently, many of the Orthodox Churches are currently in poor condition or ruined, having been looted and plundered. The Church of Avgasida has been completely destroyed, as have three chapels in Trikomo dedicated to St Demetrius, St Mamas and St Catherine. In addition, more than 133 churches, chapels and monasteries have been desecrated, 78 churches have been converted into mosques, 28 have been used as military depots and a hospital and 13 are used as stockyards; their ecclesiastical items, including more than 15,000 icons have been illegally removed and their location remains unknown.[513]

538. On 12 July 2006, the European Parliament adopted a written declaration calling on greater efforts to protect and preserve religious heritage in occupied Cyprus. The declaration, signed by 407 MEPs, condemned the pillage of Greek Orthodox Churches and the removal of their ecclesiastical items and called on the Commission and the Council of the European Communities to take all necessary actions to ensure the protection and restoration of the affected churches to their

513. *See* D. Demosthenous, *The Occupied Churches of Cyprus* (Nicosia: Monastery of Kykkos, 2000); Y. Matsis, 'International Crime: The Turkish Invasion on Cyprus and the Pillage and Theft of the Cyprus Cultural Heritage', *Cyprus Law Review* 15, 2343–2345 (1986).

original Greek Orthodox status. In 2007, two reports by the Vatican and the Onassis Foundation, respectively, confirmed that a cultural destruction of all Greek Orthodox Churches in occupied Cyprus, as well as of churches belonging to Roman Catholics, Maronites and Armenians, has been occurring; it was concluded by the reports that Turkey intends to eliminate all traces of Christianity in the occupied area through the systematic destruction of the religious cultural heritage of the Christians of the island. A more recent detailed study undertaken by the Monastery of Kykkos further confirmed the looting, destruction and pillaging of the Christian Churches in the occupied areas.[514]

539. Following a lengthy legal battle in the United States of America, the Orthodox Church has recovered priceless frescoes – the so-called Kanakaria mosaics – which had been stolen from the occupied areas. The details of the *Kanakaria* case are the following:[515] in the early sixth century, a large mosaic was affixed to the Kanakaria Church in the village of Lythrankomi in Cyprus. The mosaic depicted Jesus Christ as a young boy in the lap of his mother, the Virgin Mary, who was seated on a throne; Jesus and Mary were attended by two archangels and were surrounded by a frieze depicting the twelve apostles. The mosaic had been displayed in the Kanakaria Church for centuries and had become sanctified as a holy relic under the practices of Eastern Orthodox Christianity, being one of only a handful of such Byzantine relics to survive into the twentieth century. When the Orthodox priests evacuated the Kanakaria Church due to the Turkish invasion, the mosaic was still intact; however, the Kanakaria Church was one of the many churches plundered and reduced to a stable for farm animals, while the mosaic was looted. The Republic of Cyprus, with the assistance of many international organizations, attempted to track the fate of the stolen mosaic – as well as other stolen cultural properties – in order to recover it.

540. Through its efforts, the Republic managed to recover and return to the Church of Cyprus several stolen relics and antiquities; eventually, the frescoes and mosaics taken from the Kanakaria Church were located. Goldberg, an art dealer, enjoyed possession of four Kanakaria mosaics, each measuring about two feet square, depicting the figure of Jesus, the busts of one of the attending archangels, the Apostle Matthew and the Apostle James, respectively. After their request for the return of the mosaics was refused by Goldberg, the Republic and the Church of Cyprus brought a suit in the Southern District of Indiana for the recovery of the mosaics; it was held that possession of the mosaics ought to be awarded to the Church. Goldberg filed an appeal.

514. C. Chotzakoglou, *Religious Monuments in Turkish Occupied Cyprus* (Nicosia: Monastery of Kykkos, 2008).

515. *Autocephalous Greek – Orthodox Church of Cyprus and Another v. Goldberg and Another* 917 F 2d 278 [1990]. *See* further Cyprus Law Tribune, *Kanakaria Mosaics: The Trial* (Nicosia: 2nd ed. 1994); M. Kyprianou, 'Caveat Emptor: The Four Byzantine Mosaics and the Struggle to Good Title', in *Proceedings of the 10th Commonwealth Law Conference* 659–670 (Nicosia: 1993); W. Muir, 'La Revendication Internationale des Biens Culturels à Propos de la Décision Américaine Eglise Autocephale', *Revue Critique de Droit International Privé* 81, 1–34 (1992).

541. The United States Court of Appeal observed that the Constitution of Cyprus recognizes the existence of the Autocephalous Orthodox Church of Cyprus and grants it the exclusive right to regulate and administer its own internal affairs and property in accordance with the Holy Canons and its Charter. It further observed that under the Immovable Property Law, a religious corporation may own and register property and that the Church of Cyprus had registered the Kanakaria Church in the Land Registry Office of the Republic of Cyprus. In view of the above, the Court held that:

> As Byron's poem laments, war can reduce our grandest and most sacred temples to mere 'fragments of stone'. Only the lowest of scoundrels attempt to reap personal gain from this collective loss. Those who plundered the churches and monuments of war-torn Cyprus, hoarded their relics away, and are now smuggling and selling them for large sums, are just such blackguards. The Republic of Cyprus, with diligent effort and the help of friends has been able to locate several of these stolen antiquities; items of vast cultural, religious (and, as this case demonstrates, monetary) value. Among such findings are the pieces of the Kanakaria mosaic at issue in this case. Unfortunately, when these mosaics surfaced they were in the hands not of the most guilty parties, but of Peg Goldberg and her gallery. Correctly applying Indiana law, the district court determined that Goldberg must return the mosaics to their rightful owner: the Church of Cyprus.

542. The Court concluded that:

> Goldberg's tireless attacks have not established reversible error in that determination and thus, for the reasons discussed above, the district court's judgment is affirmed. Lest this result seem too harsh, we should note that those who wish to purchase art work on the international market, undoubtedly a ticklish business, are not without means by which to protect themselves. Especially when circumstances are as suspicious as those that faced Peg Goldberg, prospective purchasers would do best to do more than make a few last-minute phone calls. As testified to at trial, in a transaction like this, 'All the red flags are up, all the red lights are on, all the sirens are blaring.' In such cases, dealers can (and probably should) take steps such as a formal IFAR search; a documented authenticity check by disinterested experts; a full background search of the seller and his/her claim of title; insurance protection and a contingency sales contract; and the like. If Goldberg would have pursued such methods, perhaps she would have discovered in time what she has now discovered too late: the Church has a valid, superior and enforceable claim to these Byzantine treasures, which therefore must be returned to it.[516]

516. *Autocephalous Greek – Orthodox Church of Cyprus and Another v. Goldberg and Another* 917 F 2d 278 [1990].

543. Currently, the Church continues its attempts to repatriate further religious relics.[517] In addition, the Church of Cyprus has been functioning as a Centre for the Maintenance of Icons and Manuscripts since 1972, with the purpose of preserving the archaeological and cultural treasures of the Church. Moreover, an Office for the documentation of Byzantine icons functions in collaboration with the Antiquities Department of the Republic. The Monastery of Kykkos also supports a research centre, as well as a museum, aiming at the documentation of the cultural and religious history of Cyprus and the financing of relevant publications.

517. *See also* T. Hadjitofi, *The Icon Hunter* (New York: Pegasus, 2018), Department of Antiquities, 'The Looting of Cultural Heritage in Occupied Cyprus', available in http://www.mcw.gov.cy/mcw/DA/DA.nsf/All/49DAF5E76419EBAC42257C300035C4BA?OpenDocument.

Chapter 2. Religion and Media

544. The first private television channel in Cyprus belonged to the Orthodox Church, and it was named *Logos*; the Church received governmental permission to broadcast a private television channel in 1992. *Logos* first aired on 26 April 1992 with live coverage of the Christian Easter celebrations from the St John Cathedral in Nicosia. The name of the channel could be translated in English as *speech* or *reason*, but in the Christian tradition, *Logos* is identified as God. The Gospel of John identifies Jesus Christ as the incarnation of the Logos, through which everything is created. The purpose of the television channel was to:

> promote and transmit Christian spirituality, Orthodox tradition, Church's role and actions, as well as its contribution to the struggle for the liberation of semi-occupied Cyprus, without, however, neglecting the need for providing accurate, objective and direct information to the public as well as entertainment.

545. Due to financial problems, the Church decided to rent its governmental permission to broadcast to the Greek television channel *Mega* in exchange for monetary compensation. The Cypriot television channel *Mega* was, in essence, a local branch of the Greek television channel *Mega* and mainly transmitted serials, movies and other programmes also transmitted in Greece. Nevertheless, *Mega* also transmitted programmes of local interest, such as news, talk shows, or Cypriot productions. The Orthodox Church had retained, according to the Agreement to rent its permission, the right to transmit certain religious or spiritual programmes through the channel and even participate, albeit in a limited manner, in the policy decisions of the channel with respect to the Cyprus Problem. *Mega* was the third largest free-to-air private television channel in Cyprus. Whereas the Archdiocese signed a new agreement in accordance with which the Orthodox Church became the dominant shareholder and administrator of the *Mega* channel, financial problems in the Greek Channel *Mega* led to the termination of the use of the name *Mega* and the transmission of the respective Greek program. The channel was renamed TVOne in 2017, and the licence was eventually rented by the Church to a company led by right-wing businessman and former Minister Socratis Hasikos in 2018.

546. News concerning the Orthodox Church and major religious activities, such as Easter celebrations, is transmitted by private free-to-air television channels, as well as the two state-owned television channels. The Archbishop of the Orthodox Church is considered to be a significant public figure, and therefore, his views on various political, social or spiritual issues are often reproduced or commented upon in news and talk shows. In addition, the Orthodox Church currently owns a Pancyprian private radio station called *Alithinos Logos* (true reason); *Alithinos Logos* was, until 2022, a local radio station named St Demetrius. The radio station mainly focuses on religious and spiritual programmes. The Church had previously owned a leading pancyprian radio station called *Logos* for twenty-six years. *Logos* was first transmitted on 24 April 1992 and was one of the island's first private radio stations.

It focused on religious, spiritual and cultural programmes, Greek music, as well as talk shows. There are other church-owned radio stations, which, however, only transmit locally and not all over Cyprus.

547. Transmissions concerning religious or spiritual issues are also broadcast by the other major private radio stations of the island, as well as the state-owned Cyprus Broadcasting Corporation (CyBC).[518] The CyBC Law, Cap. 300A, makes a brave attempt to accommodate the various minority interests by providing access to the media and ensuring that all religious organizations enjoy a certain amount of broadcast time.[519] Section 19 of Cap. 300A specifies that the CyBC shall ensure the provision of public radio television service with unbiased attention and respect to the interests and sensitivities of the Greek Cypriot and Turkish Cypriot Communities, the Religious Groups and the various minorities in Cyprus. Furthermore, Regulations 616/2003, issued under Cap. 300A, require that, for the purpose of fulfilling its obligations to provide a balanced service, the CyBC must provide, *inter alia*, information programmes addressed to the overseas Cypriots, the Turkish Cypriots, and the minority religions, as well as programmes on the environment, art and traditional cultural activities of the communities of Cyprus, such as, for example, their activities in music, dance, poetry, pantomime painting and sculpture. The Government policy statement on public service broadcasting, issued in January 2003, further stated that:

> Cyprus Broadcasting Corporation (CyBC) provides radio and television programmes for all Cypriot communities. Special importance is placed on the significant proportion of its programming devoted to the Turkish Cypriot Community.
>
> These programmes contribute, *inter alia*, to keeping the Turkish Cypriots informed on political issues, as well as regarding the developments ahead of Cyprus' membership in the EU. It further states that … *the CyBC is generally regarded an especially reliable source of information and representation of the news.* … In this way (the public service broadcasting organization) enriches public dialogue ensuring the balanced participation of all citizens in public life.

548. The CyBC Second Programme broadcasts a multicultural daily radio programme in the Armenian language. This one-hour programme includes news coverage, extensive interviews, cultural reports and Armenian music and covers a variety of subjects, such as health, literature and religion. This programme reaches Armenians outside Cyprus, in Lebanon, Syria, Iran, Bulgaria and Greece. It is the only broadcast in the Armenian language in the area. CyBC First Programme further broadcasts a weekly one-hour radio programme concerning the Maronite Religious Group (The Voice of the Maronites), which deals with their religious and

518. *See* in detail C. Stratilatis & A. Emilianides, *Media Law in Cyprus* (The Hague: Kluwer 2nd ed. 2019).

519. *See* D. Gomien, 'Pluralism and Minority Access to Media', in *The Strength of Diversity: Human Rights and Pluralist Democracy* 57 (A. Rosas & J. Helgesen eds Dordrecht: Martinus Nijhoff Publishers, 1992).

cultural activities, as well as a half-hour weekly programme concerning the Roman Catholic Religious Group (The Latin Community of Cyprus-Yesterday and Today).

549. On television, the only programme transmitted on a regular basis concerning Religious Groups is the one-hour variety of entertainment programmes transmitted in the Armenian language and shown on CyBC television; Armenian schools participate actively in this programme with music, choir and dance groups. Other transmissions may occasionally refer to specific issues concerning the three Religious Groups of the Republic, instigated by current events or by anniversaries. There are no special issues concerning the Islamic religion of the island; however, the CyBC transmits a number of programmes concerning the Turkish Cypriot Community of the island, and transmitted in the Turkish language, including news bulletins, broadcasts, music, poetry, multicultural programmes and talk shows.[520]

550. The Cyprus Radio Television Authority (RTA) is an independent regulatory body established under the Radio and Television Stations Law (Law 7(I)/1998, as amended). It is solely concerned with regulating private radio and television stations broadcasting in Cyprus. The responsibilities of the RTA are laid down by Law 7(I)/1998 and Regulations. Law 7(I)/1998 prescribes the principles governing the broadcast of radio and television programmes and commercials. These include: (a) plurality of views and maximum accessibility of the civil society; (b) respect for the personality, dignity and private lives of persons; (c) respect for democratic principles and human rights; (d) preservation of the national identity and the cultural inheritance of the people of Cyprus; (e) protection of minors from harmful programmes such as films portraying gratuitous violence or glamorizing anti-social behaviour; (f) the right of individuals to reply or redress in the event that reports affecting them or their activities, are inaccurate or misleading; and (g) maintaining linguistic standards. All television channels and radio stations are further obliged by Law 7(I)/1998 to ensure that their transmissions do not in any way incite hatred or encourage discrimination on account of race, gender, religion or nationality. Therefore, religious hatred or preference towards a single religion to the exclusion of other religions in such a manner as to lead to discrimination on account of religion is strictly prohibited. If a transmission refers to a religious faith in a manner that is considered to be discriminatory, then the RTA may impose a fine on the television channel or radio channel.

520. Second Report Submitted by Cyprus, pursuant to Art. 25, para. 1 of the FCNM, 27 Oct. 2006, paras 35, 48 ff.

Chapter 3. Religion and Civil Society

551. Religion has a central role in the civil society of the island. Many clubs, associations or institutions on the island are either funded by the Church or related to religious activities. The Orthodox Church publishes a bi-monthly official journal named 'Apostolos Varnavas', while several other magazines promote the doctrines of the Orthodox tradition. It should also be noted that the Armenians and Maronites have their own newspapers. The Armenian Church in Cyprus brings out its own monthly bulletin, 'Keghart' in Armenian. The Melkonian Educational Institute used to publish a multilingual periodical 'Hayatsk' (est. 1998) in Armenian, Greek, English, Russian and Bulgarian.

552. Research work on religion in Cyprus focuses mostly on the foundation and development of the Orthodox Church of Cyprus and of the three Religious Groups and refers mostly to doctrinal, theological, sociological and historical aspects. In general, it could be concluded that religious identity is thus considered an intrinsic element of Cypriot identity, associated with the traditions, values and customs of Greek Cypriots. During the elections for Archbishop of the Orthodox Church of Cyprus, which were held from September until November 2006, approximately 50% of Orthodox Christians opted to cast a vote for the candidate of their choice; the elections for a new Archbishop were the main issue covered by the media during that period, a fact which strengthens the view that religion is considered as a pillar of Cypriot society. Whereas the 2022 elections for Archbishop were also heavily covered by the media and discussed by the public, only 30% of Orthodox Christians opted to cast a vote. This was partly due to the new electoral system, which diminished the importance of the popular vote since the final organ electing the Archbishop was the Holy Synod.

Chapter 4. Religion and Public Debate

553. Religion is part of the public debate of Cypriot society. As already noted in the relevant chapters, the Archbishop of Cyprus' views on the future of the Cyprus Problem are discussed by the media and political actors. The extent of involvement of religious actors in politics and of political actors in religious affairs is often debated, while issues, such as religion and family law, or church financing, are considered an essential part of the public debate. In addition to the above, there are many debates about religion as a social or historical phenomenon, while doctrinal aspects of the Orthodox religion, Christian morality, and sects are issues which interest the public and secure media attention. There is little doubt that the internal aspects of Cypriot society cannot be properly understood without considering the religious roots of its people.

Selected Bibliography

For a complete list, *see* A. Emilianides, *Digital Bibliography of Cypriot Law*, available at www.cypriotlaw.com.

I. Books

A. In Greek

Emilianides, A. *The Cypriot Law of Marriage and Divorce*. Athens-Thessaloniki: Sakkoulas, 2006.

Emilianides, A. *The Status of the Armenian Church of Cyprus*. Nicosia: Cyprus Institute of Church and State Relations, 2006.

Emilianides, A. *The Status of the Old-Calendar Church of Cyprus*. Nicosia: Cyprus Institute of Church and State Relations, 2008.

Emilianides, A. & C. Katsaros (eds). *The New Charter of the Church of Cyprus*. Nicosia: Hippasus, 2013.

Gavrielides, A. *The Ethnarchic Rights and the Referendum for Union with Greece*. 2nd ed. Nicosia: 1972.

Gavrielides, A. *Nomocanonical and Political Study on the Unfrocking of Bishops in Cyprus in Conjunction to the Exercise of Their Ethnarchical Rights*. 2nd ed. Nicosia: 1973.

Kastanas, I. *The Right to Appeal (Ekkliton) before the Ecumenical Patriarch in the Church of Cyprus*. Athens-Nicosia: Hippasus, 2021.

Konidaris, I. & A. Emilianides. *Elements of Greek and Cypriot Law on Religion*. Athens-Thessaloniki: Sakkoulas, 2016.

Mantzouneas, E. *Ecclesiastical Law of the Apostolic, Autocephalous Orthodox Church of Cyprus*. Evrichou: 1988.

Papastathis, C. *On the Administrative Organisation of the Church of Cyprus*. Thessaloniki: 1981.

Polyzoides, C. *Memorandum on the Charter of the Church of Cyprus*. Thessaloniki: 1997.

Tzortzatos, V. *The Fundamental Institutions of Administration of the Church of Cyprus*. Athens: 1974.

B. Other than Greek

Emilianides, A. (ed.). *Welfare of the Child and Beliefs of the Parents: Blood Transfusion, Religious Education and Custody*. Nicosia: University of Nicosia Press, 2010.

Selected Bibliography

Emilianides, A. (ed.). *Religious Freedom in the European Union*. Leuven: Peeters, 2011.
Emilianides, A. *Annotated Legal Documents on Islam in Cyprus*. Leiden: Brill, 2014.
Papathomas, G. *L' Église Autocéphale de Chypre dans l' Europe Unie, Approche Nomocanonique*. Katerini: Epektasis, 1998.
Serghides, G. *Internal and External Conflict of Laws in Regard to Family Relations in Cyprus*. Nicosia: 1988.
Tornaritis, C. *The Ecclesiastical Courts, Especially in Cyprus*. Nicosia: 1976.

II. Articles

A. In Greek

Chrysostomides, K. 'Cyprus Ecclesiastical Law'. In *Tribute to the Parish of Agion Panton of London*, London: 1968, 129–141.
Chrysostomos, Archbishop of Cyprus. 'Introductory Report to the New Charter of the Church of Cyprus'. *Apostolos Varnavas* 40 (1979): 375–404.
Emilianides, A. 'The Constitutional Position of the Charter of the Orthodox Church of Cyprus'. *Nomokanonika* 2 (2005): 41–54.
Emilianides, A. 'The Constitutional Framework of the Relations Between Church and State in the Republic of Cyprus'. *Nomokanonika* 1 (2006): 37–78.
Emilianides, A. 'Who Are Considered as Members of Religious Groups According to the Constitution of Cyprus'. *Lysias* (2006): 26–31.
Emilianides, A. 'The Procedure for Electing an Archbishop in the Orthodox Church of Cyprus'. *Nomokanonika* 2 (2006): 45–72.
Emilianides, A. 'Jurisdiction for Adjudicating Property Disputes Between Members of a Religious Group'. *Cyprus and European Law Review* 4 (2007): 153–170.
Emilianides, A. 'The Matter of the Hereditary Succession of Monks under Cypriot Law'. *Cyprus and European Law Review* 5 (2007): 368–378.
Emilianides, A. 'The Episcopal Territories of the Church of Cyprus'. *Nomokanonika* 1 (2008): 29–42.
Emilianides, A. 'The New Charter of the Orthodox Church of Cyprus: A First Approach'. *Nomokanonika* 2 (2011): 19–36.
Emilianides, A. 'Observations on the Case Sevastianos v. Iera Moni Metamorfoseos tou Sotiros'. *Nomokanonika* 1 (2014): 199–212.
Emilianides, A. 'Individual Rights and Internal Law of the Church'. *Nomokanonika* 2 (2015): 21–29.
Emilianides, A. 'Meletios Metaxakis and the Charter of the Church of Cyprus of 1914'. *Nomokanonika* 2 (2016): 21–38.
Emilianides, A. 'Legal Aspects of the Old-Calendar Church of Cyprus'. In *Antipelargisis. Honourary Volume for I.M. Konidaris*, Athens-Thessaloniki: Sakkoulas, 2018, 3–22.
Emilianides, A. 'The Negotiation of the Constitutional Rights of the Religious Minorities of the Republic of Cyprus'. *Nomokanonika* 1 (2022): 11–34.
Emilianides, A. 'The Possibility to Transfer a Metropolitan in the Church of Cyprus' *Nomokanonika* 1 (2023): 67–73.

Feidas, V. 'The Nomokanonical Criteria of Constituting the Holy Synod of the Church of Cyprus'. *Nomokanonika* 2 (2002): 91–100.

Georgiades, S. 'The Legal Status of Cemeteries in the Greek and Cypriot Legal Order'. *Nomokanonika* 1 (2015): 73.

Katsaros, C. 'Practical Issues Arising from the Application of the New Charter of the Church of Cyprus'. *Nomokanonika* 2 (2011): 37–58.

Mpoumis, P. 'Replacing the First of the Church of Cyprus'. *Nomokanonika* 2 (2002): 71–82.

Papastathis, C. 'The New Charter of the Church of Cyprus'. *Hydor ek Petras* 4–5 (1980): 5–17.

Papastathis, C. 'The Right of Recourse of the Church of Cyprus Before the Supreme Court According to Article 139, Paras 1 and 3 of the Constitution of the Republic of Cyprus'. *Review of Public Law and Administrative Law* 34 (1990): 321–325.

Papaphilippou, L. 'Constitutional Problems from the Representation of the Religious Groups of Armenians, Latins and Maronites in the House of Representatives'. *Cyprus Law Tribune* 4 (1991): 626–638.

Poulis, G. 'The Analogical Application of Article 59 of the Charter of the Church of Cyprus'. *Nomokanonika* 2 (2002): 83–90.

Tornaritis, C. 'The Relations Between Church and State According to Cypriot Law'. *Review of Public and Private Law* 1 (1967): 9–16.

Tornaritis, C. 'The Occupation of Secular Power by a Religious Minister According to the Law of the Orthodox Church of Cyprus'. *Cyprus Law Tribune* 2–3 (1973): 3–10.

Tornaritis, C. 'Increase of the Episcopal Territories of the Church of Cyprus'. *Cyprus Law Tribune* 1 (1979): 4–6.

Tornaritis, C. 'Is Chiliasm a Religion, Is It Permitted under the Constitution and What Measures Are Provided against It?'. *Cyprus Law Tribune* 1–2 (1981): 3–5.

Tornaritis, C. 'The Property of Monks after Their Death and Whether It Is Subject to Inheritance Tax'. *Cyprus Law Review* 1 (1983): 177–178.

Tornaritis. C. 'The Constitutional Position of the Autocephalous Greek Orthodox Church in the Republic of Cyprus'. *Cyprus Law Tribune* 4 (1990): 485–495.

B. Other than Greek

Christodoulidou, T. 'Religious Conscientious Objection in Cyprus'. *Cyprus and European Law Review* 2 (2006): 324–330.

Dizdar, K. 'The Origin and Administration of the Cyprus Evkaf'. In *Proceedings of the First International Cyprological Conference*, Vol. II. Nicosia: Society for Cypriot Studies, 1973, 63–78.

Emilianides, A. 'Interracial and Interreligious Laws in Cyprus'. *Revue Hellénique de Droit International* 11 (1958): 286–306.

Emilianides, A. 'Islamic Faith as One of the Main Religions: The Case of Cyprus'. In *Islam in Europe*, edited by M. Moravcicova. Bratislava: Institute for State-Church Relations, 2005, 220–228.

Emilianides, A. 'Religion and the State in Dialogue: Cyprus'. In *Religion and Law in Dialogue: Covenantal and Non-covenantal Cooperation Between State and Religion in Europe*, edited by R. Puza & N. Doe. Leuven: Peeters, 2006, 19–31.

Selected Bibliography

Emilianides, A. 'Il Finanziamento delle cinque Religioni: Il Caso Cipriota'. *Quaderni di Diritto e Politica Ecclesiastica* 1 (2006): 107–124.

Emilianides, A. 'Religious Entities as Legal Persons: Cyprus'. In *Churches and Other Religious Organisations as Legal Persons*, edited by L. Friedner. Leuven: Peeters, 2007, 49–53.

Emilianides, A. 'Law and Religion in Cyprus'. *Kanon* 20 (2008): 7–21.

Emilianides, A. 'Financing of Religions in Cyprus'. In *The Financing of Religious Communities in the European Union*, Peeters: Leuven, 2009, 111–117.

Emilianides, A. 'Legal Status of the Roman Catholic Community'. In *Minorities of Cyprus: Past, Present and Future*, edited by A. Varnava, N. Coureas & M. Elia. Cambridge: Cambridge Scholars Publishing, 2009, 229–240.

Emilianides, A. 'Equal Promotionist Neutralism and the Case of Cyprus'. In *Financing of Churches and Religious Societies in the 21st Century*, edited by M. Moravcicova. Bratislava: Institute for State-Church Relations, 2010, 135–144.

Emilianides, A. 'Legal Opinion on the Legal Personality of the Karpasha Church Committee of the Maronite Church of Cyprus'. *Cyprus and European Law Review* 11 (2010): 164–169.

Emilianides, A., C. Adamides & E. Eftychiou. 'Allocation of Religious Space in Cyprus'. *The Cyprus Review* 23 (2011): 97–121.

Emilianides, 'Religion in Public Education in Cyprus'. In *Religion in Public Education*, edited by G. Robbers. Trier: European Consortium for State and Church Research, 2011, 87–98.

Emilianides, A. 'Discrimination Law in Cyprus'. In *Religion and Discrimination Law in the European Union*, edited by M. Hill. Trier: European Consortium for State and Church Research, 2012, 79–85.

Emilianides, A. 'Secularism, Law and Religion Within the Cypriot Legal Order'. In *Religion, Rights and Secular Society. European Perspectives*, edited by P. Cumper & T. Lewis. Cheltenham: Edward Elgar Publishing, 2012, 169–188.

Emilianides, A. 'Immigration and Religion in Cyprus'. In *Immigration, National and Regional Laws and Freedom of Religion*, edited by A. Motilla. Leuven: Peeters, 2012: 27–34.

Emilianides, A. 'Religion in the Criminal Law in Cyprus'. In *Religion and Criminal Law*, edited by M. Kottiranta & N. Doe. Leuven: Peeters, 2013, 35–40.

Emilianides, A. 'The Mutual Role of Religion and the State in Cyprus'. In *The Mutual Role of Religion and the State in Europe*, edited by B. Schanda. Trier: European Consortium for State and Church Research, 2014, 25–31.

Emilianides, A. 'Religious Jurisdiction and Pluralism of Legal Adjudication in Cyprus'. In *Religious Adjudication and the State*, edited by R. Potz and W. Wieschaider. Granada: Comares, 2015, 39–48.

Emilianides, A. 'Public Authorities and the Training of Religious Personnel in Cyprus'. In *Public Authorities and the Training of Religious Personnel in Europe*, edited by F. Messner. Granada: Comares, 2015, 173–182.

Emilianides, A. & C. Ioannou. 'Law and Religion in the Workplace in Cyprus'. In *Law and Religion in the Workplace*, edited by M. Rodriguez Blanco. Granada: Comares, 2016, 117–126.

Emilianides, A. 'Chaplaincy and the Law in Cyprus'. In *Religious Assistance in Public Institutions – Assistance spirituelle dans les services publics*, edited by R. Balodis and M.R. Blanco. Comares, Granada, 2018, 75–82.

Emilianides, A. 'Cyprus'. In *Human Rights, Religious Freedom and Faces of Faith*, edited by G. Gunner et al. Geneva: Globethics, 2019, 119–125.

Emilianides, A. 'State and Church in Cyprus'. In *State and Church in the European Union*, edited by G. Robbers. 3rd ed., Baden-Baden: Nomos Verlagsgesellschaft, 2019, 281–296.

Emilianides, A. 'Kirche und Staat in Zypern'. In *Kirche und Staat in West-Süd – und Nordeuropa*, edited by S. Mückl und A. Uhle. Berlin: Duncker & Humblot, 2020, 213–230.

Emilianides, A. 'Disciplinary Action and Freedom of Artistic Expression' *The Cambridge Journal of Law, Politics and Art* 1 (2022): 318–320.

Emilianides, A. 'Recognized, but not fully Appreciated: The Legal Status of Religious Minorities in Cyprus'. In *The Legal Status of Old and New Religious Minorities in the European Union*, edited by M. Ventura. Granada: Comares, 2021, 97–106.

Kentas, G. & A. Emilianides. 'The Emergence and Regulation of Minority Religious Groups in Europe'. In *How Groups Matter: Challenges of Toleration in Pluralist Societies*, edited by M. Bessone, G. Galder & F. Zuolo. London: Routledge, 2013, 260–285.

Papastathis, C. 'The Legal Status of Religions in the Republic of Cyprus'. In *The Status of Religious Confessions of the States Applying for Membership to the European Union*. Proceedings of the Meeting Université Robert Schuman, Strasbourg, 2000, 197–222.

Pitsakis, C. 'La Tradition du Droit Canonique de l' Èglise d' Orient dans l' Ordre Juridique Chypriote: Histoire et Survivances Contemporaines'. *Yearbook of the Centre of Research of the History of Greek Law* 38 (2004): 151–180.

Tornaritis, C. (ed.). 'The Legal Position of the Armenian Religious Group'. In *Constitutional and Legal Problems in the Republic of Cyprus*. 2nd ed. Nicosia: 1972, 85–90.

Tornaritis, C. 'The Legal Position of the Church, Especially the Greek-Orthodox Church in the Republic of Cyprus'. *Cyprus Today* 28 (1990): 2–12.

Selected Bibliography

Index

The numbers here refer to paragraph numbers.

Index

www.ingramcontent.com/pod-product-compliance
Lightning Source LLC
Chambersburg PA
CBHW071434230926
51846CB00001B/229
* 9 7 8 9 4 0 3 5 1 7 5 8 2 *